Warriors
of
Medieval Japan

ABOUT THE AUTHOR

Stephen Turnbull, a leading authority on Japanese history, has an MA in Theology and an MA in Military History, in addition to a PhD from Leeds University for his work on Japanese religious history. He has travelled extensively in Europe and the Far East. His work has been recognized by the awarding of the Canon Prize of the British Association for Japanese Studies and a Japan Festival Literary Award. He is a lecturer in Japanese Religion at the University of Leeds and also runs a picture library.

Warriors
of
Medieval Japan

STEPHEN TURNBULL

Dedication

To Fudge, because no dog knows more about samurai!

First published in Great Britain in 2005 by Osprey Publishing Ltd.
This paperback edition first published in 2007 by Osprey Publishing Ltd,
Midland House, West Way, Botley, Oxford OX2 0PH, United Kingdom
443 Park Avenue South, New York, NY 10016, USA

Email: info@ospreypublishing.com

Previously published as Warrior 29: *Ashigaru 1467–1649*; Warrior 64: *Ninja AD 1460–1650*;
and Warrior 70: *Japanese Warrior Monks AD 949–1603*.

© Osprey Publishing 2005

A CIP catalogue record for this book is available from the British Library.

ISBN 978 1 84603 220 2

Stephen Turnbull has asserted his right under the Copyright, Designs and Patents Act, 1988, to
be identified as the author of this work.

Artwork by Angus McBride (Introduction, Part 1 and page 139); Howard Gerrard (Part 2);
and Wayne Reynolds (Part 3 & 4). All artwork © Osprey Publishing Ltd.
Page layouts by Ken Vail Graphic Design, Cambridge, UK
Index by Alison Worthington
Originated by PPS Grasmere, Leeds, UK
Printed in China through World Print Ltd.

07 08 09 10 11   10 9 8 7 6 5 4 3 2 1

For a catalogue of all books published by Osprey Publishing please contact:

Osprey Direct UK, P.O. Box 140, Wellingborough,
Northants, NN8 2FA, UK.
info@ospreydirect.co.uk

Osprey Direct, c/o Random House Distribution Center, 400 Hahn Road, Westminster, MD 21157
Email: info@ospreydirect.com

E-mail: info@ospreydirectusa.com

www.ospreypublishing.com

Editors' note
All photographs are from the author's collection, unless credited otherwise.

Contents

Introduction

The last two centuries of the times of Civil War in Japan are known to history as the *Sengoku Jidai*, or the 'Age of Warring States'. This expression is derived from the title of the Warring States Period in ancient China, although the warfare that was endemic in Japan between 1467 and 1638 was not between rival states as such. Japanese warfare was carried out between the armies of rival *daimyō* (feudal lords) who competed for dominance, and the alternative translation of Sengoku Jidai as 'the Age of the Country at War' speaks very eloquently of the nature of the times. As for the warriors of Japan's Age of Warring States, the word 'samurai' is the best known name given to them but, as this book will show, this is not the whole story. There was a considerable amount of subdivision within the samurai class, and other social groups were also involved in the fighting.

The first samurai

The word 'samurai', which literally means 'those who serve', is first encountered in the writings of the 8th century AD. The original 'samurai' were only servants in the imperial court, but the word rapidly acquired military connotations when it began to be applied instead to soldiers who were recruited by the imperial court to perform warlike duties. They tended to be wealthy aristocratic landowners and their followers who had practised the martial arts for their own protection in the distant provinces where they lived. The most important service that these men rendered was in the roles of bodyguards and policemen. Rebels against the throne, bandits and the untamed tribesmen of northern Japan soon learned what a samurai was when campaigns were conducted against them on the emperor's behalf by samurai armies. These early samurai were a military elite who rode horses and fought primarily with bows and arrows, although the legendary samurai sword was

A wounded samurai, still grasping his spear, crawls across the ground at the battle of Nagakute in 1584. His hair has been let down from its pigtail and he wears only a hachimaki on his forehead. From a painted screen depicting the battle of Nagakute in the Tokugawa Art Museum, Nagoya.

OPPOSITE

This samurai sitting under a cherry tree is wearing a yoroi-style of armour with large sode (shoulder guards) and a leather-covered breastplate. He is carrying a bow and wears a courtier's cap. By the time of the Age of Warring States this style of armour was regarded as old-fashioned, but was still worn by generals who wished to identify with their glorious ancestors.

already rapidly acquiring its later formidable reputation. An analogy between samurai and European knights is a helpful way of understanding who these warriors were and what they did.

It was not long before certain samurai families began to acquire particularly fine reputations, and by the 11th century AD their skills and confidence were such that they began to use their influence to meddle directly in affairs of state. In 1156, and again in 1180, disputes over the succession to the imperial throne saw matters being resolved through the use of force by samurai armies led by samurai generals. In 1180 the two leading samurai families of Taira and Minamoto came to blows in a civil war known as the Gempei War. When the fighting finished in 1185 the Taira had been utterly defeated by their rivals. But that was not the most important outcome for Japanese history. The Minamoto victory was so complete that the Minamoto leader, Yoritomo (1147–99), was able to assume the reins of government as Japan's first *shōgun* or military dictator. The emperor was reduced to a symbolic head of state, and the age of samurai dominance had begun.

As the centuries passed, successive dynasties of shōguns came and went. The Ashikaga family, who rose to power as a result of the Nanbokuchō Wars of the mid-14th century and ruled for almost two centuries, appear on paper to have been very successful, but the last century of their reign saw an almost total collapse of their authority. The Ashikaga had followed a policy of

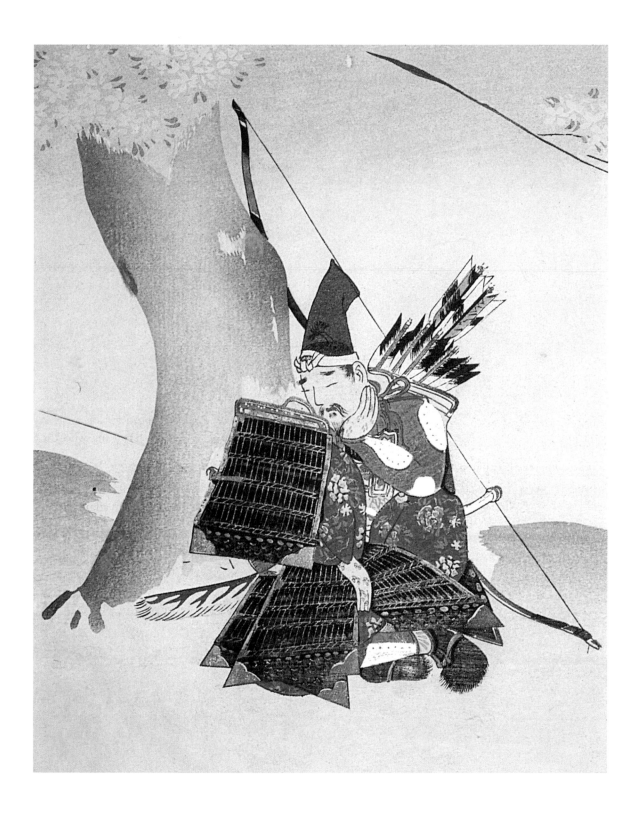

decentralization, so that military governors or *shugo* ruled the provinces of Japan on their behalf. Many shugo were samurai aristocrats who had ruled their provinces for centuries and had submitted to the Ashikaga. The system worked well until the mid-15th century, when a dispute over the succession to the shogunate led to a number of prominent shugo taking opposing sides and resorting to violence. The incumbent shōgun was powerless to control them and suffered the indignity of witnessing fighting in the streets of Kyōto, Japan's capital. The disturbances in Kyōto proved to be the beginning of a civil war known as the Ōnin War, which lasted from 1467 to 1477. Kyōto was devastated and the fighting spread to the provinces. As the shogunate had been exposed as a powerless entity, erstwhile shugo took the opportunity to create petty kingdoms for themselves in the provinces they had formerly administered. These men were the first daimyō, their title having the literal meaning of 'great names'. The Ōnin War therefore ushered in Japan's Age of Warring States, which lasted for almost two centuries until the final triumph of the Tokugawa family provided a period of stability. The Tokugawa shōguns ruled Japan with a rod of iron until the mid-19th century, when the arrival of foreign voyagers and traders forced Japan to enter the modern world.

Ashigaru on the march, showing guns in waterproof cases and naginata.

The rise of the ashigaru

As noted above, the popular understanding of the Age of Warring States is that its battles were conducted by armies of samurai, who were proud, individual mounted knights whose goal in life was to serve their lord with unswerving devotion. On the battlefield they sought out a worthy opponent whose severed head would provide the finest and most dramatic proof of their loyalty. This was the samurai ideal, nurtured by the retelling of the deeds of their ancestors, whose exploits grew in stature as the centuries went by. Yet throughout Japanese history the elite samurai were always backed up in various ways by numerous lower-class foot soldiers. Their story forms the second part of this book. They could be conscripted farmers, loyal attendants on samurai or absconding peasants, whose deeds went largely unrecognized and unrecorded until the major convulsion caused by the Ōnin War gave them a new prominence and a new worth.

The new breed of foot soldiers were called *ashigaru*, a word that literally means 'light feet'. At first they were nothing but casual and opportunistic ne'er-do-wells, attracted to an army by the prospect of loot. As time went by they began to stay with a particular daimyō and merged with the men who already worked on the daimyō's lands and served him in battle. Their final stage was their emergence as experienced operators of sophisticated weaponry in disciplined squads wearing identical uniforms, whose use on the battlefield complemented that of the samurai.

Ninja and warrior monks

The ninja are far more difficult to pin down in a simple definition. Ninja were the secret agents, the hired assassins and to some extent the 'special forces' of medieval Japan, and few military organizations in world history are so familiar yet so misunderstood as Japan's ninja. Ninja certainly existed, but much myth and exaggeration has grown up around the undoubted historical core of the subject. In this book, quotations from written accounts of ninja exploits will be confined to chronicles that are respected for their accuracy. Descriptions of items of ninja equipment will similarly be confined to implements illustrated in old 'ninja manuals' such as the 17th-century *Bansen Shukai*, or preserved in one of Japan's several (and remarkably underplayed) ninja museums. The reader will therefore find collapsible ladders, secret explosives and hidden staircases, but will have to look elsewhere for human cannonballs and ninja submarines.

In marked contrast to the samurai ideal of honourable single combat between worthy opponents, which meshed very well with the more modern notions of the manoeuvre of disciplined squads of ashigaru, the use of ninja was both underhand and dishonourable. It also represented an almost unique instance in samurai warfare of the employment of mercenaries. It is therefore not surprising that the use of ninja is shrouded in mystery. Not only did the ninja want to maintain their professional secrecy and the confidentiality of their employers, the daimyō who hired them wished to maintain the fiction of samurai honour, in which such vulgar activities played no part.

The final category of warriors belongs to the Japanese warrior monks. This is the popular translation of the word *sōhei*, which literally means 'priest soldier', and refers originally to the armies maintained by the monasteries of Hieizan and Nara from about AD 970. Unlike the samurai, their loyalty was not to the emperor, a clan leader or a daimyō, but to their temple and to the particular sect of Buddhism to which they belonged. A helpful comparison is with the military religious orders of Europe that emerged during the Crusades. Indeed, this provided a useful analogy for the only European visitor ever to make their acquaintance. The Jesuit missionary Father Caspar Vilela visited the Shingon warrior monks of Negoroji in Kii Province early in the 1560s and described them as being like the Knights of St John on the island of Rhodes.

By the time of the Age of Warring States, however, the original sōhei had been joined by other armies who shared a similar commitment to a sacred authority rather than a secular one. These were the armies of the Jōdo Shinshū

A stunt man dressed as a ninja scales the wall of the Koga ninja house.

sect, known as the *Ikkō-ikki*. The populist Jōdo Shinshū communities were very different from the monastic ones of the sōhei, and to describe the *monto* (believers) of Jōdo Shinshū as 'warrior monks' is somewhat misleading. Their communities attracted samurai, farmers and townsmen in communities of shared religious beliefs led by ordained priests. The formidable Ikkō-ikki were certainly warriors but never warrior monks. In fact the teachings of Shinran (1173–1262) with whom the sect originated, had revolutionized Japanese Buddhism by doing away with the duality of monasticism and laity and

replacing it with a new emphasis on spiritual egalitarianism. So rather than comparing the Ikkō-ikki to the Knights of Rhodes, a better European analogy would be the Hussites of Bohemia or the extreme Puritan communities that arose a century later during the Reformation. Linked by zeal for their beliefs, and under the leadership of charismatic preachers, they formed self-governing communities defended by armies. So it was with Jōdo Shinshū and their fighting monto.

The warrior monk Benkei in action with a naginata during the battle of Dan no Ura in 1185.

OPPOSITE

SAMURAI IN ARMOUR WITH STRAW RAIN CAPE
*c.*1580
In this plate a samurai of the Age of Warring States is fully armoured and partially protected from the weather by wearing a peasant's straw rain cape. His armour is a mogami-dō (multi-plate body armour made from hinged sections) laced in sugake odoshi (spaced double lacing). The armour is lacquered red. (**1**) shows how the shoulder strap of an armour fastened on to the dō using stout cords and toggles made of horn. Both his kote and haidate involve the use of closely fitting metal plates, giving him good protection. His suneate are typical of the age, and have a leather pad on each side where the legs touch the stirrups when riding. He has padded tabi on his feet, and (**2**) illustrates two of the several ways of tying the waraji to the foot. In the top right are illustrations (**3**) showing a variety of styles and mountings available for the katana, the longer tachi and the short wakizashi. There is also an aikuchi (dagger).

Chronology

1467	Ōnin War begins. Kyōto is devastated
1477	Ōnin War officially ends but fighting spreads to provinces
1480	Ise Nagauji (Hōjō Sōun) supports Imagawa
1493	Hōjō Sōun captures Izu province
1494	Hōjō Sōun captures Odawara castle
1506	Ikkō-ikki active in Kaga
1512	Hōjō Sōun captures Kamakura
1518	Siege of Arai
1524	Hōjō Ujitsuna captures Edo
1526	Siege of Kamakura
1536	Takeda Shingen's first battle at Umi no kuchi
1537	First battle of Konodai
1540	Siege of Aki-Koriyama
1542	Siege of Toda
1543	Arrival of Europeans in Japan and the introduction of firearms
1545	Night battle of Kawagoe
1546	Battle of Odaigahara
1547	Siege of Shiga
1548	Takeda Shingen is defeated at the battle of Uedahara
1549	Arquebuses used for the first time in Japan at Kajiki
1553	First battle of Kawanakajima
1554	Oda Nobunaga besieges Muraki using firearms
1555	Battle of Miyajima
	Second battle of Kawanakajima
1556	Battle of Nagaragawa
1557	Third battle of Kawanakajima
	First siege of Moji
1559	The provisioning of Odaka by Tokugawa Ieyasu shows his skill
1560	Battle of Okehazama and death of Imagawa Yoshimoto
1561	Fourth battle of Kawanakajima
	Odawara castle is besieged by Uesugi Kenshin
1562	Tokugawa Ieyasu captures Kaminojo using ninja
1564	Second battle of Konodai
	Battle of Azukizaka against the Ikkō-ikki of Mikawa
1566	Siege of Minowa
1567	Capture of Inabayama (Gifu) by Oda Nobunaga
1569	Siege of Odawara by Takeda Shingen
	Battle of Mimasetoge
1570	Battle of the Anegawa
	Battle of Imayama
	Death of Hōjō Ujiyasu

1571	Destruction of Mount Hiei by Nobunaga
1572	Battle of Mikata ga Hara
1573	Death of Takeda Shingen
1574	The Ikkō-ikki fortress of Nagashima is destroyed
1575	Battle of Nagashino
1576	Building of Azuchi castle
	Nobunaga attacks Ishiyama Honganji
1577	Siege of Nanao and battle of Tedorigawa
1578	Death of Uesugi Kenshin
	Battle of Mimigawa and the triumph of the Shimazu in Kyūshū
1579	Siege of Miki
1580	Surrender of Ishiyama Honganji to Oda Nobunaga
1581	Siege of Tottori leads to possible cannibalism
1582	Death of Takeda Katsuyori
	Murder of Oda Nobunaga at the Honnoji temple
	Battle of Yamazaki avenges Nobunaga
1583	Battle of Shizugatake
1584	Battles of Komaki and Nagakute
1585	Hideyoshi destroys Negoroji
	Invasion of Shikoku
1586	Building of Osaka castle
	Battle of Hetsugigawa
1587	Invasion of Kyushu by Toyotomi Hideyoshi
1588	Hideyoshi's Sword Hunt is completed
1589	Battle of Suriagehara
1590	Siege of Odawara and the fall of the Hōjō
1591	Siege of Kunoe – unification of Japan completed
	Separation Edict divides samurai from farmers
1592	First Japanese invasion of Korea
1593	Japanese withdraw from Korea
1597	Second invasion of Korea
1598	Death of Toyotomi Hideyoshi
	Korean War ends
1599	Death of Maeda Toshiie
1600	Battle of Sekigahara
1602	Ieyasu founds the Higashi Honganji, thus splitting Jōdo Shinshū
1603	Tokugawa Ieyasu becomes Shōgun
1614	Winter Campaign of Osaka
1615	Summer Campaign of Osaka
1616	Death of Tokugawa Ieyasu
1638	Shimabara Rebellion is defeated
1649	Publication of *Zōhyō Monogatar*

侍 Part 1
Samurai

Introduction

Samurai tradition and the Age of Warring States

The samurai tradition, by which in this context is meant the entire corpus of knowledge, belief, tradition and lifestyle associated with the samurai, was already centuries old by the time that the Age of Warring States began. It was also highly prized, largely inflexible and very nostalgic. These three attributes derived from the fact that one of the most enduring traditions among the samurai of Japan throughout the ages was an intense respect for the ancestors from whom one's family was descended. It was a concept that had its roots both in folk religion and in the Confucian doctrine of filial piety, and received its most important expression within the samurai class by an interest in, and a desire to emulate, the glorious deeds of their forebears. It is for this reason that a study like this one of the daily life of the samurai during the 16th century AD has to keep referring to precedents set by the samurai of the 12th and the 14th centuries. A particular deed of bravery, for example, might be compared to something an ancestor did during the Gempei War of 1180–85. Similar battlefield situations also invoked precedent, and on rare occasions influenced tactics. An example from recent samurai memory occurred during the second invasion of Korea in 1597. The situation at the battle of Chiksan reminded the Japanese general of the preliminaries to the battle of Nagashino in 1575, so he adjusted his dispositions accordingly.

The pages that follow will paint a picture of the daily life of the samurai of the Age of Warring States in peace and in war. The sources range from contemporary chronicles, diaries and battle reports to the curious *Hagakure* ('Hidden behind leaves'), a collection of anecdotes and moral tales compiled by a certain Yamamoto Tsunetomo in about 1710. He had retired from

samurai life to become a monk because a ban on committing suicide after a master's death prevented him from following his beloved daimyō Nabeshima Mitsushige to the grave. In these accounts we find an obsessive and almost overwhelming desire on the part of every samurai to perform deeds so glorious that he himself will enter the family pantheon and have his own name invoked for generations to come. So even though the Age of Warring States was a time when samurai warfare went through its biggest revolution in history under the influence of strategy and technology from both Europe and China, it was also a time of amazing nostalgia. In spite of the hail of bullets whizzing past his ears, and the ranks of lowly spearmen under his command, even the most modern samurai leader kept looking over his shoulders to a glorious and often hypothetical past. This golden age, in his view, had been a time when a battle consisted of a number of individual combats fought between honourable enemies who had singled each other out by the issuing and receiving of challenges. The victor would have taken the victim's head as proof of duty done, and for his reward would have been as pleased with the name he had made for himself as with any grant of rice fields he may have been awarded by his lord. We will see the strange paradox of a warrior lifestyle that embraces all that is new and efficient in the making of war, but also actively seeks out a form of individual warfare that, if uncontrolled, might even negate the achievements of the former. The supreme accolade of being the first into battle, for example, had the potential to disrupt the most talented general's plans! For a daimyō to survive and prosper therefore required him to be an extraordinarily talented individual who was capable of handling and encouraging both mass movement and personal prowess.

The happy reality of the Age of Warring States was that there seemed to be no shortage of leaders who were able to harness and direct these two contradictory sources of samurai energy. Indeed, from the time of the outbreak of the Ōnin War in 1467 we see a succession of leaders and followers who were able to move forward in samurai warfare while maintaining their own individual notions of honour and self respect.

From tradition to reality

The Ōnin War began in the streets of Kyōto, where samurai loosed arrows over the walls of poorly fortified mansions of rivals or simply set fire to them. Heroic combat took place against this savage and often indiscriminate background, and the Age of Warring States began when the fighting spread from Kyōto to the provinces. With virtually no central authority to restrain them, the shōgun's shugo became daimyō. Success bred success, so that by the early 16th century there were certain recognizable power blocs around Japan. Some were led by former shugo. Others, such as the Shimazu family of Satsuma province far to the south of Japan, bore the name of aristocratic families. These clans had dominated an area for centuries, either on their own behalf in the name of an ancient emperor or under the temporary authority of the shōgun as his largely nominal shugo. Many others were opportunistic samurai who relied on nothing more than their own military prowess. It would be very unlikely that this new breed of daimyō would invoke ancestral precedence in the proclamation of exploits. Their ancestors were as likely to have been farmers or umbrella makers as glorious samurai, and the present head of a family may well have risen to that dizzy height by murdering his former master. One of the most successful daimyō dynasties of the Age of Warring States was the Hōjō family of Odawara. Their founder, a samurai who bore the Buddhist name of

A samurai of the Takeda clan is shown in this remarkably lifelike dummy at the Ise Sengoku Jidai Mura. He is wearing an iron helmet with an antler maedate that bears the Takeda mon. The detail of how his armour is laced together is shown clearly.

The outer palisade fence at Hara castle being broken down by attacking samurai in 1638.

Sōun and was formerly known as Ise Nagauji, had appropriated the new surname from a long extinct samurai lineage because it sounded impressive. Uesugi Kenshin (1530–78) saved his former daimyō's life on condition that the daimyō adopted him as his heir and gave him the glorious name of Uesugi.

Needless to say, it was samurai like Hōjō Sōun and Uesugi Kenshin who were most successful at recruiting samurai to their standards using the methods described in the section which follows. From about 1530 onwards the Hōjō, Imagawa, Takeda and Uesugi homelands of north-central Japan became a battleground between them, with scores of smaller samurai families being alternately crushed, courted and absorbed by these growing giants. The southern Japanese island of Kyūshū witnessed similar rivalry between the samurai who fought under flags bearing the *mon* (badge) of Shimazu, Itō, Otomo and Ryūzōji, while the Mōri family steadily increased its influence along the Inland Sea.

The inevitable stalemate that resulted was only broken with the rise of 'super-daimyō', of which the most important name is that of Oda Nobunaga (1534–82). Nobunaga inherited a comparatively minor territory from his father and appeared to be heading for quick extinction when his lands were invaded by the hosts of Imagawa Yoshimoto in 1560. Nobunaga, however, took advantage of a lull in Yoshimoto's advance when the latter was enjoying

the traditional head-viewing ceremony in a narrow gorge called Okehazama. A fortuitous thunderstorm cloaked his final movements and allowed Nobunaga to take the Imagawa samurai completely by surprise. The victory at Okehazama thrust Nobunaga to the forefront of Japanese politics and samurai glory. Using a combination of superb generalship, utter ruthlessness and a willingness to embrace new military technology such as European firearms, Nobunaga began the process of reunification of Japan.

In this print we see the great samurai Uesugi Kenshin in the role of a connoisseur of swords. He is examining the detail of the workmanship on the blade by the reflected light of a fire. Note his shaven head – the mark of a samurai who was also a monk.

The march to unification

Oda Nobunaga was killed when Akechi Mitsuhide, one of his subordinate generals, launched a night attack on him in the temple of Honnoji in Kyōto in 1582. Mitsuhide had taken advantage of the absence from the scene of nearly all his fellow generals, but one of them, Toyotomi Hideyoshi (1536–98), hurried back from a distant campaign to trounce Mitsuhide at the battle of Yamazaki. Basking in the honour of being the loyal avenger of his dead master, Hideyoshi hurried to establish himself in the power vacuum that Nobunaga's death had created. In a series of brilliant campaigns Hideyoshi either eliminated or thoroughly neutralized any potential rivals, including Nobunaga's surviving sons and brothers. Over the next five years Hideyoshi conducted campaigns that gave him the islands of Shikoku and Kyūshū, and when the daimyō of northern Japan pledged allegiance to him in 1591 Japan was finally reunified.

Unfortunately for Hideyoshi, his ambitions did not stop at Japan, and in 1592 he sent tens of thousands of samurai across the sea in an invasion of Korea. This was to be the first stage of a process that would make Hideyoshi emperor of China, but the expedition was a disaster. A second attempt was made in 1597, but when Hideyoshi died in 1598 the samurai were recalled and Japan looked as though it was going to slip back into the chaos from which Hideyoshi had rescued it. His son and heir Hideyori was only five years old, but when war broke out the matter was quickly resolved at the decisive battle of Sekigahara in 1600. The victor, Tokugawa Ieyasu (1542–1616), was proclaimed shōgun in 1603. The final remnants of the supporters of Toyotomi Hideyori were defeated at the siege of Osaka castle in 1614–15. Apart from the short-lived Shimabara Rebellion of 1637–38, the Age of Warring States was over.

Recruitment, organization and command of samurai

Recruitment and retention

During the Age of Warring States the success enjoyed by a daimyō such as Oda Nobunaga depended on the quality of the men he could attract to his banner, and the elite of his army would be the samurai who had pledged to serve him to the death. They were, by definition, skilled warriors, and many had the capacity to become daimyō themselves, so recruitment of such men was never a simple matter of sending a recruiting sergeant into a village! The core of a daimyō's elite samurai would be an inner circle of very loyal and well-established vassals, whose service to the particular daimyō family could go

Oda Nobunaga was the first of Japan's three unifiers. He conquered much of central Japan through his combination of military skill and utter ruthlessness. In this modern painting we see Nobunaga mounted on a horse wearing an elaborate suit of multi-coloured armour. An ashigaru groom leads the horse, while his flag bearer follows on behind.

back for several generations. Many would have been closely bound to the family by marriage. Some, the daimyō's closest associates, would be his brothers, uncles, cousins and nephews. Other elite followers who were not related by either blood or marriage might be descended from some ancestor with a particular link to the family, such as distinguished service on a distant battlefield. They may well have served the daimyō since boyhood in the capacity of pages at his court. In addition, until Toyotomi Hideyoshi's laws began to restrict social mobility, many of a daimyō's most senior samurai simply rose from the ranks as a result of personal prowess in war. They would have been granted lands from the daimyō's own holdings as a reward, and knew that if they continued to serve him loyally and well these possessions would be regularly increased from the territories of the conquered. Beyond this inner

Toyotomi Hideyoshi, the second unifier of Japan.

circle of loyal retainers lay other samurai whose personal ties to the daimyō were not so clearly obvious. The word *tozama* (outer lords) is sometimes applied to them. A surprisingly large number of daimyō depended on samurai whose own leaders had been defeated in battle, a practice that will be discussed later in the context of the rituals of victory. The lower ranks of the samurai class were filled by men who were vassals of the daimyō, whose personal aspirations had to be restricted to the realistic ones of serving their lord in word and deed.

Jizamurai and the ikki alternative

The complex nature of the way samurai armies were put together demonstrates the fact that the social structure of the samurai class was by no means the monolithic one that is popularly supposed. Samurai could come from a very wide range of social groups with an equally wide spread of income distribution. In fact, during the early Warring States period there was only a small distinction in practical terms between a low-ranking samurai of modest financial means and

The third and final unifier of Japan was Tokugawa Ieyasu, shown in court robes in this print. Following Ieyasu's triumph the Tokugawa family ruled Japan for two and a half centuries.

a wealthy farmer who might also be a village headman. Not for him was the lowly role of an ashigaru. Instead he enjoyed considerable prestige among his own community. He could not levy taxes, but collected rent from the peasantry and resisted 'real' samurai who attempted to collect taxes from him. The name *jizamurai* is often used for them. To some extent their duties and aspirations were very similar to those of the up-and-coming daimyō. They shared a common interest of defending their territory and collecting revenue from it in an efficient manner.

The difference between the warriors who fought for jizamurai and those who fought for daimyō occurred in the growth of internal structures. The daimyō sought to recruit warriors under their standards and under their direct command. Their samurai would fight for them and be rewarded in various ways, but whereas a daimyō aspired towards a vertical vassal structure in a hierarchy of which the daimyō was the apex, the lowlier jizamurai had an alternative, which was the formation of an *ikki* (a league or organization). When an ikki was created, potential allies whose individual power bases were limited joined forces in a

This modern bronze equestrian statue of Yamauchi Kazutoyo is interesting in that it represents his horse in the correct scale of the smaller breeds of horse that would have been used in the Age of Warring States. Kasutoyo, the daimyō of Kochi, stands outside Kochi castle holding his long spear.

mutual protection association, and such a grouping of equal but highly committed allies often proved to be a match for a daimyō's tight pyramid of samurai. The religiously motivated 'single-minded league' of the Ikkō-ikki merely provides the largest example in Japanese history of such a creation, but there were many others. For example, in 1485 samurai and 'peasants of all the province of Yamashiro' gathered for a meeting to agree to drive out the troops of the two shugo who had been battling over the area. The resulting Yamashiro ikki was under the leadership of local samurai, but the organizations of the villages sustained it. Needless to say, ikki formation cut right across the vertical vassal structures that ambitious daimyō were trying everywhere to create, and in some cases this caused considerable conflict of interest. Some samurai retained membership of their ikki even after they became vassals of daimyō, and weaning them away from such ties was very difficult if membership of the ikki involved staunch religious beliefs.

Through their membership of ikki, samurai created alliances beyond their immediate kinship circles under the formal pledge of mutual loyalty. The structure of an ikki was therefore broadly democratic and its rules stated explicitly that any conflict among its members should be resolved at a meeting where the majority decision would apply. Nowhere was this democratic structure more dramatically illustrated than in the ritual that marked the initial formation of an ikki or the resolution of a major problem such as a decision to go to war. The visible proof that an agreement had been reached would take the form of a document. Inscribed upon it was a set of written rules to which the members' signatures were added. The signatures were often written in a circle to show the equal status of the members and to avoid quarrels over precedence. Next, a ritual was celebrated called *ichimi shinsui*, ('one taste of the gods' water'), when the document was ceremoniously burned. Its ashes were mixed with water and the resulting concoction was drunk by the members. The ritual was considered to symbolize the members' like-mindedness that was the outward sign of their solidarity.

The complex nature of contemporary samurai social structures is neatly illustrated by the example of the villages of Hineno. At the beginning of the Age of Warring States the population of Hineno had to deal with three power blocs, each of which was competing for their loyalty and their revenue. First was Kujo Masamoto (1459–1516) their absentee landlord, who resided at the imperial court in Kyōto. The aristocratic family of Kujo had ruled Hineno for centuries, and the Hineno villages had paid Masamoto and his forebears a fixed tax every year since 1417. His authority was a traditional one but was in decline, and changing circumstances had forced Masamoto to leave the capital and reside in Hineno. This was a desperate move for a court aristocrat, to whom the notion of country life was unspeakably vulgar. Second in influence was the shugo who nominally ruled the area for and on behalf of the shōgun. He threatened Masamoto's long standing autonomy, but was himself under threat from the growing anarchy that followed the Ōnin War. But there was also a third force involved in the persons of the sōhei of Negoroji, and when they decided to invade Hosokawa territory in 1502 Hineno lay in the way of their forces. Nothing daunted, the villagers opened negotiations with Negoroji for the protection of their village, which was secured by a large cash payment. Kujo Masamoto paid only one fifth of the sum. The rest was supplied by the villagers themselves. In addition, the temple granted the villagers the power to punish any soldiers who were found guilty of misconduct within the area of Hineno. So, in this one tiny area of Japan, aristocrats, samurai and warrior monks had to listen to the demands of the lower classes, who were asserting themselves more and more.

Samurai and social separation

The social organization of the samurai class only really changed with the rise of Japan's 'super-daimyō', in particular the first two unifiers of the nation: Oda Nobunaga and Toyotomi Hideyoshi. Nobunaga's greatest rivals were not fellow daimyō but the peasant and lowly samurai armies of the Ikkō-ikki, so he pursued a policy of disarming the rural population from which the Ikkō-ikki had traditionally drawn their strength. This went a long way towards separating the farming class from the samurai class, a development that is usually regarded as having begun with Toyotomi Hideyoshi's 'Sword Hunt' of 1588. So, for example, in 1575, when the Ikkō-ikki of Echizen Province had been subdued, we read of regulations forbidding peasants to seek new masters or to leave their villages and ordering them to confine themselves to tilling the soil. In 1576 Nobunaga's general Shibata Katsuie conducted a Sword Hunt of his own in Echizen, just to make sure.

Nobunaga's successor Toyotomi Hideyoshi enacted two laws that were to change completely the face of Japan and the nature of the samurai class. He had realized that one reason why organizations such as the Ikkō-ikki had been able to challenge samurai rule so easily was because of the ready supply of weapons. The resulting Sword Hunt of 1587 was designed to disarm anyone who might oppose Hideyoshi's control. Over a short period of time Hideyoshi's troops entered villages and confiscated all swords, spears and guns. But the process did not stop at the peasantry. Minor daimyō whose loyalty was questionable, village headmen, temples and shrines were all relieved of their offensive weaponry. It was a far-reaching and very ruthless programme akin to Henry VIII's dissolution of the monasteries, and even extended to the coasts, where any seafarer who was tempted to engage in piracy had his military means curtailed.

The Separation Edict that followed in 1591 enshrined in law the increased professionalism of armies that had been developing for at least 20 years. The trend had meant that untrained peasants given a spear or a gun could be more of a hindrance than help, and now this informal move towards a separation between the military and agricultural functions was made both legal and rigid. No longer could someone like Hideyoshi enlist as a foot soldier and be promoted to general. If you were classified as a farmer then your function in life was to grow food while others did the fighting. We will see in the section on ashigaru the far-reaching effects that these measures had.

The final unifier of Japan, Tokugawa Ieyasu, completed the process by classifying all his subjects as samurai, farmers, merchants or others, the final section being a catch-all category that included priests and actors. All the daimyō in Japan swore allegiance to him, and were liable to be called upon to fight on the shōgun's behalf. Under the Tokugawa, therefore, the four categories of warriors covered by this book were clearly defined and rigidly controlled. All samurai were ultimately followers of the shōgun and the ashigaru were officially classified as the lower ranks of the samurai class. Warrior monks no longer existed, and the ninja families were now in Ieyasu's exclusive employment to guard his castle of Edo. 'Samurai' now had a more precise meaning than ever.

Appearance and equipment of the samurai

As the elite of a daimyō's fighting force, the samurai were expected to set an example to the lower classes by the dignity of their appearance. It could safely be concluded that a dishevelled or unkempt samurai in any situation other

To the background of cherry blossoms, the eternally poignant symbol of the samurai, Toda Ujikane points his war fan in the direction of the enemy. He is wearing a typically practical suit of armour embellished by a lavish helmet with a large maedate. This statue of him is outside Ogaki castle.

than a battlefield was a man who was unemployable, unwanted or had abandoned himself to crime or to drink. *Hagakure* tells us in 1710 that:

> The samurai of fifty or sixty years ago would bathe, shave their foreheads, put lotion in their hair, cut their fingernails and toenails, rubbing them with pumice and then with wood sorrel, and without fail pay attention to their personal appearance. It goes without saying that their armour in general was kept free from rust, that it was dusted, shined and arranged.

A bas relief depicting Date Masamune and his samurai on the plinth of his statue in Sendai. Masamune is shown with his characteristic crescent moon maedate. His spearmen have smaller versions on their helmets. They are all wearing the yukinoshita-dō style of armour with its bullet-proof breastplate.

A samurai's personal pride was apparent from the moment of first contact. When out of armour he would wear fine clothes of a particular traditional design. Above a *kimono*, a garment that resembled a dressing gown, he would wear various types of clothing that reflected the situation in which he found himself. Formal duties in a daimyō's castle demanded the *kamishimo*, the traditional combination of wide *hakama* (trousers) and either a formal jacket with shoulders that stuck out like wings, or a looser *haori*. The two parts of the kamishimo were of identical colour and design and bore the daimyō's mon on the breast and on the back. Tight *kobakama* (breeches) were more informal attire. Thrust into the belt of the hakama were the two swords that were the recognized badge of the privileged samurai class. Particular care was lavished on the samurai's hair. It would be combed and drawn back into a pigtail which either stuck out behind or was folded forward on itself. It was fashionable to have the front part of the head shaved. When in battle the hair would be let down and tied simply with a *hachimaki* (headband) – hence the illustrations on Japanese prints of battle scenes showing samurai with their hair streaming in the wind. *Hagakure* recommended that samurai should grow moustaches so that their severed heads would not be mistaken for those of women. Full beards were most unusual, and Kato Kiyomasa's penchant for facial hair was remarked upon.

Samurai armour

The clothes worn under armour would have been of much simpler design, although an embroidered *yoroi-hitatare* (armour robe) would look splendid on a senior samurai. On a more mundane level, *Hagakure* recommends underwear made from badger skin, which would eliminate lice infestation, a frequent problem on campaign. Samurai armour has been adequately described elsewhere, so for the purposes of this book we will simply note that Japanese armour was predominately of lamellar construction, in other words it was made from small scales of metal fastened together rather than from one large armour plate. Unlike European armour the small armour plates were lacquered as a precaution against rust. The individual plates were fastened to each other by rawhide cords to make horizontal sections, a number of which were combined vertically by silk suspensory cords. Various combinations of plates provided a complete suit of armour. There was a *dō* (body armour) from which hung a row of *kusazuri* (tassets) making an armoured skirt. Sleeve armour (*kote*) was worn, as were larger shoulder plates (*sode*) and a *nodowa* (throat protector). Beneath the *dō*, *haidate* (thighguards) and *suneate* (shinguards) provided protection for the legs. The only examples of true plate armour appeared above the neck, where a *mempo* (facemask), often embellished with features and horsehair moustaches, provided a secure anchor point for the heavy iron bowl of the *kabuto* (helmet). A lamellar *shikoro* (neckguard) hung round the helmet's rim, while the helmet's crown was often used to enhance the samurai's martial appearance by the addition of weird and wonderful decorations. Antlers, golden horns, imitation sword blades, rows of feathers, and conch shells carved in papier mâché were all to be found transforming a sombre and practical battledress into a glorious fantasy. The popularity of wooden buffalo horns meant that many samurai actually did wear the horned helmets so cherished in our erroneous image of Vikings!

The samurai's allegiance was proclaimed by the wearing on the back of his armour of an identifying device known as a *sashimono*. This was often, but not exclusively, a small flag bearing his daimyō's mon, but just as in the case of the helmets the choice of design of the sashimono provided the opportunity for a little creativity. Golden fans and plumes of feathers could replace the small flag, while the most spectacular form of sashimono was the curious *horō*. This was a cloak stretched over a bamboo framework and had supposedly originated as an arrow catcher, but by the time of the Age of Warring States it had become a decorative appendage for a daimyō's elite samurai who acted as his bodyguards or messengers. The horō filled with air as the samurai rode across the battlefield, and the bright colours made him easily recognizable to friend and foe. It was customary that when a horō-wearing samurai was decapitated his head was wrapped in the horō for presentation as a mark of respect.

Samurai armour changed very little during the Age of Warring States. The main developments were caused by the need to make armour bullet-proof once

In the Nishimura Museum in Iwakuni we find this excellent example of a multi-coloured armour of haramaki style (opening at the back), which was popular in the Age of Warring States.

firearms had become established. We therefore see the introduction of solid plate breastplates for the dō, and also solid iron plates for the horizontal sections of skirts and shoulder guards. This had the additional advantage of saving time for the armour-maker, whose craft was in high demand. *Hagakure* adds a few details about armour:

> For soldiers other than officers, if they would test their armour, they should test only the front. Furthermore, while ornamentation on armour is unnecessary, one should be very careful about the appearance of the helmet. It is something that accompanies his head to the enemy's camp.

Samurai weapons

By the time of the Age of Warring States the influence of the use of large numbers of lower-class troops had forced the samurai to evolve from being a mounted archer to being a mounted spearman. The occupation of the archer operating from horseback had become limited to those who had sufficient skill to act as mounted sharpshooters. They were still in great demand, because the alternative missile weapon, the arquebus, was not the best thing to operate from horseback. Towards the end of the period we see matchlock pistols being introduced, but again they were of very limited capacity.

The samurai's *yumi* (bow) was of made from deciduous wood faced with bamboo. The rattan binding reinforced the poor adhesive qualities of the glue used to fasten the sections together and the whole bow was lacquered to weatherproof it. The arrows were of bamboo. The nock was cut just above a node for strength, and three feathers were fitted. Bowstrings were of plant fibre, usually hemp or ramie, coated with wax to give a hard smooth surface, and in some cases the long bow needed more than one person to string it. The archer held the bow above his head to clear the horse, and then moved his hands apart as the bow was brought down to end with the left arm straight and the right hand near the right ear. To release the string the fingers supporting the thumb were relaxed, at which the bow, having discharged the arrow, rotated in the hand so that it ended with the string touching the outside of the bow arm.

The *yari* (spears) carried by the mounted samurai bore little resemblance to a European knight's lance. They were lighter and shorter and were not carried in a couched position. Their blades were short and very sharp on both edges, with their tangs sunk into stout oak shafts. This made the yari into a weapon unsuitable for slashing but ideal for stabbing – the best technique to use from

In this scene we see a daimyō attended by his samurai. An attendant sits next to him holding his sword. His visitors have removed their katana before being allowed into his presence. This diorama is in the museum in Hagi.

a saddle. A useful variation was a cross-bladed spear that enabled a samurai to pull an opponent from his horse. If a samurai wished to deliver slashing strokes from horseback then a better choice than a yari was the cumbersome *naginata*, a polearm with a long curved blade, or the spectacular *nōdachi*, an extra-long sword with a very strong and very long handle. Yari would also be the samurai's primary weapon of choice when he had to fight dismounted, and a whole field of martial arts techniques existed for teaching its correct use.

After the spear there was, of course, the famous samurai sword. Much has been written about this legendary weapon, of how its secrets were passed down from master to pupil and of the complex and clever way it was made. Japanese swords could be objects of great beauty, but to the samurai of the Age of Warring States function was more important than form. The finest swords, often presented as gifts to a worthy warrior, were of superb finish. They were perfectly balanced for the two-handed style of fighting that they demanded. The samurai never used shields. Instead the *katana*, the standard fighting sword, was both sword and shield, its resilience enabling the samurai to deflect a blow aimed at him by knocking the attacking sword to one side with the flat of the blade and then following up with a stroke of his own. The cutting edge was able to take a razor-like quality, while the surrounding body of the sword blade allowed the necessary flexibility to absorb the shock of parrying an enemy's blow. The wavy line running along the blade showed where the two halves of the blade were welded together.

The katana blade would be mounted in a wooden handle bound with silken cords over a layer of *same* (the skin of the giant ray). The scabbard would be lacquered, often very decoratively, and the whole ensemble was completed with an attractively carved iron *tsuba* (sword guard) and other ornaments. A shorter

This room inside the Mōri mansion in Hofu gives an excellent indication of the interior design of a daimyō's yashiki. There is simple and subtle decoration of natural polished wood and tatami mats. A painted scroll hangs in the tokonoma, while the shoji have been slid to one side to afford a glimpse of the garden.

sword, the *wakizashi*, joined the katana to make a pair known as a *daishō*, the wearing of which was the badge and exclusive privilege of a samurai. The two swords were sometimes worn while in armour, but it was more usual for the katana to be suspended with its blade downwards from a sword belt and accompanied by a *tanto* (dagger) instead of a wakizashi.

Daily life and training of samurai

From *Hagakure* we read that a samurai should rise at four in the morning, bathe and arrange his hair daily, eat when the sun comes up and retire when it becomes dark. Within this tidy framework the samurai of the Age of Warring States led a full and busy life from a very early age. *Hagakure* even has advice for the parents of young samurai:

> There is a way of bringing up the child of a samurai. From the time of infancy one should encourage bravery and avoid trivially frightening or teasing the child. If a person is affected by cowardice as a child, it remains a lifetime scar. It is a mistake for parents to thoughtlessly make their children dread lightning, or to have them not go into dark places, or to tell them frightening things in order to stop them from crying.

In another section Yamamoto Tsunetomo recommends an active life up to the age of 40, and to have 'settled down' by 50.

Kiyosu castle, the seat of Oda Nobunaga, looking from across the river. We see the keep and gatehouse in a layout typical of a Japanese castle.

The samurai's built environment

Up until the time that the Separation Edicts of Toyotomi Hideyoshi achieved a rigid distinction between samurai and farmer, a samurai's daily life would have been conducted between the two poles of the daimyō's castle and the samurai's own estates. The extent to which the samurai was merely an estate manager or an actual worker on the land depended on the resources he possessed, which in turn depended on his prowess in the daimyō's service. Service to one's lord, either on the battlefield or off it, produced reward, but also increased his obligation. To some extent this was an unending progression, because a samurai's wealth was measured in terms of the yield of his rice fields. This figure was then translated into the number of men he was required to supply in the daimyō's service. More lands could be farmed, and more food could be produced to feed one's own followers, so more followers were required when danger threatened. Towards the end of the period actual grants of land were replaced by a rice stipend. The professional samurai would now spend most of his time in the service of his daimyō in the daimyō's own headquarters while his own men worked the fields on his behalf, just as he had once done for the daimyō.

The keep of Uwajima castle, seat of a branch of the Date family on Shikoku island.

The sparse and completely functional interior of a castle's keep contrasts sharply with the opulence of the yashiki. This is the entrance room of Uwajima castle, from which a steep wooden staircase leads to the upper floors.

The daimyō's base would be centred on a castle. The castle's role as an economic centre encouraged the growth of *jōkamachi* (castle towns) which spread around the castle's walls. Many of modern Japan's prefectural capitals were once the castle towns of daimyō. Over the two centuries covered by this book the Japanese castle evolved from being a simple stockade on top of a mountain – the original *yamashiro* (mountain castle) to the huge fortresses like Osaka and Himeji, where graceful buildings soared into the sky above massive stone bases. The outer walls of such castles sheltered the buildings, which were virtually barracks, where the samurai lived. The quality of the buildings he occupied depended upon the samurai's rank, as did their location. The closest retainers of the daimyō were settled in the buildings nearest to the centre of the castle where two key complexes would be found. The first was the keep. This was the heart of the military and defensive function of the castle. It provided a lookout tower and also a place for a last-ditch stand at the time of war. The final evolution of the castle keep produced the stunning examples that still exist to this day in places like Hikone and Matsumoto. They are often of four or five storeys in height with graceful tiled roofs, heavy doors and windows and clever defensive elements such as trap doors that act like machicolations, as well as spikes and concealed sally ports.

Because a keep was essentially a military structure it was unusual for the building to be highly ornamented inside. Instead it would be solidly built with plain decoration and polished wooden floors. Any ostentation in the castle was to be found in the daimyō's *yashiki* (mansion), which would usually lie in the inner courtyard beside the keep. This would be the living quarters and administrative area for the daimyō and the samurai who were his closest retainers. The yashiki would be a one-storey building that reflected the unity

This view is of the classic layout of a samurai's yashiki. The floor area is effectively one large room subdivided using opaque sliding screens or the translucent shoji. Beyond the outer corridor we can see the garden. The floor is covered with tatami mats. This is the yashiki of Kochi castle.

of style of Japanese architecture. Wooden corridors (in some cases made deliberately noisy to warn of intruders) connected sets of rooms subdivided one from another by sliding screens. The *shoji* (translucent paper screens) on the outer walls of rooms could be slid back to reveal gardens and ponds, while the inner screens were decorated with pictures of landscapes and animals. Rooms were of various sizes depending upon their intended function, from tiny little spaces for an intimate tea ceremony to large and impressive reception areas. A stage for the performance of the Noh drama might well be included in the yashiki complex.

Inside the rooms furniture was minimal. Low wooden tables or desks, an arm rest, a lamp stand and a sword rack would be all that would be normally visible. Subtle decoration was provided by a *tokonoma*. This was an alcove in the corner of a room where a hanging scroll could be displayed or a flower arrangement placed inside some beautiful pottery vase. Just as in traditional Japanese inns today, bedrooms had no beds. The bedding would be packed away in concealed cupboards and only brought out for sleeping. There was no heating other than the warmth provided by an open fire in the middle of a room, or a box of warm charcoal.

A kitchen would occupy a space on the outside of the building. Here food would be prepared over a number of ranges and carried into the living quarters on trays. A bath house provided the best relaxation of all. Toilet facilities were private and heavily guarded, as this was the only place where an assassin might hope to encounter a daimyō on his own.

The further down the social scale a samurai lay the simpler his accommodation became. His house might have only one room and a tiny kitchen area, but all could expect hygiene and cleanliness in the castle environment. This would also be found out in the countryside. Here the simple samurai's mansion would be a farmhouse thatched with rice straw surrounded by a vegetable patch rather than an ornamental garden. Fish might be drying in the sun, and frogs would croak in the rice fields that occupied every square inch of cultivable land.

Food and drink

A samurai was brought up in a tradition that emphasized frugality, and this was reflected in his diet. The chronicle *Azuma Kagami* tells us how the first shōgun, Minamoto Yoritomo, gave a New Year banquet that consisted of only one course: a bowl of rice and a cup of *sake* (rice wine). Tokugawa Ieyasu is recorded as reprimanding a retainer who brought him fruit out of season as a special treat, although this may have had more to do with Ieyasu's concern over his personal health.

Most of the time samurai food was sparse and simple, consisting mainly of rice, vegetables, soy bean products, fish, seaweed, salt and fruit, but it was always highly nutritious. Vegetables would be freshly gathered except for certain pickles, of which pickled plums and pickled ginger were very common. Giant radishes and fresh mountain greens, a form of spinach, were popular. Burdock, aubergines, cucumbers, chestnuts, mushrooms and other root vegetables were also eaten.

This is the kitchen of the Ogawa samurai house in Kochi. The earthenware range heats two cooking pots which have wooden lids. The wooden workbench to the right is for food preparation.

Food fit for a samurai. The fare includes rice, shellfish, shredded daikon and sashimi.

A great deal of use was made of products derived from soy beans. Soy sauce was produced commercially, as was *miso* (fermented soy bean paste) which could be made into soup. *Tofu* (soy bean curd) was an important protein source. Rice had become a regular part of the samurai's diet only since the 14th century, but polished rice was a luxury item. Husked rice was far more common, and this could be augmented by millet or a mixture called *gemmai*, which was husked rice and wheat. Rice could be either boiled in a pan, mixed with vegetables and seaweed, steamed, baked or made into rice cakes. *Mochi*, the most common form of rice cakes, were made from rice flour or a mixture of rice and wheat flour.

The products of hunting, such as wild duck, venison or boar, would occasionally augment the protein intake. Samurai were enthusiastic hunters and enjoyed delicacies such as bears' paws, badger, and the crackling from the skin of wild boar. Meat could be preserved by salting and drying strips of it. The produce of the sea provided much more for a samurai's table. Every conceivable sea creature was caught and eaten, from shrimps to whales! Horse mackerel, tuna, squid and sea bream all appear on menus in samurai history, with the preferred means of preparation always being *sashimi*, whereby fish was cut into strips and eaten raw with soy sauce and *wasabi* (green horseradish paste). Shellfish, including the delicacy *awabi* (abalone), were much used. Many different kinds of seaweed were also eaten. *Wakame* gave flavouring to dishes and provided a base for stock. The deep purple *nori*, used nowadays in the preparation of *sushi*, was another commonly eaten seaweed. Deep-fried *tempura*, nowadays regarded as traditionally Japanese, was introduced by the Portuguese during the 16th century. At the time of the samurai tea performed the same function as brewing in Europe: it made water safe to drink. For alcoholic refreshment there was sake, a drink of considerable potency.

The serving of a meal inside a daimyō's yashiki would be attended by considerable ceremony. The guests would sit on the floor and eat using chopsticks from a low table, either one large one or individual smaller ones. The meal would be brought to them on a lacquered tray, with each individual dish presented immaculately on a lacquer or pottery vessel. Rice would be taken from a large rice pot and etiquette demanded that one should never pour sake for one's own consumption. A meal in a lowly samurai's barracks would be less exquisite in appearance, but would be attended by the same meticulous etiquette. Hygiene was of a very high standard.

The martial arts

The samurai existed as a fighting man, so much of his time had to be given to increasing his prowess in fighting techniques. These skills gave rise to the modern martial arts of Japan, so *kenjutsu* (sword techniques), for example, became modern *kendo* (literally 'the way of the sword'). Schools of swordsmanship were developed during the Age of Warring States. They were led by experts known by the title of *sensei*, a word that can be translated simply as 'teacher', but implied such a tremendous respect verging on awe that the word 'master' gives a better idea of its meaning.

The mythology and mystique that has grown up over the centuries around the martial arts of Japan has tended to lay too great a stress on the transmission from master to pupil of secret techniques. The author of *Hagakure* recognized this trend by the end of the 17th century, when he writes of a dying sensei, who told his best disciple:

> I have passed on to you all the secret techniques of this school, and there is nothing left to say. If you think of taking on a disciple yourself, then you should practise diligently with the bamboo sword every day. Superiority is not just a matter of secret techniques.

No matter how skilled a revered a sensei was, he was of course hampered by one almost inescapable fact: that realistic practice with such a sharp and deadly weapon as a samurai sword was almost impossible. The slightest mistake on behalf of one of a pair of sparring students would have led to a death, so various teaching methods were developed to get round this problem. The usual scheme was for an aspiring student to learn first of all the basic techniques. If no opponent was involved then this could be done with real swords. Set techniques using a practice sword and an opponent followed. As the student progressed he would move on to using a *habiki* (edgeless sword) which was a real sword with a completely blunt blade. The final stage involved the use of a real edged weapon.

One variety of practice in the first stage was *suburi*, a drilling method whereby the sword was swung over and over against an imaginary opponent. Although similar to shadow-boxing, suburi had real value in that it taught the samurai good balance with a real weapon and developed his muscles. A student could also perform *kata*, a standard practice method still found in the Japanese martial arts today, which is the performance of set moves or forms in a precise and prescribed manner. The student could also practise kata with a partner. In this case each knew precisely what the other's next move would be, so real swords were an option. Like suburi, the repetitious kata could become boring, and required great dedication from the student. But in the Age of Warring States the prize was not a gold medal in a competition. It was survival on a battlefield and the achievement of the simple goal of doing one's duty to the daimyō, and that, theoretically at any rate, was all that the samurai lived for.

The substitution of dummy weapons for real ones allowed a certain amount of contact between opponents. For *yarijutsu* (spear techniques) the samurai used a *tampo yari*, a practice spear with a round padded end, and for sword fighting they used *bokutō*. The word bokutō consists of the two characters for 'wood' and for 'sword', as that is what bokutō were – wooden swords made with the overall shape of a real sword and with a real sword's approximate weight. To compensate for the higher density of steel the blade was made about an inch thick, and was practically identical to the modern bokutō, also called *bokken*, used in present-day *aikidō*. Samurai fighting with bokutō would not wear protective armour but fought instead with unmasked faces and unprotected sleeves. The result was that even if mortal wounds and disablement were avoided, very savage blows could still be sustained leading to severe bruising and the occasional broken limb.

The inside of the walls of Kochi castle show several important defensive features. There are bow and gun ports. The flat horizontal wooden beams are there to allow planking to be laid across them to provide an extra storey for firing. The tree will serve to hide the interior of the castle from prying eyes.

SAMURAI TRAINING WITH PRACTICE SWORDS
c.1580
Prowess at swordsmanship required endless practice in a dojo with real weapons, blunted swords or wooden practice swords. Here a sensei is taking on a promising pupil. Both are dressed in practical kimono and hakama, but the pupil has fastened back the sleeves of his kimono using a tasuki. The pupil has his hair tied back in 'tea whisk' style. The bandages on the other pupils show that quite severe blows could be sustained using the practice weapons shown in the corner behind them.

Towards the end of the 16th century a new practice weapon called a *shinai* was introduced and was developed for friendly encounters. The original shinai, almost identical to the weapon used in modern kendo, consisted of a number of light bamboo blades tied together. If some form of protective armour was worn blows could be delivered with the light shinai using all the power in a samurai's forearms, and enabling what one might term 'full-contact kenjutsu' to be practised, thus making a simulation of actual combat more realistic. It was introduced by the sensei Kamiizumi Nobutsuna, and first used by him in a duel against Yagyū Muneyoshi. A century later, in about 1711–14, the sensei Chōshō Shiroemon began to use protection for the face and forearms similar to modern kendo armour for practising the martial arts, but shinai and armour were always abandoned for serious contests and bokutō used instead. The

By means of a Japanese garden a samurai sought to bring nature within the walls of his castle or mansion. This is a winter view of one of the finest existing Japanese gardens at Suizenji in Kumamoto. The conical hill represents Mount Fuji.

samurai swordsman of the Age of Warring States had to be tough as well as skilful, so a few bruises were fully acceptable. The third stage of training using blunted swords must have caused even more physical damage.

Bokutō were also used for duels between rivals and it was the accepted practice that before two men began such a fight they exchanged documents which said that neither cared for mortal wounds. In some contests the fighters would use a method of pulling their punches before the opponent was actually struck, thus giving one a victory 'on points'. This technique, also used in sword practice sessions, was called *tsumeru*. To be praised for one's tsumeru, especially in the heat of a contest, was one of the greatest compliments a swordsman could receive. This was, however, always difficult to achieve, and it was equally difficult to judge when a victory had been gained in the split second that the decisive blow was laid. This is very well illustrated in a famous scene in the film *Seven Samurai*. The duel is based on an incident that is supposed to have occurred in the career of the swordsman Yagyū Mitsuyoshi. The supposed loser in a fight with dummy swords was so convinced he had won that he made his opponent fight again with real swords. His rival, convinced of his own superiority, was reluctant to agree, and only fought with real swords when his opponent started to goad him. His skills were demonstrated beyond any doubt when he killed the man in the process.

Tsumeru techniques were of course the only acceptable form of 'full contact' when the final stage of a swordsman's training using real swords was reached. Tsumeru was brought to perfection by Miyamoto Musashi, who was an expert at tsumeru with real swords. According to one of the many stories told about him, he could so perfectly control the blow from a katana that he could sever a grain of rice placed on a man's forehead without drawing blood. Such self-control would establish a swordsman's skills beyond any doubt, but for lesser mortals sword practice in the Age of Warring States with dummy swords did lead to some rather odd-looking and unsatisfying contests. The need to avoid death or injury also placed sensei in a quandary when it came to assessing their pupils' progress. Prowess at tsumeru with real swords was probably the best guide to a budding samurai's attainment, but his entire mental and physical attitude would be under review, and an experienced sensei knew exactly what to look for.

There was one way in which a samurai could practise some of his swordsmanship skills in a real-life situation. This was by the execution of criminals. In *Hagakure* Yamamoto Tsunetomo records that 'last year I went to the Kase Execution Grounds to try my hand at beheading, and I found it to be an extremely good feeling.' Formerly, he tells us, all the young samurai were expected to have carried out a beheading by the age of about 15, and even five-year-olds could use swords to kill dogs. A more merciful alternative was to hack at bundles of bamboo or tatami mats.

The above techniques presupposed a situation where both opponents had drawn their swords and were facing squarely on to each other safely out of striking distance. But there was another set of sword techniques that laid the emphasis on drawing the sword and cutting in a single stroke. This was *iai*, whereby a series of moves were practised time and again to allow a samurai to draw the sword from his scabbard and deliver a deadly blow all in one rapid movement.

Practice with missile weapons allowed far freer range and more realistic simulation of battle situations. Hours would be spent at ranges loosing arrows and firing guns. The sublime skill of horseback archery could be honed by the practice of *yabusame*, the colourful sport still demonstrated at shrine festivals today. Dressed in hunting gear, the samurai would loose arrows from a galloping horse against a small wooden target. Practice in shooting at moving targets could be provided by shooting dogs, a speciality of the Hōjō family that drew scorn from Toyotomi Hideyoshi in 1590 when he confronted them with firearms.

Spear techniques from the saddle must have been practised, but there is a dearth of references as to how this was actually done. The nearest form of martial art to equestrian yarijutsu would appear to be *dakyū*. This was the Japanese equivalent of polo, and is said to have the same roots in Central Asia. Dakyū was played between two teams of five riders each. There was only one goal post, on which either red or white flags were raised when a team scored a goal. The game concluded when 12 balls had been played. Although popular in the Nara Period, dakyū went into a decline until being revived by the Shōgun Tokugawa Yoshimune (1677–1751) who was an enthusiast for the martial arts. Dakyū riders wielded a long pole with a net at the end, making the action more like mounted lacrosse than Western polo, but the benefits for training a mounted samurai are obvious.

Rest and relaxation

Samurai did not spend all their time fighting or practising for it. There was ample opportunity for rest and relaxation, and several of the samurai most renowned for their martial prowess were also famous for being patrons of the arts. The great swordsman Miyamoto Musashi, for example, was also famous as a practitioner of *sumi-e* (ink painting). Hōjō Sōun's testimony to his sons included the statement that the literary and martial arts were to be practised always, because letters were the left hand and military matters the right hand, so that neither should be neglected.

To some extent these two apparently opposite poles were quite closely connected. The administration of one's domains required much more than an ability to lead men into battle, and it is interesting to note how the activities chosen by samurai when 'off duty' reflected the primacy of their martial calling. For example, a visit to a castle by a travelling *biwa* player promised much more than mere entertainment. Such men specialized in retelling through epic poetry stories such as *Heike Monogatari*, the great *gunkimono* (war tale) that tells the story of the decline and fall of the Taira clan. A performance inside the inner chambers of a daimyō's yashiki would be an uplifting moral experience for a young samurai, who would hear the stories of the deeds of the samurai of the past. *Hagakure* stressed the correct mental attitude at this time. Inspiration to action was more important than any contemplation:

> There is something to which every young samurai should pay attention.
> During times of peace when listening to stories of battle, one should never

In this painted scroll we see a group of samurai enjoying a performance from the Noh theatre. (Yamauchi Shrine, Kochi)

say, 'In facing such a situation what should a person do?' Such words are out of the question. How will a man who has doubts even in his own room achieve anything on the battlefield?

Similar historical and exemplary themes occurred in the plays of the Noh theatre. The actors, dressed in period costume and with amazing masks and head dresses, provided an additional visual experience that would enhance a samurai's education about who he was and where he had come from. The game of *go*, whereby opposing armies of white stones attempt to surround and capture black stones on a board, was a lesson in strategy, not just a pastime. *Shogi* (Japanese chess) added a tactical dimension that made it into a war game.

Of all the pastimes in which a samurai could indulge none had more lore and tradition associated with it than the performance of the tea ceremony. Tea had originally been introduced to Japan as a means of keeping Zen monks awake for their nocturnal devotions. But in addition to its ubiquity as a beverage, tea drinking developed in this one highly specialized way that encompassed much of what a samurai valued in terms of aesthetic appreciation and sensitivity. The Way of Tea centred on the drinking of a bowl of green tea with like-minded companions in an artistically pleasing and aesthetically inspiring manner. The ceremony would take place in a tea room, which was often located in a teahouse set within a tea garden. The décor of a teahouse was traditionally very simple and rustic, although Hideyoshi, whose flamboyance in artistic matters was renowned, was known to make use of a tea room where the wooden beams were plated with gold. The guests would enter from the

One common form of entertainment for samurai was the chanting songs of a blind player of the biwa. Here Uesugi Kenshin is listening to a performer along with his closest retainers who are privileged to be with him. The biwa player may well be recounting tales from Japan's glorious samurai past.

SAMURAI RELAXING WITH A GAME OF GO
*c.*1600
Almost all the pastimes associated with the samurai had a direct relevance to their martial calling. The game of go, being played here in earnest, had obvious connections to strategic planning. It is played on a heavy wooden board using black and white stones, kept here in wooden bowls. The samurai in the centre, smoking a pipe, is wearing the standard kamishimo, which consists of hakama and a kataginu, the sleeveless jacket with projecting shoulders. It bears the mon of the Mōri family. On his head is an eboshi, a stiffened cap. Beside him is a lacquered hibachi containing smoker's implements. The samurai on the left is wearing a kamishimo of a more relaxed day-to-day variety. The standing samurai is wearing the 'shorts' known as han-bakama.

garden and take their places, after which the tea master, who was sometimes the daimyō himself, would join them through a separate door made deliberately low so that the tea sensei was forced to express his humility by crouching very low. A meal of exquisite design and quality might be served, but the centre of the meeting was always the tea ceremony itself, whereby the master boiled the water and served the tea in a strict formality that allowed his guests to appreciate every gesture and factor involved. They would admire the quality of the pottery used in the vessels, the reflection of the seasons in a flower arrangement or a hanging scroll in the tokonoma, the play of light in the garden outside, partially visible through the sliding screens. But most of all they would be enthralled by the motions of the tea master as his hands moved in a 'kata of tea' that would be reminiscent of the greatest exponent of swordplay.

The political pay-off from the tea ceremony was considerable. Information gathered from guests, political support confirmed by attendance, bonds of comradeship forged by fellow enthusiasts, gifts of priceless tea bowls and many other spin-offs arose from these gatherings. Nor should the socially competitive nature of the tea ceremony be overlooked. The Way of Tea sorted the aesthete from the boor and distinguished the patient man from the over-hasty. It revealed areas of self-control that would stand a samurai in good stead on the battlefield. It exposed his weaknesses under pressure. In the tea ceremony a samurai practised the inner martial arts where he had no sword but his wits, and no defence to a challenge but to draw on the fund of aesthetic knowledge he was required to possess.

A lesser-known pursuit of the samurai class, and one that had little connection to the martial arts, was the curious *kemari* (courtly football), an ancient game originally introduced from China that had been popular among court aristocrats in the Nara and Heian Periods. Oda Nobunaga was particularly fond of kemari, and there are several references to games in his contemporary biography. Kemari was non-competitive and involved passing the ball from one player to another and keeping it in the air. The ball, about eight inches in diameter, was made of deerskin and stuffed with sawdust. There could be a varying number of players, usually between two and eight. There was no tackling. When a player received the ball he was allowed to kick it in the air as many times as he liked in order to show his skill, shouting 'Ariya' every time he tapped it. Then he would pass the ball to another player with the cry 'Ari!' Kemari was played on a pitch called a

The most exquisite form of entertainment that a samurai could pursue was the performance of the Japanese tea ceremony, which had its origins in the complex contemplative world of Zen Buddhism. Here we see the thatched teahouse in the garden of the Kodaiji temple in Kyōto. The room actually used for the tea ceremony is in the foreground and has a circular window. To its right is the entrance that the host will use. As it is extremely low he has to crouch to enter, thus showing his humility.

The finest and most historic example of a daimyō's yashiki is the Hiunkaku pavilion. It was built by Toyotomi Hideyoshi and formed part of Fushimi castle. It was transferred to the Nishi Honganji temple in Kyōto. This is the view from the ornamental pond garden.

kikutsubo that was marked out by trees. The Heian aristocrats would grow trees in specific areas in their gardens so as to have a permanent pitch. Others grew trees in pots so that they could mark out the pitch in a way dependent on the number of people playing. The four trees used to mark out the pitch were normally a cherry tree, a maple, a willow and a pine.

There were simpler pursuits as well, of course. The more literate samurai composed poetry or whiled away their time in innocent pastimes like 'guessing the incense' or tea tasting. Stronger beverages provided a more boisterous outlet, and drinking dens flourished in castle towns. Prostitutes were readily available and a welcome relief for samurai hundreds of miles away from home.

Belief and belonging

Shintō, Buddhism and sacred warfare

The samurai was brought up in a world in which religion was all-pervading. Prayers were offered at the start of battles and banners were emblazoned with invocations of the gods of war, who were believed to take part in a righteous cause. On several occasions during the invasion of Korea a Japanese victory was ascribed to the intervention of supernatural forces. If a defeat ensued then blame could be directed towards the anger of the gods.

This wonderful example of a samurai's Zen-inspired garden is in Saigo Keiichiro's house in Chiran, near Kagoshima. The use of large rocks and clipped bushes, together with the 'borrowed scenery' from the buildings next door, creates an atmosphere of perfect tranquillity.

Zen Buddhism was noted above as a major influence on the tea ceremony, but this was just one sect among one of Japan's 'five formative traditions' (Shintō, Buddhism, Confucianism, Taoism and folk religion) that have intermingled over the centuries to produce a system that can be understood as an entity. Not only did the various religions mingle, but Japanese people have always participated in rituals from a number of different traditions. The one exception was Christianity, introduced by St Francis Xavier in 1549, and this attitude was partly to blame for its persecution. The willingness to accept different traditions is also recognizable in the attitude that Japanese religion is as much about doing as about believing. There is a strong ritual basis to Japanese religion, which was not separated from everyday life in traditional Japan. There were rituals for planting rice and rituals for harvesting it, as well as a host of other activities. In such ways the samurai, particularly those who still farmed on a part-time basis, remained close to the passing of the seasons and their religious roots.

Shintō was the name given during the 19th century to the indigenous religious beliefs of Japan that centred around the worship of a huge number of *kami* (deities), who were enshrined in shrines known as *jinja*, easily recognizable by the presence at their entrance of the characteristic *torii* (gateway). The Japanese have historically been quite content to do without precise conceptions of what kami are, its vagueness expressing something of true kami nature, a concept totally contrary to Western thought. Some kami are, however, quite precisely defined. Emperor Ojin, who reigned during the 3rd century AD, was deified as Hachiman the kami of war, whose veneration was associated strongly with the Minamoto family.

Samurai would not attend weekly religious services in temples and shrines. Instead, like Japanese people nowadays, they would visit a shrine when they had a need for prayer, such as at departure for war. When Oda Nobunaga set out on the march that led to his victory at Okehazama in 1560, he wrote a prayer for victory and deposited it at the great Atsuta shrine near present-day Nagoya. The kami would then be expected to aid him in his coming campaign. Rewards would be forthcoming if they did, and retribution in the form of burning a shrine was not unknown when prayers for victory were not answered.

Buddhism came to Japan by way of China in the middle of the 6th century AD. It was a profoundly different religious system, but Shintō and Buddhism had become so intertwined that the samurai of the Age of Warring States would have recognized little difference between the two, each of which made its own contribution to the religious milieu along with the other traditions. For example, from Shintō came a stress on purification and the avoidance of pollution, which causes offence to the kami. Death in battle required Shintō ceremonies to purify the site, as at the battle of Miyajima in 1555, which was fought on an island that was itself regarded as a Shintō shrine. A samurai's funeral, however, would be conducted according to Buddhist rites in the family temple.

By the time of the samurai, Japanese Buddhism existed as a number of different sects, and although much is made nowadays about the dominant influence of Zen Buddhism, a samurai of the Age of Warring States would be every bit as likely to belong to another sect. The original Nara sects tended to come under the patronage of the imperial court, while the Tendai and Shingon sects were esoteric in their approach. Their monks undertook arduous mountain pilgrimages and performed long mysterious rituals in their temples. Their centres were the holy mountains of Hieizan and Kōyasan respectively and were associated with the warrior monks described later in this book rather than with the samurai class.

The populist sects of Jōdo and Jōdo Shinshū, again associated with a link between religious belief and military activity, had numerous members among the samurai class. The latter drew in lower-ranking samurai through their tradition of ikki formation, which could cause serious conflicts of interest when a samurai was also a daimyō's vassal. A prime example was the situation that faced the young Tokugawa Ieyasu in the early 1560s. The Ikkō-ikki of Mikawa Province were among his greatest rivals, but several of his retainers were monto who embraced the Buddhist sect of Jōdo Shinshū and had various ties to its community, so when issues of armed conflict arose such men were placed in a quandary. For example, in the *Mikawa Go Fudoki* account of the battle of Azukizaka in 1564 we read that:

Tsuchiya Chokichi was of the monto faction, but when he saw his lord hard pressed he shouted to his companions, 'Our lord is in a critical position with his small band. I will not lift a spear against him, though I go to the most unpleasant sorts of hells!' and he turned against his own party and fought fiercely until he fell dead.

The Nichiren or Lotus Sect attracted several famous samurai including Kato Kiyomasa (1562–1611), who emblazoned the sect's motto on his banner. Nichiren, named after its founder, expressed a form of fanaticism akin to that of Jōdo Shinshū's Ikkō-ikki. Zen, by contrast, presented an image of detachment from the world and the achievement of enlightenment within oneself. The elements of detachment and separation had obvious echoes for a samurai who was going into battle and might not return, so it is fascinating to see that Zen's other influence on the samurai lay through the performance of the tea ceremony and the enjoyment of a garden. The tea ceremony also had overtones of Taoism, where the emphasis was on 'the way' of doing things, a concept also paramount in understanding the martial arts and their later expression as *bushidō*, the 'Way of the Warrior'.

Zen, Confucianism and the samurai

Confucianism, along with Zen Buddhism, was one of the main philosophical influences on the samurai. The adoption of Confucian ethics provided the model for the relationship between master and follower and ultimately for the Tokugawa shogunate, because Confucianism valued an ordered society where everyone knew his place. In Confucian eyes good government was based on virtue and example rather than on sheer military might. The most important ethical demands made by Confucianism were *ko* (filial piety) and *chū* (loyalty), both of which were fundamental to the ideals of the samurai. Another strong influence was the stress laid by certain Confucian scholars on the necessity to act and the primacy of action over thought. This laid the basis for the fanaticism that was to characterize much samurai behaviour at the time of the transition to modern Japan.

In applying Confucianism to swordsmanship the approach was to stress the ethical meaning of sword fighting, linking prowess in swordsmanship with the warrior's need to serve his master. Here Confucianism met that other great philosophical influence on samurai: the self-denying Buddhism of the Zen sect. Zen Buddhism related swordsmanship directly to the Buddhist goals of attaining enlightenment and moving towards the achievement of selflessness. By the blending of self and weapon through action the swordsman moved towards the goal of complete emptiness which was the aim of all Zen practices. Much has been made of the links between Zen and swordsmanship. In fact swordsmanship was the possession of no one philosophical system, and to Confucianism and Zen can be added the influence of the ancient Chinese classics, all of which came together to give the 'Way of the Sword', and with it the 'Way of the Warrior'.

The samurai and the ancestors

The most important way in which Japanese folk practices were expressed by samurai was through the importance they gave to the preservation of the memory of their ancestors. Through ancestor veneration the structure of social relationships within a samurai's family unit was extended to encompass the dead. This continuity was assured by a complex series of rituals designed to keep the ancestors peaceful and content in the successive stages through which they would pass. As we noted earlier, the samurai had the greatest respect for the deeds of his forebears on the battlefield who provided both a model and a source of inspiration.

In early Japan, however, the dead were treated with a mixture of fear and respect. The corpse was a major source of ritual pollution and required Shintō rites of purification, but the spirit of the dead person was also frightening, as it could linger in the realm of the living. These spirits of the dead were venerated and, to some extent, manipulated, along the journey they had to take in order to become an ancestral kami. The process was carried out through the rituals of Buddhism, and may be summarized as follows. The *shirei* (spirit of the recently dead) became a *hotoke* (Buddha). After a period of years there was a transformation to *senzo* (ancestor) and finally to a kami, as part of the collective spirits of the locality. These ancestral kami remained eternally in the land, and continued to work for its prosperity and that of the samurai family. This process was regarded as continuing as long as there was living memory within the family, otherwise it was lost, and the ancestral kami then had to be treated as a collectivity. There was, however, a class of wandering spirits known as *muenbotoke* (Buddhas of no affiliation), who either had no descendants to worship them, or were victims of violent or untimely death, and thus 'remain possessed by the worldly passion in which they died'. It was spirits such as these, often dead samurai slaughtered on battlefields, who provided the rich material for the numerous ghost stories and plays that made up the Noh dramas that many samurai must have enjoyed with a shudder.

The samurai on campaign

The military command structure

When peace was replaced by war the system of social organization described above was mobilized into a system of military organization and command. The closest retainers became the daimyō's officer corps. Takeda Shingen's celebrated 'Twenty-four Generals' acted in this role on a battlefield. Every daimyō also had an elite corps of samurai known usually as the *umamawari*, which literally means 'horse guards'. Oda Nobunaga furnishes the most colourful example,

Tokugawa Ieyasu and his closest retainers appear on this woodblock print. The Tokugawa mon is shown on the maku behind the great shōgun.

because his umamawari wore either red or black horō on their backs, making them instantly recognizable. Maeda Toshiie and Sasa Narimasa are but two famous names whose military careers involved service in Nobunaga's elite units. As one would expect from such a ruthless pragmatist as Oda Nobunaga, his horse guards were chosen according to military merit and not because they possessed any impressive ancestors. Several therefore hailed from quite modest backgrounds and rose to fame and fortune along with their master. When off duty, they enjoyed a privileged position in his inner circle, and while their military role was primarily to provide Nobunaga's bodyguard they would also lead attacks. As bodyguards they protected Nobunaga's field headquarters along with his pages and ashigaru archers and gunners. In 1568 they led the attack on Mitsukuri castle with their horō billowing in the wind.

The call to arms

When a call to arms took place the samurai such as the umamawari who inhabited the castle complex were immediately transferred from guard duty to campaign duty. For others some form of muster had to take place, and various documents survive to show how daimyō converted their part-time samurai into full-time fighters. The process depended on the degree of professionalism within a daimyō's system and the closeness of the ties between him and the vassals being summoned. An interesting example is provided by the samurai of Chosokabe Motochika (1539–99), who conquered the whole of Shikoku island using samurai who were also farmers. His followers were known as the *ichiryo gusoku* (owners of one suit of armour) which indicated their comparative poverty. They would tend their rice fields up to their knees in mud but with the boxes containing their precious suits of armour lying on the paths between the paddy fields and their spears thrust into the ground with their straw sandals dangling from them. When the alarm sounded they downed tools and became samurai once again. These 'minutemen' were sufficient when all that Motochika had to face were similarly equipped samurai in neighbouring provinces, but they proved to be no match for Toyotomi Hideyoshi when he invaded Shikoku in 1585. 'Their horses are large, long bodied and fierce-looking,' reported the keeper of a castle in Awa Province to Motochika, 'but we ride Tosa ponies that are mere dogs in comparison. Our saddles are made of wood. Our worn-out armour is stitched together with hemp yarn. I do not think we can win.'

Hideyoshi's own mobilization was a far more complex affair. He could call on his own virtually professional samurai, but as his conquests proceeded he was also able to summon other daimyō who had accepted vassal status to serve under him. The preparations for the invasion of Korea in 1592 provide some excellent examples. Goto Sumiharu, who held the fief of Fukue on the Goto islands, had an assessed income of 140,000 koku, which by the sliding scale in operation required him to supply 840 men for the Korean campaign. He actually provided only 705, broken down as shown in the following table:

Goto Sumiharu in person	1
Bugyo (army commissioners)	5
Messengers	3
Inspectors	2
Mounted samurai	11
Foot samurai	40
Samurai's armed attendants	38
Ashigaru	120
Priests, doctors, secretaries	5
Labourers	280
Boatmen	200
Total	705

The figures therefore include 220 fighting men but more than double that number of non-combatants who acted in a supportive function.

The samurai on the march

When an army was ready to march off, the samurai would be inspected and would watch and wait as their leader performed a number of rituals of departure. The most important act was to pray for victory. Certain Buddhist deities were particularly favoured as bringers of victory and destroyers of evil. One's enemies were of course evil by definition, so powerful gods like Fudo 'the immoveable one' would be enlisted to smite them down. Buddhist priests would offer up such prayers on a daimyō's behalf either by chanting or writing prayers on wooden sticks called *goma* which were ceremonially burned. Just before the fifth battle of Kawanakajima in 1564 Uesugi Kenshin offered up a prayer for victory at a nearby Hachiman shrine. The text, which has been preserved, consists largely of a catalogue of Takeda Shingen's misdeeds, beginning with the forced exile of his father. Kenshin lists seven categories of Takeda wrongdoing including several failures of a religious nature. Shingen, he states, had been remiss in overseeing religious ceremonies and had assigned secular authorities to supervise temples and shrines when he invaded Shinano. The prayers then posed a question and a challenge to Hachiman:

> Now that Shingen has destroyed Shinano's temples and shrines and exiled their priests, who could possibly respect the authority of the kami if they allow him to continue gaining victories?

The traditional farewell meal of *kachi guri* ('victory' chestnuts), *kombu* (kelp) and *awabi* washed down with sake was the last ritual of departure before the

A group of cheerful defenders of Hara in 1638 enjoying a well-earned meal break. They are sitting round two large rice tubs, eating their rice from bowls without chopsticks and drinking water from ladles. The solid palisade is shown in detail, but the total involvement of the community is illustrated by the presence of an undoubtedly female body outside the walls.

daimyō took his signalling fan and shouted 'Ei! Ei!' to which the samurai replied 'Oh!' As an example we may take the grand departure from Sosaengp'o castle in 1598 of Japan's great hero general Kato Kiyomasa:

> Kiyomasa put on his black laced armour, tightened the cords of his helmet…and taking along fifteen pages, fifteen messengers, twenty guns and thirty-five foot soldiers, jumped into a small boat, set up his standard and shouted 'Ei! Ei!'

An army on the march was a spectacular sight. The best-known images of thousands of samurai marching by come from woodblock prints of the Edo Period, where martial processions were required by the shōgun's part of the Alternate Attendance System. We see them armed to the teeth on their way to pay their respects to the shōgun, with flags flying and spears shouldered. A march to war a few decades earlier cannot have looked much different, and was attended by very strict discipline. Tokugawa Ieyasu's orders for behaviour during the advance to Odawara in 1590 run to 12 articles and include admonitions about marching order and prohibitions against letting horses stray loose in camp. The document ends with a warning that the 'gods and Buddhas will blast transgressors', but Ieyasu's own officers did quite a bit of blasting themselves. Gamo Ujisato noted that one samurai with a rather distinctive helmet was not keeping his place and ordered him to do so. On a further turn of inspection the man was out of place again, so Ujisato calmly drew his sword and lopped off the man's head. He gave the splendid helmet to someone else.

The night before a battle would be a lonely one for a samurai. These supposedly super warriors were only human after all, and felt fear. During the 14th century one samurai wrote to his wife and told her that he felt 'so alone' now that battle was imminent. It was a time for prayers to one's own personal choice of kami, and an opportunity to purify oneself by abstaining from sex, or by not eating venison, a meat that was regarded as ritually harmful. Alternatively a samurai could simply get drunk.

OPPOSITE PAGE
SAMURAI ON CAMPAIGN WITH ACCESSORIES
c.1590
This samurai, whose sashimono identifies him as a retainer of the Honda family, is dressed in the tosei gusoku (modern armour), the classic 'battledress' armour that became universal towards the end of the Age of Warring States. His body armour is an okegawa-dō, of which the breastplate, although composed of small plates, has been lacquered over to give an almost perfectly smooth finish. This was the basis of the armour issued to ashigaru. The sashimono is attached to the rear of armour by a hinged support (**1**). His helmet, the only trace of flamboyance in his otherwise sombre costume, is a momonari kabuto (peach-shaped helmet). The lacquered finish on all his armour plates is russet iron. (**2**) is a detail of the parts of Japanese armour that resemble brigadine. Small metal plates are sewn into hexagonal patterns inside a cloth bag. His weapon of choice is an arquebus, unusual perhaps for a samurai, but as he would have a man to keep him reloaded and supplied it was a perfectly practical proposition. About his person he carries a bamboo canteen, a powder flask and bullet pouch, a sleeping mat and ration bags. Behind him and to his left are a selection of personal items including feeding implements, a spare pair of sandals and a comb.

The samurai's experience of battle

When the day of battle dawned (and dawn attacks were quite common) the samurai moved into action. If the battle was not a sneak attack he might have been surprised to see crowds gathering to witness the spectacle. When Tachibana Muneshige assaulted Otsu castle in 1600 on behalf of Tokugawa Ieyasu the local townspeople turned out to watch. The slopes of Mount Hiei beside the temple of Miidera provided an excellent vantage point out of range of stray bullets, so they took along picnic boxes and settled down to enjoy the show.

Samurai combat

When a samurai entered battle he moved on to a stage to play the role for which his entire life and training had prepared him. Superman or coward, the samurai was about to move from theory to reality. He strove first to achieve an unclouded mind so that he could focus totally on the situation. His training in Zen meditative techniques would be helpful, as was the samurai lore he had absorbed. *Hagakure*, for example, advised that a samurai 'in approaching for the attack…does not forget to wait for the right moment. In waiting for the right moment he never forgets the attack.' But at least he knew he was not alone. He was surrounded by his comrades as he sat on his horse, or stood with spear in hand. His officers would have organized him, and somewhere near the spot where the largest flags were flying was his daimyō whom he had pledged to serve. Would he be thinking about the examples he had heard of his

The view from the courtyard of a samurai's country house in Chiran near Kagoshima. The roof is thatched with rice straw.

illustrious ancestors in similar situations in the past? How would he acquit himself? Would he take a head, or was this the day he died?

Perhaps the desire to be the first into the attack was uppermost in his mind? This was a potent source of samurai glory testified by many ancestral anecdotes. Suicidal advances and even cheating were readily enlisted to win this accolade for a particular samurai. At the battle of Uji in 1184 two samurai raced their horses across a river to be first into battle, and 400 years later the same obsession ruled. At the siege of Chinju in 1593 Kato Kiyomasa's standard bearer threw his master's standard over the wall to claim a place. On occasions carefully thought-out battle tactics had to be changed in case any rivalry negated the attack, the classic instance being the crucial move against Gifu castle as part of the Sekigahara campaign. Ieyasu entrusted its capture to a co-operative attack by Fukushima Masanori (1561–1624) and Ikeda Terumasa (1564–1613). It was agreed that both should advance together, but when Terumasa got a little ahead the two leaders almost came to blows. On the very night before the battle Masanori challenged Terumasa to a duel, but a sensible compromise was reached whereby Masanori attacked the front gate and Terumasa assaulted the rear.

The first battle of a young samurai's career was always a challenging and exciting experience. The young warrior would have absorbed all that he had been taught, and would be inspired by ideals such as those expressed in writing at the end of the Age of Warring States by the author of *Hagakure*:

> When on the battlefield, if you try not to let others take the lead and have the sole intention of breaking into the enemy lines, then you will not fall behind others, your mind will become fierce, and you will manifest martial valour. This fact has been passed down by the elders. Furthermore, if you are slain in battle, you should be resolved to have your corpse facing the enemy.

The baptism of fire happened for Takeda Shingen at the age of 15 at the siege of Umi no kuchi. His father eventually abandoned the siege and marched the army away, but in the early hours of the morning young Shingen, who was in charge of the rearguard, turned his detachment round and returned to the castle. As he had rightly anticipated, the garrison were off their guard and when Shingen attacked the castle fell. This was quite an outcome for a first encounter: to disobey your father's orders and win a battle on your own!

Takeda Shingen was however an unusually talented individual, and in taking account of the samurai's experience of combat we have to recognize that warriors differed greatly in their skills. A superior swordsman entering battle was in a totally different position from a poorly trained part-time farmer. A certain Maehara Chikuzen no kami would have had enough self-confidence to allow him to translate into the battle situation the following skills he had exhibited in his lord's castle:

Maehara Chikuzen no kami seated himself in a corner of a room and five or six men threw fans from a distance of about half a dozen paces. No sooner had he picked up his wooden sword than he cut down the fans before they could hit his body... He could also smash a sixty-two plate helmet...

The latter demonstration would have been the one most useful to repeat on the battlefield. In the press of battle the swinging of a sword was greatly restricted, and Japanese armour gave good protection, so it was rare for a man to be killed with one sweep of a sword blade unless the blow was so powerful that it would split an opponent's helmet in two. Sword fighting from a horse was not easy, because the normally two-handed katana then had to be used in one hand, but this disadvantage was somewhat overcome by the samurai's position above a foot soldier and the momentum of his horse. The process was helped by the curvature of the sword's blade, which allowed the very hard and very sharp cutting edge to slice into an opponent along a small area that would open up as the momentum of the swing continued to cut through to the bone. Historical records show that some samurai survived multiple cuts from sword blades. One victim was still alive after 13 strokes found their mark, and on a separate occasion a horse endured seven slashes.

The painted screens and scrolls of the period show much more use being made of spears from horseback than of swords. Ashigaru are run through, while rival horsemen are transfixed through the neck and lifted off their saddles like kebabs. At the battle of Kawanakajima in 1561 Takemata Hirotsuna was knocked off his horse with such force that his helmet was dislodged from his head. Other polearms were also used to great effect. At the battle of Anegawa in 1570 Makara Naotaka covered the retreat of the Asakura army by wielding a nōdachi with a five-foot-long blade from horseback. At the siege of Ulsan in 1598 Reizei Motomitsu spun his naginata 'like a waterwheel' to kill at least 15 Chinese soldiers.

The noise and confusion of a Warring States battle was considerably greater than had attended the fights of the Gempei War four centuries earlier. Armies were much larger and the introduction of firearms had added greatly to the cacophony. A vivid impression of the confusion of a battle is provided by Okochi Hidemoto's account of the siege of Ulsan in Korea in 1598. To divert the Chinese attack, a gate of the castle was opened and a sally was made on to the Ming flank:

But as friend and foe were all mixed up we could not fire our guns. A soldier who had sallied out and taken a head halfway down the slope had achieved the exploit of *yarishita* [being first to take a head with a spear], then our troops, without the loss of a single man, began to pull back.

Chosokabe Motochika, whose army of part-time samurai called the ichiryo gusoku enabled him to conquer the whole of Shikoku island, but proved to be no match for the professional army of Toyotomi Hideyoshi in 1585. This waxwork is in the Sakamoto Ryoma Memorial Museum in Noichi near Kochi.

As the two armies separated, firing began again and this finally drove back the Chinese. 'No brush could be equal to the task of painting a picture of this particular battle,' wrote Okochi Hidemoto, who added a note of sadness that this great battle fought in a distant land could not be personally witnessed by Hideyoshi himself. His master Ota Kazuyoshi, naturally, comes in for the most effusive praise:

Afterwards they performed the head inspection ceremony for the men's eleven meritorious heads. Kato Kiyomasa's men had taken one head.

Asano Nagayoshi's men had taken one head, but Ota Kazuyoshi's men had taken a total of nine heads. Everyone inside the castle noticed this and praised him, saying, 'While Kiyomasa owns half of Higo province, and Nagayoshi owns the whole province of Kai, they only took one head each, yet Kazuyoshi is a person of low degree and has taken nine heads. Indeed, he conducts himself as a fine, brave samurai.

Keinen adds that Ota Kazuyoshi received a bullet through his arm, which caused him great pain.

The clouds of smoke from arquebuses would have obscured a samurai's view in a way unknown to his ancestors, and would therefore frustrate him in the samurai's other legendary pursuit of seeking a suitable opponent for single combat. The wearing of distinctive sashimono went some way to correcting the trend, however, so that at Nagashino a samurai who took the head of a Takeda follower wearing a flag sashimono with an obviously personalized design believed he had killed a victim of some importance. This was confirmed after the battle when the head was identified as being that of Mochizuki Nobumasa, the cousin of the Takeda daimyō Takeda Katsuyori. During the Korean campaign high-ranking Chinese or Korean officers stood out because of the quality of their armour and became prime targets for glory-seeking samurai.

A fitting conclusion to this section is the rich account of samurai behaviour on the battlefield that occurs in Okochi Hidemoto's description of the capture of Namwon in Korea in 1597. Several of the points mentioned above appear in this vivid report. He begins by telling us how ashigaru scoured the nearby fields, cutting the rice crop which would otherwise soon have been harvested and tying the stalks into large bundles which were thrown into the moat at a chosen position. So many were collected that a huge and unsteady mound extended to the level of the ramparts. While arquebuses raked the walls with fire, bamboo scaling ladders were added to the pile ready for a determined assault. As the ramp neared completion fire arrows were loosed at the nearest tower, and when this was set alight the samurai rushed on to the huge heap of rice bales. We then see the traditional competition to be first into battle. Kishi Rokudayu, later to be credited with taking the first head at Namwon, was among the leaders, to be passed on his progress along the ramp by Okochi Hidemoto, who became the first actually to touch the wall. He heaved his body on to the parapet while behind him swarmed the ashigaru, whom Hidemoto refers to as 'our inferiors'. He shouted for the flags to be brought up as quickly as possible and, led by his lord Ota Kazuyoshi, dropped down into Namwon. Every warrior proclaimed his name like the samurai of old, even though their intended victims could not speak Japanese, and numerous single combats began as the civilians huddled in their homes. Okochi Hidemoto killed two men, and:

Graciously calling to mind that this day was the fifteenth day of the eighth lunar month, the day dedicated to his tutelary kami [Hachiman] Dai Bosatsu, he put down his bloodstained blade and, pressing together his crimson-stained palms, bowed in veneration towards far off Japan. He cut off the noses and placed them inside a paper handkerchief which he put into his armour.

Very soon the Japanese assault party was faced with a counterattack from mounted men, yet even in all this confusion and danger the personal credit for taking a head was all important:

Okochi cut at the right groin of the enemy on horseback and he tumbled down. As his groin was excruciatingly painful from this one assault the enemy fell off on the left-hand side. There were some samurai standing nearby and three of them struck at the mounted enemy to take his head. Four men had now cut him down, but as his plan of attack had been that the abdominal cut would make him fall off on the left, Okochi came running round so that he would not be deprived of the head.

Nearby a bizarre encounter took place between a group of Japanese and a giant Korean swordsman seven feet in height. He was dressed in a black suit of armour, and as he swung his long sword a samurai thrust his spear towards the man's armpit, only to catch his sleeve instead. At the same time another Japanese caught the man's other sleeve with his spear, ensuring that the warrior was now pinioned like a huge rod-operated puppet. He continued to swing his sword arm ineffectively from the elbow 'as if with the small arms of a woman', but the reduction of this once formidable foe drew only scorn from Hidemoto. Impaled on two spears, and waving his arms pathetically, he reminded Hidemoto of the statues of Deva kings in Buddhist temples with their muscular bodies and glaring eyes. With contempt and ridicule from his attackers the helpless giant was cut to pieces.

Soon Hidemoto himself became a casualty. He was attacked by a group of Koreans and was knocked to the ground. As he was getting up, several sword cuts were made to his chest, leaving him crouching and gasping for breath. His comrade Koike Shinhachiro came to his aid while Hidemoto parried five sword strokes with the edge of his blade. A sixth slash struck home, cutting clean in two the middle finger of his bow hand, but he still managed to rise to his feet and quickly decapitated his assailant. Advancing more deeply into Namwon's alleys, Hidemoto encountered another strong man dressed magnificently in a fine suit of armour on dark blue brocade. Hidemoto 'was cut in four places on his sleeve armour, and received two arrow shafts that were fired deeply into his bow arm in two places', but in spite of these wounds he managed to overcome

The details of a samurai's most elaborate costume, together with delicate lacquerwork utensils, are shown in this waxwork in the Date Masamune Historical Museum in Matsushima. It depicts Date Masamune at the time of his wedding.

the man and take his head. No one on the Japanese side was able to identify it, but after a short while it was shown to some Koreans who had been captured alive. 'They were taken aback, and as they looked at it in anger tears began to flow' when they identified it as none other than the Korean commander.

Wounds, death and suicide

Samurai were tough characters. A messenger during the siege of Hara in 1638 received a bullet in his pelvic region, but immediately rose to his feet and delivered the message. He was then shot again and died. A seriously wounded samurai, however, would be likely to die on the battlefield because medical treatment was either primitive or unavailable, although doctors do appear on the muster lists for some campaigns. The cuts produced by samurai swords must have led to hundreds of warriors simply bleeding to death. Minor cuts could, however, by treated by applying *yomogi* (mugwort), a known coagulant. Acupuncture was also available. A medical manual of the 14th century quoted by Thomas Conlan includes the following recommendation for dealing with abdominal wounds:

Cover the intestines with dried faeces, then close the wound with mulberry root sutures and spread cat-tail pollen over the area. Activities to be avoided were anger, laughter, thought, sex, activity, work, sour foods and sake.

Somehow one imagines that a recuperating samurai might not have much trouble avoiding laughter, but it is interesting to note the use of horse faeces two centuries later. According to *Hagakure*, Amari Tōzō of the Takeda army was faced with a samurai who had received a deep wound and whose blood would not clot. Tōzō ordered him to drink the faeces of a red-haired horse mixed with water. The man was most reluctant to take his medicine until Tōzō set the useful example of drinking some first.

There is an extraordinary comment by Yamamoto Tsunetomo in *Hagakure* that 'even if one's head were to be suddenly cut off, he should be able to do one more action with certainty'. Only when a samurai's corpse was lying still on the ground could he be considered no longer a danger, and dead samurai whose corpses were left on a battlefield were likely to be buried in mass graves. Local priests would often undertake this necessary task.

Some anonymous individuals might have grave markers erected for them to help them on their way to becoming a kami, but prominent samurai had none of these problems. A daimyō was surrounded by so many bodyguards that for a man of his status to be killed in action was a very unusual occurrence. A far more likely fate for a defeated daimyō was for him to commit suicide, and there were many historical examples to inspire him. For example, the suicide of Minamoto Yorimasa when he had been defeated at the battle of Uji in 1180 was always valued for the precedent it had set. Yorimasa had chosen to disembowel himself rather than fall into the hands of the enemy, and had performed the act of *hara kiri* with great finesse. He had retired to a quiet temple, and wrote a farewell poem on his war fan before cutting himself open. During the battles of the Age of Warring States Yorimasa's death was always there as a folk memory to provide the perfect example of how a defeated warrior should take his leave of the world, and the battlefields of Japan were to see hundreds of similar acts performed. Several outshone Yorimasa by some very dramatic variations, so Yorimasa's act of hara kiri therefore became remembered more for its precedence that for its means of execution.

Most surviving descriptions of hara kiri relate to samurai who had been ordered to kill themselves as an alternative to a degrading execution. In these cases the deed was performed off the battlefield, so there was time, and enough peace and quiet, to allow it to be carried out with sufficient finesse. Akechi Mitsutoshi, for example, committed hara kiri in 1582 and wrote a farewell poem on the door of the room using the blood from his severed abdomen. The isolation of the inner rooms of a castle keep under siege provided the only real privacy in a battle. It was in the keep of Fushimi castle that Torii Mototada cut himself open in 1600. His blood, including a handprint, stained the floor, which was then preserved as a trophy by making it into the ceiling of a temple.

In the situation of a field encounter the most a defeated samurai could hope for was to kill himself quickly while his most loyal followers protected the place with a hedge of spears. At the battle of Awazu in 1184 Imai Kanehira dived off his horse with his sword in his mouth. Alternatively the samurai who was resolved to die could simply charge headlong into the enemy lines and be met by a hail of arrows or bullets. The samurai's personal retainers might then choose to follow him in death. When the above-mentioned Reizei Motomitsu was killed at Ulsan his three closest retainers had become temporarily separated from him. When they found he had been killed they immediately committed suicide on the same spot.

The fate of the vanquished

Contrary to the popular image of all samurai fighting to the death or committing mass suicide when a battle was lost, most battles had many survivors. There are several example of entire armies, including defeated generals, being absorbed into a victor's ranks with little moral concern. The one frequent and tragic exception was the actual defeated daimyō and his immediate family. They might well be put to death or forced to commit hara kiri so that there was no focal point left for a revival of the family. This practice is perfectly illustrated by Oda Nobunaga's report on his defeat of Asakura Yoshikaga in 1573. It includes the words: 'I forced Yoshikaga to commit suicide and sent his head up to the capital. I took the majority of his troops into my service.' A generous alternative was to allow the defeated daimyō to renounce the world and become a monk. Kōyasan, the holy mountain of Shingon Buddhism, was a common destination for such religious exile, but there was always the danger that when circumstances changed the former daimyō might return to reclaim his inheritance. When the Amako family were defeated by Mōri Motonari, their leader Amako Yoshihisa became a monk. His former retainer Yamanaka Yukimori, however, was unwilling to give up the struggle, but Yoshihisa was unwilling to return, and in fact lived peacefully until 1610. Instead Yukimori persuaded Amako Katsuhisa, Yoshihisa's second cousin, to renounce his own monkish vows and return to lay life. As an alternative to a monastery the place of exile might be a distant island. Ukita Hideie, who commanded the Japanese forces during the Korean expedition, chose the losing side at the battle of Sekigahara in 1600 and was banished to the tiny island of Hachijōjima. He lived to be 90 years old, dying in exile in 1662.

Below daimyō level there were no moral qualms on either side about defeated warriors fighting for a victor, and the Takeda family provide an excellent example. Several of Takeda Shingen's celebrated 'Twenty-four Generals' entered

Takeda Shingen's service in this way, and when Shingen's heir Takeda Katsuyori was in his turn defeated by Tokugawa Ieyasu in 1582, many of his former followers joined the Tokugawa. Individual survivors of a lord who was either dead or disgraced might fare less well. A samurai who had lost his lord was known as a *rōnin* ('man of the waves'), and was readily available for re-employment. The 'seven samurai' in the famous film are all rōnin who are recruited to defend a village against bandits. The reality of the Age of Warring States meant that rōnin did not have to be contented with such lowly employers but could sell their service to any ambitious daimyō.

The one stark reality that militated against such a tidy transfer of allegiance was the enduring samurai tradition of taking an enemy's head as proof of duty done. Every samurai who went out to fight appreciated that, to paraphrase the words of Tokugawa Ieyasu before the battle of Sekigahara in 1600, there were two alternatives: either to come back with an enemy's bloody head in your hands, or to come back minus your own.

Head collecting is a tradition found throughout samurai history. For example, in the chronicle *Yamamoto Toyohisa Shiki*, which refers to the Osaka Campaign of 1614–15 we read: 'That night twenty three heads were taken. At dawn on the seventeenth day twenty four men were summoned before

This detail from a painted screen depicting the battle of Nagakute depicts a quite unusual event. A samurai is taking a defeated enemy prisoner and tying his hands behind his back. This would normally only happen with high-ranking enemies whom a victorious daimyō sought to humiliate by a public execution.

ABOVE LEFT

Great ritual attended the collection and presentation of heads. In this scroll in Ogaki castle we see the task of dressing and preparing a head. This was normally done by women, and in this case is taking place on a battlefield. A dead warrior's sword and armour lie at the rear. A paper label attached to the pigtail identify the victim and the brave samurai who has taken the head.

ABOVE RIGHT

In another section from the Ogaki scroll a woman contemplates two severed heads brought to her for her attention, while other trophies hang from a rack in the background.

Hideyori…and received rewards of gold.' It was a practice that probably has roots in folk tradition because the handling of a corpse went wholly against the purity dictated by Shintō. When a battle was won the taking, recording and presentation of these ghastly trophies was as systematic and as thorough as the battlefield situation allowed. In an ideal situation of a clear-cut victory the heads would be viewed in a highly ritualized ceremony by the victorious daimyō, who was seated on a camp stool and surrounded by his closest retainers. He would not wish to be presented with a bloody trophy, so the heads were carefully cleaned and dressed, the hair combed, and the resulting trophy made presentable by cosmetics. They would then be mounted on a spiked wooden board with labels for identification.

This routine was a task traditionally done by women, and there exists a rare eyewitness account that was recorded by Oan, the daughter of a samurai. She experienced the horror of sleeping beside a collection of severed heads in Ogaki castle at the time of the battle of Sekigahara in 1600. The castle was under constant attack from the superior forces of Tokugawa Ieyasu, and her description of her work with heads is as follows:

My mother and I, as well as the wives and daughters of the other retainers, were in the castle's keep casting bullets. Severed heads taken by our allies were also collected in this area of the castle. We attached a tag to each head in order to identify them properly. Then we repeatedly blackened their teeth. Why did we do that? A long time ago, blackened teeth were admired as the sign of a distinguished man. So, we were asked to apply a generous coat of black dye to any heads with white teeth. Even these severed heads no longer held any terror for me. I used to sleep enveloped by the bloody odour of those old heads.

Two samurai appear on this painted scroll in the Ishikawa Prefectural History Museum to show a typical costume worn out of armour. They are wearing tight fitting trousers and loose haori (jackets). They have wide straw hats, and their two swords – the mark of a samurai – are thrust inside their belts.

The identification of the head and the name of the samurai who had taken it was a crucial factor if credit for the deed was to be correctly ascribed. This was a change from the situation in the 12th century, when quantity had mattered more than quality and a wounded man who survived to daybreak on a battlefield was a very lucky fellow. By the time of the Age of Warring States the samurai who decapitated an abandoned or anonymous corpse became an object of scorn, and the heads of ashigaru taken in the heat of battle might often be discarded.

If the head-viewing ceremony was to be held with no time for preparation, the heads could be presented on an opened war fan with a paper handkerchief or some leaves to soak up any dripping blood. But it was unwise to rush, and sometimes a victorious general was too ready to relax and enjoy the head inspection after his victory. On one celebrated occasion this led to a victory being turned into a defeat. Imagawa Yoshimoto was viewing heads taken from a captured fortress as he rested in a narrow wooded gorge near Okehazama in 1560. A few minutes later he was surprised by Oda Nobunaga and was himself beheaded.

There were, however, times when head collecting was very difficult or even had to be discouraged. When Hōjō Ujiyasu was preparing for the night attack that saved Kawagoe castle in 1545 he issued orders forbidding the taking of heads so that his samurai would not be distracted from the primary aim of the campaign. A less draconian measure was to allow heads to be taken but then discarded, with rewards being subsequently granted on the basis of reliable eyewitnesses. Head collecting also presented problems if it was found that once a samurai had taken a valuable head he would abandon the fight, secure in his proof of duty accomplished. This was hardly conducive to the achievement of victory. It was also found that a battle could be disrupted because a samurai trying to take a head attracted five or ten enemy samurai to try and stop him. One samurai during the 14th century returned with a piece of his victim's armour because the press of battle was too great to allow him to hack off the man's head.

TSUGARU NOBUHIRA TAKES POSSESSION OF HIROSAKI CASTLE, 1610

The Tsugaru family became the dominant family in the far north of Japan, a position they strengthened by their support for the Tokugawa family at the time of Sekigahara. In this plate Tsugaru Nobuhira (1586–1631) marches proudly through the snow to take possession of his newly built castle of Hirosaki. The most prominent motif is their mon of a swastika, which appears on the jingasa and breastplates of the lowly ashigaru and in gold upon the red sashimono of the samurai. Red swastikas also appear on the numerous white nobori flags. The ō uma jirushi uses different religious symbolism as it is a huge three dimensional shakujo, the metal-ringed rattle used by the wandering yamabushi to drive away wild animals from the route of their mountain pilgrimages. Tsugaru's shakujo is lacquered gold. His lesser standard is a gold disc on white. The ashigaru standard bearer with the shakujo has it tied firmly to his back using a specially strengthened sashimono holder. Two of his comrades hold a steadying rope each, while the standard bearer holds a further two.

This well is in the courtyard of the preserved samurai house called the Ogawa House in Kochi on Shikoku island.

The invasion of Korea presented the logistical problem of shipping heads home to their commander-in-chief Toyotomi Hideyoshi. Hideyoshi's increased irrationality made him demand proof that his generals were carrying out his wishes, so a compromise was reached. When Namwon, the first objective of the 1597 invasion, was captured, out of the 3,726 heads counted that day only the head of the Korean general was kept intact. The others were discarded after the noses had been removed, the beginning of the process of nose collection in lieu of heads that was to become a horrible feature of the second invasion. Toyotomi Hideyoshi began to receive a steady stream of shipments of noses pickled in salt and packed into wooden barrels, each one meticulously enumerated and recorded before leaving Korea. In Japan they were suitably interred in a mound near Hideyoshi's Great Buddha, and there they remain to this day inside Kyōto's least-mentioned and most often-avoided tourist attraction, the grassy burial mound that bears the erroneous name of the Mimizuka, the 'Mound of Ears'. The largest contribution to the Mimizuka came after the battle of Sach'on in 1598 when the noses were sliced off 38,700 Korean and Chinese heads.

The final ritual of victory was the recording of the exploits. The record of heads taken during a battle was a very important document. The following extract from Okochi Hidemoto, which refers to the siege of Namwon, is an excellent example. The heads are listed in four sections relating to the four walls of Namwon and it is not surprising to find that Okochi begins with the exploits of his own unit under Ota Hida no kami Kazuyoshi. Unlike the practice on a Japanese battlefield, only one of the heads is actually identified:

First. The retainers of Ota Hida no kami in the vanguard:
Resident in Echizen province – Kutsumi Heizo – two heads taken
Resident in Mikawa province – Ōkōchi Shigeza'emon – three heads, including the General and Magistrate of Kwangju, a general of 20,000 horsemen
Resident in Ōmi province – Kiyomizu Yaichirō – one head
Resident in Ise province – Toyoshima Kinza'emon – one head
Resident in Kii province – Danzuka Genshirō – one head
The first head at Namwon, [was taken by]
Resident in Kii province – Kishi Rokudayū – one head
Hida no kami's total heads – 119.

Head viewing did not only take place on the battlefield. It could be delayed until a more dramatic occasion presented itself. The classic instance is the New Year's banquet thrown by Oda Nobunaga in 1574, where the *coup de théâtre* was the presentation by his closest retainers of the heads of Asakura Yoshikaga, Asai Hisamasa and Asai Nagamasa. All had been taken in the previous year, and each had been preserved by being lacquered and coated in gold dust.

足軽

Part 2
Ashigaru

Introduction

The antecedents of the ashigaru may be traced to one of the earliest attempts by a Japanese emperor to control and systematize the owning and use of military force. To this end, Emperor Tenmu (reigned 673–86) envisaged a national army that was to consist largely of conscripted foot soldiers, but as they often absconded from duty the programme was eventually abandoned. By the 10th century the government began instead to rely on the military service provided by the landowning classes, whose possession of horses had already guaranteed their position as the 'officer class' of the conscript armies. These men were the first samurai, who were supported in their endeavours by scores of lower-class troops who at other times worked on the land. Some foot soldiers had long connections with a particular family or geographical area, and would tend to act in the capacity of *genin* (warrior's attendant). They would carry a samurai's equipment or act as grooms, and would also perform the important function of collecting the severed heads, each of which counted to their master's total. The genin would fight if necessary, particularly if the samurai's life was in danger, but samurai combat was largely regarded as a private duel in which the rival genin provided only a supportive function. Their service was valued nonetheless, and loyal genin occasionally received promotion to samurai status.

In a typical army there were other foot soldiers, however, to whom such ties of social obligation and personal service were either weak or non-existent. These men were often hastily recruited, badly trained and poorly armed. To the compilers of the epic chronicles of samurai warfare, they were almost invisible and invariably anonymous, and it is only through careful reading of the texts that their presence on the battlefield becomes apparent. Curiously, the neglect

of the foot soldier in the written accounts of battle is not to be found in the artistic works, such as scroll paintings and screens, which have survived from these times. The *Heiji Monogatari Emaki*, for example, includes numerous vignettes of soldiers who fight on foot. The artist has clearly taken great pains to show the contrast between the foot soldiers and the elite mounted samurai, whose armour is more extensive and more elaborate. In physical appearance too, the foot soldiers are painted as coarse, rough characters, with whiskered faces and with a noticeable lack of delicacy compared to their betters. Other examples show the contrast between samurai and foot soldiers in terms of the functions they perform. The samurai demonstrate prowess at mounted archery, while the mob of foot soldiers sets fire to buildings.

Foot soldiers appear occasionally in the early accounts as either combatants or victims. For example, in the chronicle *Azuma Kagami* for 1221 we read: 'Eastern warriors filled the neighbouring provinces, seeking out foot soldiers who had fled the battlefields. Heads rolled constantly, naked blades were wiped over and over.'

The first ashigaru

In 1274 and 1281 elite samurai, supported by foot soldiers, drove back the two Mongol invasions. Japan then enjoyed many years of comparative peace until an ill-fated attempt at imperial restoration led to the Nanbokuchō Wars, which were fought in the name of two rival emperors and lasted for much of the 14th century. Many of the actions of these wars were fought from defended positions in mountainous areas, and a new way of using archery was developed. Instead of single arrows being fired at targets by elite mounted samurai, huge volleys of arrows were launched into the enemy ranks by foot soldiers, a technique that had been used against the Japanese by the Mongols. The *Taiheiki*, the chronicle of the Nanbokuchō Wars (the 'Wars between the Courts'), refers to these lower-class archers as *shashu no ashigaru* (ashigaru shooters), the first use of the term 'ashigaru' in Japanese history. Out of 2,000 men who fought for the Sasaki at the battle of Shijo Nawate in 1348, 800 were these 'light archers'.

A century later the word 'ashigaru' appears again in the different context of the disastrous Ōnin War of 1467–77. The daimyō who rose to power needed fighting men, and for a landless peasant dissatisfied with his lot the lawlessness of the times offered a sellers' market. The name 'ashigaru' (light feet) indicated their lack of armour, footwear, or even weaponry until all three were looted from a defeated enemy. Such men found it easy to attach themselves casually to samurai armies, and then fight, pillage and ultimately desert.

An ambitious daimyō was therefore able to increase the numbers of his foot soldiers tenfold by the addition of such a loose and uncertain rabble. Unfortunately, it often turned out that men who had been casually recruited

would just as easily disappear to till the fields or swell the armies of an enemy. Untrained peasants attracted only by personal gain were also not the ideal candidates to fight in organized groups and wield increasingly sophisticated weapons. There was therefore a need for continuity, for the development of skills, and above all for the inculcation of the loyalty that was already expected from the daimyō's own men. Both these trends developed as the Age of Warring States continued and battles, sieges and campaigns grew larger in scale.

The final conclusion was a recognition that, although the ashigaru, whatever their origin, were different from the elite samurai, their fighting skills could be complementary. The successful daimyō was one who used foot soldiers in a combination of arms, controlled by samurai who valued the contribution they could make toward victory.

Here a gang of casual ashigaru overpower a defeated samurai who has crawled away from a battlefield. They wear a typical mixture of looted armour, and they seem set to add one more suit to their collection. (E. G. Heath collection)

Disciplining the ashigaru

Evidence of the increasingly important role of ashigaru is found in the numerous surviving suits of armour made for them. Known simply as *okashi gusoku* (loan armour), ashigaru armour was of plain construction, consisting of little more than a dō with kusazuri, together with a simple helmet called a jingasa. The existence of such armour shows that the daimyō who provided them now valued the service of the ashigaru sufficiently to give them armour rather than expecting

A wounded foot soldier falls to the floor with an arrow protruding from his eye socket. From the *Kasuga Gongen* scroll. (Courtesy of the Imperial Household collection)

them to turn up with their own. Also, nearly all okashi gusoku had the daimyō's mon stencilled on the front of the dō. A simple heraldic device was sometimes additionally carried on an identifying sashimono flying from the rear of the ashigaru's armour. Some, notably the Ii clan from Hikone, dressed all their troops in the same coloured armour. The combined effect of these moves was to transform the ashigaru costume into a military uniform.

The ashigaru's improved military status, however, was largely due to a change in the choice of weaponry allocated to them. During the heroic days of the Gempei War (1180–85) the primary samurai weapon was the bow, and prowess at archery was the most prized samurai accomplishment. Yet by about 1530 we see ashigaru used regularly as missile troops while the mounted samurai fight with spears rather than bows. From the 1550s onwards the ashigaru bows were augmented by firearms, but for these to be effective they had to be placed at the front of an army, the position traditionally occupied by the most loyal and glorious samurai. There was much honour attached to being the first to come to grips with an enemy. To place the lowest-ranking troops in such a position was a challenge to samurai pride, even allowing for an overall tactical plan that envisaged the ashigaru's fire merely breaking down enemy ranks ready for a spirited charge by samurai, at which point the ashigaru politely held back.

The development of ashigaru warfare

By the 1590s arrangements that placed the ashigaru at the front of an army had become commonplace, showing a profound difference in military attitude. Not everyone approved, and there exists a scornful comment in a later chronicle

From the time of the Ōnin War between 1467 and 1477 the power of the shōgun declined and samurai warlords began to assert their independence. This provided the opportunity for peasants to join armies on a casual basis, and such men were the original ashigaru. In this illustration is a peasant farmer whose only military equipment is a sword and shinguards. He retains his sickle and carries a sharpened bamboo pole as a spear. Men like these became ashigaru in the daimyō armies.

which laments that instead of ten or 20 horsemen riding out together from an army's ranks, there is now only this thing called 'ashigaru warfare'.

A major step forward was made in 1575 with Oda Nobunaga's victory at the battle of Nagashino. Nobunaga, who was faced by the prospect of a devastating cavalry charge against him by the renowned samurai of the Takeda clan, lined up all his arquebus squads into three ranks protected by a loose palisade. Under the iron discipline of his most experienced samurai the ashigaru gunners fired controlled volleys into the horsemen, killing or disorientating so many that they became prey for the samurai swords and spears. The firearms alone did not win the battle, which lasted for eight hours of bitter fighting, but Nagashino showed that victories could be won by a combination of samurai and ashigaru under firm leadership.

Under the rule of Toyotomi Hideyoshi (1536–98), the ashigaru became almost as professional as the samurai. Hideyoshi, who had risen from the ranks, understood ashigaru warfare better than most other daimyō. His father was an ashigaru in the service of Oda Nobunaga's father Oda Nobuhide. During a battle he was shot in the leg and forced to withdraw from all combat duties. As a result he lost the relationship he had with the Oda family and returned to the fields. His son, by contrast, rose through the ranks as he gained the confidence of Oda Nobunaga. After Nobunaga's death Hideyoshi fought a series of brilliant campaigns and went on to rule the whole of Japan, but once he had achieved his goal Hideyoshi began to pull up behind him the ladder of promotion that he had scaled so successfully. In 1588, when his conquest of the country was almost complete, he ordered the 'Sword Hunt', a nationwide confiscation of all weapons from the peasantry. It was an audacious move that no national leader had ever attempted before, but such was Hideyoshi's power that it was largely successful.

Following the Sword Hunt, the supply of casual ashigaru for hire virtually dried up, forcing all the daimyō in Japan to rely on their own men to form their armies, and then in 1591, with all the daimyō now acknowledging his suzerainty, Hideyoshi produced the Separation Edict to set this distinction in stone. It forbade any change in status from samurai to farmer, or from farmer to anything, whether merchant or ashigaru. This edict is extremely important in understanding the evolution of the ashigaru.

If there should be living among you any men formerly in military service who have taken up the life of a peasant since the seventh month of last year, with the end of the campaign in the Mutsu region, you are hereby authorized to take them under surveillance and expel them…

If any peasant abandons his fields, either to…become a tradesman or labourer for hire, not only should he be punished but the entire village should be brought to justice with him…

No military retainer who has left his master without permission shall be given employment by another…

Whenever this regulation is violated and the offender allowed to go free, the heads of three men shall be offered in compensation…

The final evolution of the ashigaru was to a uniformly dressed infantryman, as shown in this excellent illustration from *Zōhyō Monogatari*. Note how the ashigaru has thrust his two swords through his uwa-obi (belt) before putting his armour on. The two tube-like sleeves are tied at the front and rear. His long trousers are fastened in at the knee and the ankle. The two shoulder straps on the armour with their toggles, and the tying cords for the side, are clearly illustrated. His cloth tube of provisions is shown on the ground. Each tied section is a day's ration of rice.

The ashigaru of the defeated daimyō were therefore forbidden to return to the soil, and the newly disarmed farmers were finally and legally cut off from following in Hideyoshi's own illustrious footsteps. From 1591 onwards, therefore, we have a vastly different situation from the one that existed before. A peasant called up for service would in future be only a labourer, and any ashigaru carrying a heavy bullet box on his back could think himself lucky that, despite his lowly status, he had at least one foot on the rungs of the samurai ladder.

The process of implementing the Separation Edict was a long one, and was only completed by Hideyoshi's successor Tokugawa Ieyasu (1542–1616). The ashigaru were already recognized as the 'other ranks' of a Japanese army, without whom victory could not be gained. With the establishment of the Tokugawa hegemony there came a rigid separation of the social classes of Japanese society. At the top were the samurai, and the ashigaru were there among them, being from then on officially defined as the lowest ranks of the samurai class.

With this acknowledgement of the ashigaru as samurai came a further recognition in a remarkable and unique book produced by a leading commander of the time. This work, entitled *Zōhyō Monogatari*, which translates literally as 'The Soldier's Tale', was written in 1649 by a serving samurai who had command of ashigaru and wished to pass on to posterity his own tips on how to get the best out of them. The author was Matsudaira Nobuoki, the son of Matsudaira Nobutsuna who commanded the shōgun's forces during the

ASHIGARU LOOTING DURING THE ŌNIN WAR, 1467
The first men to be called ashigaru during the Age of Warring States are seen in this plate which illustrates a scene during the Ōnin War in 1467. The source is a painted scroll entitled *Shinnyodō Engi*. In typical fashion, this collection of ne'er-do-wells, who owe allegiance to no one but themselves, are looting houses and stores in Kyōto. They are rough characters, and have been helping themselves to looted sake. They first attached themselves to an army (whose it was they neither knew nor cared) during a recent raid, and have now slipped away from the main scene of the fighting to collect their reward in the form of unauthorized pillage.

Their equipment has been picked up from previous battlefields. Only one has any armour. It is already bloodstained and damaged, and the silk cords lacing the parts together are now so heavily cut that the whole ensemble is falling to pieces. The others appear to be wearing only a short kimono, a loincloth and a headband. Spears are used as levers to prise up floorboards in search of hidden treasures, while outside their more inebriated companions scatter documents and carry off strongboxes.

A jingasa, made of lacquered papier mâché, bearing the mon of the Tachibana.

Shimabara Rebellion of 1638, the last action in which samurai armies were to be engaged. As the Shimabara Rebellion was conducted by renegade Christian samurai and disaffected farmers, Matsudaira Nobuoki may have learned several lessons from observing the tenacity and fighting skills of his opponents. The real significance of *Zōhyō Monogatari* lies in the fact that it was written at all. The wars of the 12th century produced a literature that concentrated almost exclusively on the individual prowess of named samurai. *Zōhyō Monogatari* is a handbook for the commanders of ashigaru, a class of fighting man whom the writer of the *Heike Monogatari*, for example, preferred to regard almost as non-existent. By 1649 the ashigaru were recognized for the immense contribution they could make to samurai warfare.

Ashigaru recruitment

The history of the ashigaru is that of a move from a casual, poorly trained infantry arm towards a more professional organization with continuity of service, and nowhere is this better illustrated than in the methods of recruitment. The casual nature of ashigaru activity during the Ōnin War ensured that the rate of desertion often matched the rate of enlistment, and on some occasions an army could be swelled by bands of opportunistic ashigaru without the commander actually knowing they were there. Such men prowled around the extremities of a campaign like vultures, and were practically indistinguishable from the ghoulish peasants who roamed battlefields by night, finishing off wounded samurai and stealing their possessions.

In addition to this uncertain way of recruiting, the daimyō also drew foot soldiers from the men who worked his own lands. As the years went by, and such daimyō territories became more widespread, so the means of recruiting ashigaru became less haphazard and more systematic. The final stage in this evolution was the transformation of ashigaru into full-time soldiers.

Until about 1580 the pressure on resources ensured that most daimyō had to use their ashigaru in the dual roles of soldiers and farmers, and it was only when campaigns began to be of longer duration that problems arose with this system. It was then inevitable that the wealthier landowners, who could spare men for fighting without affecting agricultural production, would develop both economically and militarily. Success also bred success, because a victorious daimyō would attract followers for both purposes, thus making it even easier to arrange a division of labour. Some of the increase in numbers came from the opportunistic ashigaru who a century before would have moved on after a battle and now chose to stay, while a few managed to leave an unsuccessful daimyō for a more promising master. In some cases there was a wholesale movement of allegiance when defeated enemies were absorbed into a victor's hegemony.

The ashigaru barracks at Kochi. This building was once the outer limits of Kochi castle next to the river.

The call to arms

For most of the daimyō, therefore, the recruitment of ashigaru consisted simply of a call to arms among their part-time soldiery, tearing them away from their farms when danger threatened. The excitement of war, the very real prospect of promotion, and the break from the routine of agricultural work made up an inviting prospect to many. But a successful response to a call to arms depended on much more than the allure of a break from farming duties and had its basis in the feudal structure of Japanese society. A well-organized daimyō knew in minute detail the extent of the territory he owned, because registers of landholdings listed the lands granted to retainers, who held them in a system of mutual obligation. These men, who were of the samurai class, received lands from the daimyō, and in return were 'retained' in his service, hence the word 'retainer'.

The most important aspect of this retained service was, of course, to serve in the daimyō's army both in a personal capacity and also to provide other troops in the lord's service. This is how the ashigaru entered the story. The samurai knew exactly how many men he was required to take with him on campaign. Some would be other samurai who were usually related to him. The rest would be jizamurai or farmers who may not have had long family connections, but as the years went by and casual recruitment became less common, a family tradition of service to a particular samurai family would develop.

With promotion dependent almost entirely on performance, and performance being assessed in terms of the number of heads taken, the loyal and brave ashigaru could achieve at a personal level what Hideyoshi was to formalize in 1591 at a legal level, namely, the integration of the ashigaru into the samurai class as its lower ranks. The existing overlap between a poor landowning jizamurai and a well-rewarded ashigaru, therefore, became increasingly blurred until Hideyoshi and Ieyasu abolished the distinction by making them both 'samurai'. To misquote Napoleon, 'every ashigaru carried a general's war fan in his knapsack'.

Yet while there was an overlap between the ashigaru and the samurai above them, until 1591 there was an additional overlap between the ashigaru who carried equipment for a daimyō and the huge numbers of people who could be virtually press-ganged into an army when extra labouring work was needed. Hideyoshi's Separation Edict ensured that the only active service that peasants could now supply was as labourers, because weapon use was officially forbidden to them. Yet this was no drawback for a general, as the advances in military technology meant that, without training in group fighting with long spears and arquebuses, a peasant would be a liability in an army rather than an asset.

Prior to 1591, therefore, we see labouring and fighting duties being mixed up and allotted according to experience and need. An enhanced use of labourers and carriers is particularly apparent for campaigns of long duration such as sieges, when considerable demands were made on the population in numbers required and in the range of services offered. For example, the Takeda family operated a number of gold mines and the miners were ideal for tunnelling under an enemy's castle walls. A detailed muster list for similar non-combatant service is provided in the records of the Shimazu family of Satsuma in southern Kyūshū. In 1576 the Shimazu attacked the fortress of Takabaru, and in their call to arms listed many labouring duties in addition to fighting.

ASHIGARU OPERATING CATAPULT ARTILLERY, 1468

These ashigaru are operating catapult artillery during the Ōnin War on behalf of the Hosokawa. These are not casual troops; in times of peace they would work on the Hosokawa estates, so they are naturally loyal, if poorly trained. The cohesive nature of their employment is an asset for the task to which they have been allotted, which is to launch delayed action firebombs by catapult, a task requiring both discipline and timing. Such men would have to supply their own armour and equipment. For the job of pulling on catapult ropes, however, armour would get in the way, so they have abandoned it for now. Pulling simultaneously on long ropes on a Chinese-style catapult, they fling large soft-cased fireball bombs into the Yamana lines under the eagle eyes of a samurai guard and a foot soldier. Another man, who probably supervised the making of the bomb, drags a fireball into position for it to be loaded and the fuse lit.

This plate is based on detailed contemporary descriptions of such operations, with a number of assumptions being made. Medieval illustrations of the use of traction trebuchets in Europe suggest that the crew pulled the ropes vertically downwards to launch a projectile. By contrast, Chinese illustrations usually show a very large number of ropes, which would have been impracticable unless the haulers stood away from the machine and pulled in a roughly horizontal direction. This is the arrangement deemed appropriate for this reconstruction. The other assumption is that a man would have given tension to the sling by holding on to the projectile until the last moment, hence the extra operatives shown here.

The development of permanent ashigaru units

At the other end of the ashigaru social scale were the elite ashigaru who were kept almost permanently 'under the colours', a state of affairs that was confined to a daimyō's personal bodyguard for much of the period under examination. A good example is provided by the Hōjō family. The Hōjō, who were based around the area of present-day Tokyo, prospered as successful daimyō over five generations until their castle of Odawara surrendered to Toyotomi Hideyoshi in 1590. A samurai called Okamoto Hachirōza'emon Masahide belonged to the Hōjō's umamawari based at Odawara castle, and had to supply his own personal service with horse, plus four unmounted samurai, six ashigaru spearmen, two ashigaru flag bearers, and two others who would act as reserves.

Both Okamoto and the ashigaru under his command were based permanently in Odawara castle. Not only is the weaponry of his followers recorded, but also their names, indicating the continuity of service that was later to become universal. The names of his men do, however, show one fundamental difference between samurai and ashigaru, because the four samurai have surnames, while the ashigaru have none. Any ashigaru who fought his way to samurai status soon took a surname, of which one of the written characters was often derived from the surname of his master or an admired ally. This neat illustration of class distinction reminds us that even though the ashigaru service was definitely valued, the samurai still regarded them as their social inferiors.

In contrast to Okamoto's contribution to a permanent unit, another retainer of the Hōjō called Ōtō Nagato no kami was called upon to supply a contingent of 252 men at the time of the Odawara campaign in 1590. The numbers

Ashigaru with guns, from a scroll in Shinshiro Museum.

This illustration is from a modern Japanese comic book by the accomplished manga artist Junko Miki, and it shows a group of ashigaru resting on a battlefield. Their long spears and cloth sunshades are well depicted.

were made up from 75 mounted samurai, 36 foot samurai, 115 ashigaru and 26 labourers. Most of these men would still be part-time farmers, showing how far behind the Hōjō were in military development compared to their rival Toyotomi Hideyoshi.

An earlier example of a Hōjō 'call to arms' is the document issued in about 1560 by Hōjō Ujimasa (1538–90), which shows how a farmer on standby could quickly become an ashigaru:

1. All men, including those of the samurai class in this country district, are ordered to come and be registered on the 20th day of this month. They are to bring with them a gun, spear, or any kind of weapon, if they happen to possess one, without fearing to get into trouble.
2. If it is known afterwards that even one man in this district concealed himself and did not respond to the call, such man, no matter whether he is a commissioner or a peasant, is to be beheaded.
3. All men from 15 to 70 years of age are ordered to come; not even a monkey tamer will be let off.
4. Men to be permitted to remain in the village are those whose ages are above 70 years, or under 15 years, and too young to be used as messengers, but the others are all ordered to come.

5. It will be good for the men to prepare for the call by polishing their spears and preparing small paper flags to be taken with them. Those who are fitted to be messengers, and desire to do that service, will be so permitted.

6. All the men covered by this order are to come to Katsukui on the 4th day and register before the lord's deputy and then return home. If the appointed day happens to be rainy they are to come the first day the weather is settled. Men must arrive at the appointed place properly armed with anything they happen to possess, and those who do not possess a bow, a spear or any sort of regular weapon are to bring even hoes or sickles.

7. This regulation is generally applicable, and even Buddhist priests who desire to do their duty for their native province are ordered to come.

It is ordered to pay strict attention to the implications of the above seven articles, and if there be anyone who disregards this ordinance and neglects his duty, such a one is to be severely punished; while the man who is careful and eager to be loyal to his lord will be rewarded with the grant that is reasonable and suitable to him.

Rapid response

The invasion of one's province by an enemy did not allow the leisurely assembly described above. In such a situation the farmers not only needed to become ashigaru within hours rather than days, which implied considerable readiness and preparation on their part, but the clan itself needed an efficient internal communications system to enable the call to arms to be transmitted rapidly. The most successful daimyō to tackle this problem was Takeda Shingen (1521–73), one of the greatest military leaders of his age, who established a series of fire beacons known as *noroshi* throughout his territories. The noroshi were elaborate devices mounted on a three-storey wooden tower. The watcher, who was probably an ashigaru, stationed himself on the upper platform, while the beacon itself consisted of an iron bucket mounted at the end of a long tree trunk pivoted in its centre from a bracket fastened to the upper storey. On spotting the signal from the next beacon along, the watcher would hurry down the ladders and set fire to the combustible materials already prepared in the bucket. By pulling on ropes, the beacon bucket would be swung high into the air. The system allowed observers on the edges of the Takeda territories to communicate directly with Kōfu, the Takeda capital, by a series of beacon chains.

Fire beacons were supplemented by fast horses ridden by scouts who passed the call on to local runners. By such means the population of the Takeda territories was transformed into a fighting machine, multiplying tenfold the

small permanent garrisons of samurai and ashigaru as well as the large, 3,000-plus unit that made up Takeda Shingen's personal bodyguard. In later years, of course, practically an entire daimyō's army would be permanently 'under the colours', but in the mid-16th century the basis of ashigaru use was the call to arms from part-time soldiers.

Organization and command of ashigaru

Once the daimyō began to realize that their ashigaru were a precious asset that should not be forgotten at the end of a campaign, systems of organization were introduced that paralleled the move towards structured systems of recruitment and retention. The organization of ashigaru took two forms: a hierarchical command structure, which was invariably headed by samurai, and a horizontal specialization of the three weapon groups of arquebus, bow and spear.

The overall command of the specialized ashigaru units was vested in respected and reliable samurai who were usually known as *ashigaru taishō*. Evidence that they were as highly regarded as commanders of purely samurai units is provided by the appearance of men bearing the rank of ashigaru taishō within the elite of the Takeda family who were known as the 'Twenty-four Generals'. Saigusa Moritomo, killed at the battle of Nagashino in 1575, was an ashigaru taishō, as was Hara Toratane who, it was said, could make ten ashigaru fight like 100 samurai.

The highest of the actual ashigaru ranks was the *ashigaru kashira* ('captain'). The ashigaru kashira would have command of an ashigaru company, which was more than likely to be homogeneous in terms of weapon function. The one exception to this was the inclusion of archers among the arquebus corps to keep up the fire during reloading, as illustrated by the *Kōyō Gunkan*, which notes a unit of 'ten arquebuses and five bows'.

Beneath the ashigaru kashira were the *ashigaru ko gashira* ('lieutenants'). In the *Kōyō Gunkan* one ashigaru kashira has five ashigaru ko gashira serving under him to command his company of 75 archers and 75 arquebusiers, so that every ko gashira has responsibility for 30 men. The ashigaru ko gashira was a vital element in the chain of command because the ordinary ashigaru in their weapon squads served directly under him. The *Zōhyō Monogatari* notes how a ko gashira was selected:

> In the firearms squads they were chosen on the basis of marksmanship and speed of fire, the possession of a calm spirit, one who would not disengage when the enemy bullets began.

Weapon specialization – arquebuses and bows

The sideways division of the ashigaru was by weapon speciality, between arquebus, bow and spear. In 1592 the Shimazu army that went to Korea included 1,500 archers, 1,500 arquebusiers and 300 spearmen, while in 1600 the Date family supplied the Tokugawa with 200 archers, 1,200 arquebusiers and 850 spearmen. One trend that can be readily identified is an overall increase in the

Ashigaru on the march. The daimyō is being carried in a palanquin.

Oda Nobunaga is attended by ashigaru spearmen who are wearing okegawa-dō (smooth-surfaced breastplates) with the kusazuri tied up so as not to impede their progress in wooded countryside, from *Ehon Toyotomi Gunki.*

The teppō ko gashira were the lieutenants of the firearms squads. This man (from *Zōhyō Monogatari*) would have direct command of the arquebusiers. His badge of office is his red-lacquered 'swagger stick', which is a bamboo tube in which is concealed a sturdy ramrod. The swagger stick could be used by an arquebusier should his own ramrod break. The ko gashira also has a spare length of fuse wrapped round his left arm.

OPPOSITE RIGHT

An ashigaru armed with his arquebus. He has placed a set of spare ramrods in a cloth in his belt like a quiver of arrows, lest one should break. His fuse is tied around his left wrist.

number of firearms possessed, even if the proportion of them to other arms varies considerably. By 1530 missile weapons in the form of bows had already tended to become the province of the lower-class warrior, leaving the samurai free to engage in spear fighting at close quarters with a worthy opponent. It was, therefore, only natural that the new missile weapon, which had an even greater range, should be similarly regarded. We read in the *Jōsen Kidan*:

> As a rule, on the battlefield, it is the job of the ashigaru to face on to the enemy and fire arquebuses in volleys into the midst of the enemy. As for the arquebuses owned by samurai, they are for shooting and bringing down an enemy of importance.

The Korean campaign saw devastating use made of massed arquebuses, leading one general to write home to argue that any soldiers who were sent to Korea should bring guns with them. No other weapon was needed.

The firearms squads were supplied with an arquebus that was based on the design introduced to Japan by the Portuguese in 1543. It was fired when a smouldering match fastened into a serpentine was dropped on to the touch hole and, unlike primitive hand guns, the model had reached a sufficient degree of sophistication for this process to be operated from a sprung trigger. To prevent premature discharges, the touch hole was closed until the point of firing by a tight-fitting brass cover. In 1549 the Shimazu clan of Satsuma became the first samurai to use arquebuses in battle.

One disadvantage of the arquebus was its slow loading time compared to the bow, making it necessary for archers to provide cover while reloading took place. The experience of the battle of Nagashino confirmed volley firing as the most effective way of using arquebuses, but it also illustrated the iron-hard discipline needed to make it work. Rain was of course an enormous problem, but it was one that affected friend and foe alike in a field battle, and fuses were weatherproofed by boiling them in various mixtures, such as tooth-blackening powder!

The arquebus men were under the direct command of a *teppō ko gashira* (lieutenant of the firearms squad). Judging by their representation on painted screens, a firearms unit would comprise a series of groups of gunners, at least five per group, with each group accompanied by an archer. A number of these groups (between one and six) would be answerable to an individual ko gashira, but the exact number varied enormously from daimyō to daimyō. The ko

The firing of reproduction arquebuses at a re-enactment of the battle of Kawanakajima in Kōfu.

gashira was recognizable by his possession of a length of red-lacquered bamboo reminiscent of a swagger stick, in which was kept a strong ramrod in case any gunner's ramrod broke during action.

Large numbers of ashigaru archers were also employed throughout the Age of Warring States. Some may have been highly trained sharpshooters like the samurai archers and used as skirmishers or for sniping, but their most important role was to fire volleys of arrows. The bow was identical to a samurai's longbow. It was made from bamboo and rattan and lacquered for protection against damp. Even though they had a shorter range than the arquebus, and required a more practised operator, their rate of fire was more rapid and enemy arrows could be re-used. Archers were supported by carriers who were at hand with large quiver boxes containing 100 arrows. The preferred range for firing was from between 30 and 80 metres, and the bow had a maximum effective range of 380 metres.

The training that both sets of missile troops required must have been quite extensive. Even though the training required for the simple operation of an arquebus looked far less than that required to produce a marksman archer with the necessary muscular strength to draw the bow, any 'training dividend' that this produced was countermanded, as in Europe, by the extra training that arquebusiers needed for speed in reloading and the discipline of firing rotating volleys.

Spearmen

The other specialized arm were the spearmen, who almost always outnumbered missile troops within an army. Oda Nobunaga, who was probably the first to introduce disciplined ashigaru spear units, possessed a contingent that made up 27 per cent of his fighting force, compared to 13.5 per cent for the arquebusiers. In 1575 the Uesugi had ten spearmen for every arquebusier, and by about 1570 the breakdown of weaponry within the Hōjō armies included between 33 per cent and 50 per cent of all men (samurai and ashigaru) armed with spears. Within the Takeda clan, the proportion was between 50 per cent and 66 per cent.

The earliest ashigaru spears had been the same length (about three or four metres) as samurai ones, and were wielded just as freely in the conflicts of the Ōnin War. A noticeable lengthening of the shaft of the ashigaru weapon follows from about 1530, producing the *nagae yari* (long-shafted spear) which was more akin to a pike. A call to arms issued by Hōjō Ujimasa in 1587 includes the words: 'They are to bring with them any of the following three weapons: a bow, a spear or a gun. However, a spear, whether its shaft is made of bamboo or wood, is useless if it is shorter than two ken [about four metres].' The increase in length came about because a very different technique was developed for ashigaru spear fighting as distinct from samurai spear fighting. The samurai were regarded as individual spearmen who would engage in single combat with their weapons. The ashigaru spearmen were trained to fight as a group formed up in a line of two or three ranks with their spear points even, thus showing certain similarities to European pikemen.

The shaft of a nagae yari was of composite construction, with a core of hardwood such as oak, surrounded by laminations of bamboo. Like the bows, the whole shaft was lacquered to weatherproof it. The total length of nagae yari differed from clan to clan according to the general's preference but the length of shaft was usually about three ken. At the start of the Age of Warring States one ken was equivalent to 1.6 metres (the dimensions changed later to 1.8 metres), so the length of the spear shaft would have been 4.8 metres. The Takeda used a nagae yari shaft of three ken. Uesugi Kenshin used a shaft of two-and-a-half ken, while his successor, Kagekatsu (1555–1623), used three ken at about the time of Sekigahara, as did Toyotomi Hideyoshi. The Tokugawa also used a three-ken shaft.

This detail from *Ehon Toyotomi Gunki* showing the siege of Inuyama in 1584 gives a rare glimpse of ordered ashigaru ranks in action. Arquebuses are fired and spears dropped to the horizontal as the spearmen advance. The enemy front line stand ready with spears held vertically.

Oda Nobunaga used the longest spears of all, with a giant three-and-a-half ken (5.6 metres) shaft. This would appear to be a development Nobunaga adopted quite early in his career, because there is a reference in the *Shinchōkoki* dated at April 1553 to '500 three-and-a-half ken long spears'. His father-in-law Saitō Dōsan expressed amazement at Nobunaga's long shafts, which meant the user required as much training as a gunner.

Serving a samurai

An army would also have several other ashigaru employed to carry the personal possessions of a samurai and to serve him like the genin of the Gempei Wars. For example, the *zori tori* (sandal bearer) carried a samurai's footwear, among other duties equivalent to an officer's batman. Spare footwear was important, because Japanese straw sandals do not last long, and a particular treatise on Japanese armour states, 'An extra pair of sandals must be carried at your waist; this is quite as important a thing as carrying provisions.' Quite early in his career the great Toyotomi Hideyoshi, who had proved his worth as a fighting ashigaru, was promoted to the position of Oda Nobunaga's sandal bearer, and endeared himself to the latter by warming his master's sandals inside his shirt in cold weather.

A zori tori would also be found among that exclusive body of men who attended the daimyō himself. The greatest honour in this regard was attached

The ashigaru spearmen were the third of the three specialized ashigaru units described in *Zōhyō Monogatari*. Two types of spears are found, the long nagae yari which were akin to European pikes, and the shorter mochi-yari (hand spears). The character on the viewer's right appears to have acquired three trophies of war: two swords, which he has tied on to the shaft of his mochi-yari, and the severed head of their former owner. Note how the cords of the skirts of the armour are draped over the scabbards of his own swords, thus allowing them to be drawn in katana style (blade uppermost), unlike the samurai practice of slinging them tachi style, with the blade downwards, from a sword hanger.

to being the lord's *mochiyari gumi* (spear bearer). This man carried the samurai's personal polearm, and was a highly valued bodyguard, as the *Zōhyō Monogatari* tells us:

> As for the spear bearers, we invariably find them, and there is no place for cowards among their ranks, they serve with great devotion, and it is work of great merit. It is a tremendous thing to be used as a spear carrier, and a thing of ambition to serve the lord's needs.

Other ashigaru carried his bow, his arquebus or his naginata, and many illustrations also show ashigaru carrying an assortment of spears with very elaborate scabbards. For example, Kimata Morikatsu, who was not himself a daimyō but merely a senior retainer of the Ii family of Hikone, was personally attended by the following men of ashigaru rank in 1600:

Personal ashigaru (including a sandal bearer)	4
Bearer of the cross-bladed spear	1
Bearer of the personal nobori	1
Groom	1

Kimata would also have had to supply samurai, each of whom was in turn served by a smaller group of attendants, plus a number of specialist ashigaru who would fight in the Ii weapon squads.

Signals and flag bearers

Other ashigaru would have the responsibility of operating the signalling devices used on a battlefield. The most commonly recorded is the *horagai* or shell trumpet. Drums were also used frequently. Smaller ones were carried on an ashigaru's back while a comrade beat the drum. Larger ones were suspended from a pole carried by two men, while the largest of all were mounted on a wooden framework, or built into a tower in a castle. Bells and gongs were also used. There was an agreed system of commands for advance or assembly, and armies marched to the beat of a drum.

The shift from a pattern of warfare between individuals to one of organized movements between groups is best illustrated by the large numbers of ashigaru who were employed in carrying flags. The vast majority would carry the long vertical nobori banners which were used to identify the locations of various units. Painted screens indicate that long rows of identical nobori would be found with each unit.

The most prominent positions of all fell to the carriers of the *uma jirushi* (literally 'horse insignia'). This was the device, often a flag, but sometimes a three-dimensional object, which acted as a samurai's standard and indicated his personal presence rather than that of a unit. A daimyō would possess an enormous *ō uma jirushi* (great standard), which was the nucleus of the army on the battlefield and attracted the heaviest fire. Smaller devices (including the *ko uma jirushi* or 'lesser standard') were carried in a leather bucket fastened to the ashigaru's belt, while large ones were strapped securely into a carrying frame worn on the back. Ropes were provided for the ashigaru standard bearer to steady his flag in a wind or on the run, and in the case of the large examples two comrades would hold two separate ropes to keep it steady.

The Sanada ashigaru in march formation, with their family banner bearing the mon of six coins – the fee payable to the boatman who conveys souls from earth to heaven.

Certain other ashigaru roles are not reflected in muster lists. For example, ashigaru would have the responsibility of operating the Takeda fire beacon chain, and a daimyō with his own navy, or one who acted as admiral, used ashigaru as sailors and marines. While some rowed the clumsy warships, others fired arquebuses from portholes, launched firebombs and wielded grappling hooks. Throughout the Age of Warring States there is also a steady development of a specialized artillery arm. Exploding firebombs launched from catapults are recorded as early as 1468. Each catapult was fired by a team of 40 ashigaru pulling simultaneously on ropes to swing a lever arm. By 1615 such teams had been replaced by gun crews operating European culverins to bombard Ōsaka castle.

Campaign life of the ashigaru

The ashigaru assembled through the muster system are now ready to set off on campaign, and we may imagine them leaving the castle gates in an orderly procession, with arquebuses, bows and long spears carried tidily on their shoulders. But whereas the function of the specialized ashigaru units is self-evident from their titles, the role of certain other ashigaru only becomes

The most vulnerable men in an army were the ashigaru who carried flags. The ashigaru shown here has a hata-jirushi (flag streamer, fixed to a cross piece) which he carries in a leather bucket at his right side. Bravest of the brave were the men who carried the daimyō's ō uma jirushi, which denoted the presence of the lord and attracted the fiercest fighting.

apparent when examined in the context of campaign life. As an example of the additional retinue that a high-ranking samurai might have been expected to have, the servants and general bearers who were in attendance on Kimata Morikatsu in 1600 are listed below, but it is important to make a distinction between ashigaru such as these and labourers who could be press-ganged into a daimyō's army.

Item	Number of men
Lantern carriers – 4 chests	4
Maku (field curtain) and standards in one large chest	2
Kitchen utensils – 2 chests	2
General porters – 2 packs	2
Food bearers – 2 packs	2
Packhorse leader	1
Fodder bearers – 3 packs	3
Grooms with spare horses	2
Gunpowder – one chest	1
Cloaks etc. for rainy conditions – 2 large chests	4
Bodyguard samurai armour – 2 large chests	4
Bodyguard ashigaru armour – one large chest	2
Another large armour chest	2
Kimata's own armour – one chest	1
Footwear bearer – one chest	1
Arquebuses and tools (bullet moulds, etc.) – one large chest	2
Bullets, powder, arrows – one large chest	2

The large chests referred to were like small palanquins and were slung from a pole and carried by two men each, while a 'pack' is of bamboo and straw. Bales of rice were also carried on men's backs, on pack horses, or on two-wheeled carts pushed and pulled by bearers. Larger carts, pulled by oxen, were also used and were particularly handy for transporting heavy cannon. European cannon were usually supplied only as barrels, and without a carriage.

Discipline was the key to a successful march. In the earlier section on the samurai we noted that when Tokugawa Ieyasu advanced on Odawara in 1590 he issued a number of strict regulations concerning keeping order in ranks and the avoidance of disruption to the civilian population. There was to be no looting. This may seem a very noble sentiment, but they were his own territories through which his army was marching! Weapons also had to be carried according to set rules and horses had to be controlled. When going on campaign, food supplies for men and horses were of paramount importance, as made clear by the *Zōhyō Monogatari*:

> Normally take food for ten days but no more. If continuing on a road for ten days distance, use pack horses, and do not leave them behind… As for the horse's food, store it safely in a bag when raiding enemy territory, do not abandon anything, and if suffering from hunger in a camp eat the vegetation. The horse can stick to dead leaves. It will also eat refined pine bark… As for firewood 80 monme is sufficient for one

An illustration from a modern Japanese comic book by Junko Miki. The picture shows the steady but rapid advance of ashigaru across rice fields. The dramatic effect is considerable.

person for one day, and all can gather it together. If the place has no firewood take dried horse dung and use it as firewood.

As for rice, for one person allow six go, and one go of salt for ten people, for miso allow for ten people two go, but when there is a night battle and so on the amount of rice should be increased.

Horses could be particularly trying. 'When taking horses on a raid,' says the *Zōhyō Monogatari*, 'you must be very careful. Young horses may break free and will get excited. Because of this an army could be defeated, so this must be strictly forbidden. Keep them well tied up to avoid this.'

Looting, pillage and the treatment of civilians

When not fighting on a battlefield or marching to war, the enduring image of the common soldier in all cultures contemporary with the ashigaru is that he

was the agent of pillage, destruction, arson and other havoc. We noted earlier that the origin of the ashigaru at the beginning of the Age of Warring States were the ne'er-do-wells who joined the armies for the prospect of loot. Now that ashigaru were integrated fully into the samurai army, did such activities continue on an official basis as an instrument of war?

Looting was sometimes necessary if a campaign proved to be of long duration in an enemy territory, and it was then usually regarded as fair game. The wise counsels of the *Zōhyō Monogatari*, however, took the view that looting could be avoided if the army was properly prepared:

> Nowadays 45 days' allowance can be taken, but no more than three or four days should be forced on to a horse, but whether in enemy territory or that of allies there should be no unpreparedness. In such cases take food with you or you will have to seize food from allies, which would be foolish and also theft.

These are sentiments which tally with Tokugawa Ieyasu's orders before Odawara, but if looting could not be avoided, then it may as well be successful, as the *Zōhyō Monogatari* says:

Neither of the two grooms shown in this illustration from *Zōhyō Monogatari* wears any armour except for the jingasa helmet. The figure on the left has a wooden drinking cup thrust through the belt of his jacket. The groom on the right holds on to the horse. He has a spare bit and bridle slung around his neck and has a whip in his belt. The details of the horse's saddle are well illustrated. The knot on the pommel is the place where the saddle girth was tied.

The Korean campaigns saw many actions directed against civilians. In this illustration from *Ehon Taikō ki*, samurai and ashigaru loot a Korean village. One soldier steals a vase, another takes rolls of cloth, while a woman is the prize for a third.

Food and clothing may be buried inside houses, but if it is buried outside it may be concealed in a pot or kettle. When such things are buried in the ground, visit during an early morning frost, and at the places where things are buried the frost will disappear, and many things may be discovered.

However, the ashigaru foragers are warned to be careful of booby traps left by an enemy:

Remember that a dead person's blood may have contaminated the water supply you drink. You should never drink the water from wells in enemy territory. It may be that faeces have been sunk to the bottom. Drink river water instead. When provinces are exchanged take care with the water. In camp it is a good idea to drink water which has been in a pot with apricot kernels in silk, or put into the pot some freshwater snails brought from your own province and dried in the shade, and that water supply will be good to drink.

坂井右近
堅田浦
浅井朝倉が
兵根と
奪ふ

In many cultures, of course, foraging and looting go hand in hand with acts of unnecessary cruelty to the civilian population, and in one very important respect the Japanese situation was different from that in Europe. Nearly all its wars were civil wars, so an oppressed peasant could theoretically cross a provincial border to till the fields of an enemy, making cruelty against civilians most inadvisable. In support of this benevolent view it must be admitted that the most dramatic example of a peasant uprising against a cruel daimyō occurred two decades after the civil wars had ceased. This was the Shimabara Rebellion of 1637 to 1638, directed against the tyrant Matsukura Shigemasa, who was given to tying peasants inside straw raincoats and setting fire to them. From this it may be argued that if Matsukura had lived at a time when one's neighbour was by definition one's rival, then self-interest alone would have prevented him from acting in such an outrageous manner.

When Takeda Shingen was repulsed before Odawara castle in 1569 he burned the town of Odawara before retiring, and when Toyotomi Hideyoshi took Kagoshima in 1587 and Odawara in 1590 there was nothing that remotely resembled the sack of a European town. It may simply be that the compilers did

In this section from *Ehon Toyotomi Gunki* ashigaru are carrying straw bales packed with rice. The operation is being carried out under cover of darkness, as shown by the pine torches carried by their comrades. There were many carrying duties associated with the ashigaru role, but their numbers were also augmented by labourers.

The preserved ashigaru house in the Nagamachi quarter of Kanazawa.

not think that such matters were worth recording, but a more likely explanation is that these daimyō in these campaigns needed to win hearts and minds. A very different picture emerges when the victims are regarded as worthless vermin who need to be eradicated if the daimyō is to flourish. The worst example is Nobunaga's campaign against the Ikkō-ikki, where the distinction between soldier and non-combatant was practically non-existent. Nobunaga took Nagashima in 1574 by building a palisade round it and burning the entire complex. Forty thousand people perished in the conflagration and the massacre. In 1575 the eradication of the Echizen Ikkō-ikki was carried out in cold blood when between 30,000 and 40,000 were executed and an unknown number taken prisoner.

The Korean campaign of 1592–98 added a further dimension to the situation to produce the worst example of methodical and sustained cruelty against non-combatants in samurai history. Here there was no prospect of an ill-treated peasant joining the Japanese army (although some Korean renegades managed to benefit from the situation). The Japanese troops took what they wanted from Korean fields and towns as an act of war to supply their own needs, so we must undoubtedly accept a role for the ashigaru in pillage and plunder. As for unnecessary violence to civilians, there was one other important difference from the Japanese theatre of war. In Korea the fortified town often replaced the isolated castle as a battle site, and many civilian deaths must be inferred from the huge number of heads taken at such conflicts as Chinju and Namwon.

The most powerful evidence of Japanese atrocities in Korea comes in the form of a unique and little-known document, the diary of a Japanese

The eating area in the ashigaru house in Kanazawa.

Buddhist monk called Keinen, who accompanied the daimyō Ota Kazuyoshi as his personal chaplain and physician. Keinen secretly recorded his observations and feelings about the human suffering inflicted on the Korean population. His entries covering the fall of Namwon castle in 1597 include a chilling description of mass slaughter. Keinen reveals that the notorious (and incorrectly named) Ear Mound in Kyōto contains the noses not only of dead soldiers but also of thousands of non-combatants: men, women and children. He also reveals that many hundreds more people were sent as slaves to Japan.

Another revealing point from Keinen's diary covers the cruel treatment that the samurai meted out to their own people. In this case, the victims were the Japanese labourers press-ganged into the invading army to complete the building of Ulsan castle:

> There are beatings for the slightest mistake in performing such tasks as tying knots. In many cases I have witnessed this becomes the last occasion on which the person gets into trouble… Hell cannot be in any other place except here.

In another section Keinen describes how a group of labourers were sent into the forests to cut timber and had to stay behind to trim the tree trunks. They were caught by a Chinese patrol and beheaded. He also describes labourers 'brought from thousands of miles away' bent double under the weight of the goods they were unloading at the ports for the Japanese war effort.

Apart from the shock of reading of such cruelty, Keinen's diary provides a remarkable illustration of the consequences of Hideyoshi's Separation Edict of 1591. There is now a complete distinction between the armed and uniformed ashigaru and the unarmed and despised peasant labourer. One need only consider that Toyotomi Hideyoshi, who masterminded the invasion, had begun life as a peasant to appreciate how impossible such a rise through the ranks would now be for a member of this wretched press gang. It is therefore not surprising to hear of some peasant labourers concluding that they would be better off with the Koreans than their fellow Japanese, and absconding from the fortified camps. This is confirmed in the diaries of Admiral Yi Sun-sin, who interrogated some Japanese peasants captured by Korean soldiers. The diaries reveal that the peasants had been taken along into the army by the Shimazu family and had run away because of their ill-treatment.

Field remedies and wounds

Yet whether a man was a samurai, an ashigaru or a labourer, anyone could be laid low by the rigours of a long campaign or a terrible siege. The rigours of campaign life provided many challenges, for which the most dramatic advice in the *Zōhyō Monogatari* concerns the treatment for snake bite in a bivouac:

> When lying down in a camp in a field or on a mountain, if an adder bites don't get over excited, speedily apply one monme of gunpowder to the spot. Set fire to it and the virulence will quickly disappear, but if it is delayed it will not work.

The treatment of wounds was an important issue. The most gruesome account in the *Zōhyō Monogatari* concerns the methods for extracting arrowheads:

> Tie the hair up in a bag and use chopsticks to pull the arrow out. If it is not possible to pull the arrow shaft out using the hands, pincers may be employed. With these it should be possible.

For removing an arrow stuck through the cheek the method is a little more stringent:

A samurai attended by ashigaru arquebusiers, a groom, a standard bearer and a baggage carrier, from *Ehon Toyotomi Gunki*.

The head must not move, so fasten him [the casualty] to a tree, and with the head tied to a tree like a crucifixion the work can begin. The arrow can be pulled out gently, but while doing this the eye socket will be filled with blood.

The *Zōhyō Monogatari* also offered the following, somewhat naive, advice for conditions where a padded haori jacket or a peasant's straw rain cloak was insufficient to keep the cold at bay:

The most bizarre illustration from *Zōhyō Monogatari* is this painful account of field surgery, which at least shows that the Japanese did not abandon their wounded, nor insist on hara kiri. The victim has an arrow lodged in his eye socket. One comrade ties his head securely to a tree, while the other advances menacingly with a pair of pliers. The torn armour of the 'surgeon' suggests that he too has been in the wars. Note that the arquebus in the foreground has been sheathed in a leather cover.

Concerning pepper grains, in both summer or winter take one each in the mornings, this will ward off the cold and encourage warmth. This can be varied by taking umeboshi [pickled plums]. If you apply squashed red peppers from the hips to the tips of the toes you will not freeze. It is also good to daub it on your arms too, but avoid the eyes and the eyeballs.

Yet some conditions went far beyond a remedy from eating pepper grains. The bitter cold of the Korean winter deprived men of hands and feet from frostbite, and an eyewitness of the siege of Ulsan in the bitter winter of 1597–98 noted how death from hypothermia made no distinction between samurai, ashigaru or labourer:

29th day, and both friend and foe are silent. Nevertheless inside the castle we have maintained our defences by day and night without any sleep. Here and there inside the castle, at the sunny places on the walkways and

at the foot of towers, without differentiating between samurai, ashigaru or labourers, 50 or 30 men at a time are bowed under the unbearable hunger, thirst and cold. Also, besides this, there are a number of men who let their heads drop and lie down to sleep. The soldiers take their spears and patrol, but it is a fact that there are some men who have not moved all day, and when they try to rouse them with the butt end of a spear, the ones who are completely bent over have been frozen to death.

At the fourth battle of Kawanakajima in 1561 ashigaru carry water to their wounded comrades using their helmets as bowls.

The ashigaru's experience of battle

The ashigaru had a vital role to play on the battlefield, and this topic will now be examined from two directions: the theoretical and the practical. The theory involves such materials as modern experiments on firearm effectiveness plus Matsudaira's recommendations in the *Zōhyō Monogatari*, which, although written in 1649, was based on first-hand experience of ashigaru warfare. The practical sections identify accounts of ashigaru warfare from the chronicles and

The arquebusiers could not pick up their enemies' missiles as could the archers, so bullet carriers, like this man who wears a heavy box on his back, kept the firearms squads supplied.

diaries of the period. These accounts are quite rare, and often we have to tease out the ashigaru involvement from the context, such as the use of firearms or the controlled use of spears.

One of the most important areas of military theory in 16th-century Japan was the existence of numerous models of battlefield layout. Most were based on old Chinese models, but all had certain features in common: the general to the rear centre, surrounded by his bodyguard; the cavalry units ready to charge; a vanguard of brave samurai and ashigaru missile troops protected by ashigaru spearmen; and a sizeable flank and rear contingent. The baggage train would

The main means of transporting bulky loads on campaign was by pack-horse battery. This illustration from *Zōhyō Monogatari* shows a pack horse, with two rice bales on its back. The horse also carries a small flag as an identification of the unit.

be guarded to the rear. Different units would communicate with one another through the highly mobile *tsukai ban*, the elite mounted samurai who acted as messengers. Other messengers would operate between allied contingents, who occupied different positions on the field.

The presence of allied contingents, and the definition of what constitutes an 'ally' rather than a subordinate commander, begs an important question with regard to ashigaru warfare. If two or more allied armies were present on a battlefield, did they combine their ashigaru weapons troops into, say, one large arquebus unit, or did they continue to operate separately?

In answering this question we must first appreciate the difference between a typical Japanese battle formation and the contemporary European pike and shot 'squares'. For example, at the battle of Fornovo in 1495 the Swiss packed 3,000 men into a 60-metre square. Nowhere do Japanese records imply such formations. The impression is always given of a much looser structure from which defence could quickly convert into lively offence. The way in which a Swiss pike square could make its steady and crushing advance while keeping formation also bears little resemblance to a Japanese army's 'charge', 'charge' being one of the most frequently used words in battle descriptions.

Within a particular daimyō's army a pooling of weaponry certainly took place. The examples noted earlier of Okamoto in the Hōjō army and Kimata in the Ii army indicate the men they were required to provide, not the men they were required to use. Both samurai would have retained the service of their personal attendants, but the arquebusiers and spearmen included in their muster requirements would serve in the specialist ashigaru squads. At the time of the Gempei Wars in the 12th century, however, the equivalent to Kimata would have had personal leadership of his own band of horsemen and foot soldiers in a very loose military structure. In the Warring States Period such command was subordinated to the greater good of the daimyō's army through a more systematic arrangement based on group fighting and weapon specialization.

It is also apparent that the greater the social homogeneity in a daimyō's army, then the more precise and ordered were its tactics. Thus the fourth battle of Kawanakajima in 1561 involved very complex manoeuvring by night, but both armies were either Takeda men or Uesugi men, all of whom knew each other and had trained and served together. At Nagashino, Oda Nobunaga set up a very precise linear formation from troops who were either his vassals or those of one other allied army, the Tokugawa. The 3,000 arquebusiers selected for the volley firing were drawn from troops who fitted into an existing rank and social structure. The best example is the Shimazu, whose total social homogeneity allowed them to perfect the very difficult tactic of a false retreat.

The opposite situation, that of a coalition of allies, is seen to best effect at Sekigahara. Here Ishida Mitsunari commanded some very doubtful contingents, and the fact that Kobayakawa Hideaki was able to order his entire army to turn against their erstwhile comrades is proof that there was no pooling of weapon types across the whole command. However, there seems to have been little 'sharing' on the other side either, as we read of an advance by the 'Ii contingent', who were among Tokugawa Ieyasu's closest retainers, and would surely have been more than willing to pool their ashigaru along with others. In some cases we may also envisage different contingents, whether allies or subordinates, drawn up in very similar formations side by side, with only the change in the design on the flags being displayed indicating that this was not one complete army but several joined together.

This Japanese arquebus has an external brass spring. The trigger releases the serpentine, which drops the glowing match onto the touch hole. A brass cover protects the firing pan. The barrel is fitted with a backsight and a foresight. Note the short stock: the weapon would be hand-held rather than rested on the shoulder.

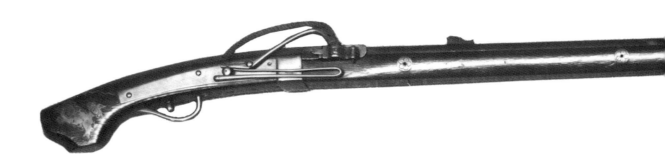

The deployment of allies or subordinates as separate armies was occasioned by the vast scale of engagements like Sekigahara. The advantage was that different contingents could cover a wide area of possible activity. The disadvantage, however, was that weapon effectiveness was reduced, and that some contingents could change sides when they saw how the battle was going. The notorious Tsutsui Junkei, who fought at Yamazaki in 1582, only decided that he was for Hideyoshi when he saw the tide of battle going Hideyoshi's way. Up to that point he had simply watched and waited on a well-positioned hill.

Arquebus troops

Whatever the layout adopted, the growing importance of firearms meant that the first exchange of fire in a battle would probably be between the rival arquebus troops firing at a maximum range of about 100 metres. The firing would be controlled by the teppō kashira who commanded through the teppō ko gashira. Like the spearmen and archers they would be under the overall command of the samurai who bore the rank of ashigaru taishō. He would usually be stationed in the most forward position of all the samurai officers, and would thus be in the best position to judge when the firing had disorientated the enemy sufficiently for a charge to be ordered. At the ideal moment, the ashigaru spearmen advanced and the samurai attacked vigorously on foot or horseback. While this was going on the ashigaru missile troops reorganized themselves under the protection of other ashigaru spearmen. In some situations the ashigaru archers supplied a volley of their own while the arquebusiers reloaded.

The response to arquebus fire varied enormously. Controlled volleys like those used at Muraki in 1554 and Marune in 1560 showed their effectiveness against a fortified position. The experience of the Takeda at Nagashino, where they were almost broken by it, was an object lesson about the use of the arquebus from a fortified field position that was not wasted on other daimyō.

Sometimes such volleys produced unexpected results, as when the poorly disciplined rōnin of Osaka castle were goaded into action by gunfire at the battle of Tennōji in 1615.

In a recent practical assessment of an arquebus's range, five bullets were fired at a target in the shape of an armoured samurai from distances of 30 metres and 50 metres respectively. At 30 metres each of the five bullets hit the target area of the chest, but only one out of the five struck the chest when the target was moved back to 50 metres. Even at 50 metres, however, a bullet that struck home could do considerable damage, as shown by the results of a further experiment where a bullet pierced a one-millimetre iron plate at 50 metres. The scales of a typical lacquered *dō maru* were of similar thickness.

A third experiment showed that an experienced Japanese arquebus enthusiast could perform the sequence of load, prime, aim and fire in as little as 15 seconds, a speed comparable to that of a flintlock musket. Other studies of arquebuses have shown that the need to keep the smouldering match out of the way while the pan is primed slows the process down to a more realistic rate of between 20 and 30 seconds, or in clumsy and inexperienced hands no better than one shot every minute. As we know that Nobunaga selected his 'best shots' for the line at Nagashino the rate of fire was probably quite high.

Modern European experiments have revealed that operating an arquebus is a hazardous business. The force of the explosion has been found to dislodge the match, a problem the Japanese solved by inserting a tiny bamboo peg through holes in the serpentine. This would not, however, greatly add to safety, because the only sure way of preventing premature discharge was to remove the burning fuse completely away from the weapon.

The recommendations for successful ashigaru warfare in the *Zōhyō Monogatari* are arranged according to weapon group. Beginning with the arquebus, we see that there was great responsibility placed upon the shoulders of the ko gashira. His first duty was to distribute the bullets, which were carried in the bullet box by an ashigaru and then transferred to the bullet pouch worn at the gunners' belts. The leather bag in which the arquebus was carried was then carefully put to one side. When the enemy began to appear the fuse was inserted into the serpentine. If it was dropped in quickly or fitted badly the fire might go out, so a number of spare lighted fuses were kept on a metal stand thrust into the ground. Sound ramrods were another absolute necessity for the arquebusier:

Use a ramrod that is made from oak, but even these will sometimes break. Without a ramrod the gunpowder cannot be forced down, so in most cases one man will have two or three, but the ko gashira carries a case in which a particularly sturdy ramrod is kept, and when there is difficulty getting the bullets in one can use it.

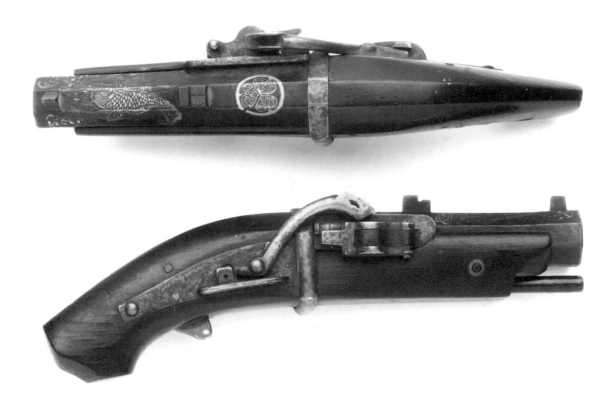

Illustrations show spare ramrods being thrust through an ashigaru's belt. Ramming itself could be hazardous to one's comrades:

> When ramming do it up and down as far as the brim of the jingasa. If it is done out to one side there is a danger to the eyes of one's comrades, because other people's ramrods may be stuck in eyes, so it is best to lift it straight up and down.

There was also the factor of the fouling of a barrel after a number of shots had been fired. In the case of an 18th-century French flintlock, for example, fouling reduced the firing rate from one shot every 12 seconds to one shot every 45 seconds. Arquebuses were no different, and this is noted in the *Zōhyō Monogatari*, which states that: 'when five or six arquebus bullets have been fired there will be scorching inside the barrel and there will be difficulties with bullets getting stuck or with loading'.

The order to fire would be given when the enemy came within sufficient range. Nagashino provides the best example, as the precise locations of both the Takeda cavalry and the Oda arquebusiers are known. The arquebuses used at Nagashino had a maximum range of 500 metres, a distance at which even

Detail of the trigger and touch-hole mechanism of an arquebus, as shown on a miniature example.

125

As time went by, cartridges were introduced for the arquebus, which greatly speeded up the process of firing. In this painting from *Nakajima-ryū jutsu densho* in Kyōto University Library, the final stages of the process are shown. On the right the gunner is withdrawing his ramrod having rammed the bullet home. The next figure takes his priming powder flask, which the third man tips into the pan. The fourth figure cocks the serpentine against the external spring, while the final man takes aim. Note how the ramrods appear to have been tucked into the back of the armour, and how the position adopted by the gunners has the body weight thrown back on to the rear leg. The gunners wear their cartridges as a bandolier.

volley firing could be expected to do little damage. The maximum effective range for causing casualties was 200 metres, which was just a little less than the distance from the fence to the woods out of which the Takeda cavalry began their charge. It is highly unlikely that Nobunaga would have allowed any firing at this range, because the slight wounds caused would not have interrupted the flow of the charge and would have wasted at least one of the volleys. At 50 metres, which was approximately the distance from the fence to the little river called the Rengogawa that provided Nobunaga's outer line of defence, the effects would be more pronounced. Writing with the benefit of experience, the author of the *Zōhyō Monogatari* in 1649 recommends:

> As for the enemy, after beginning with the horses it is good to attack the riders. On these occasions fire at those riding the horses so that they fall off and also at the horses. It will disturb many of the enemy.

In spite of all the noise, confusion and danger, an arquebusier would have had to give his total concentration to the business of reloading, ensuring that the touch hole was clear, that the bullet was correctly rammed down, and that there was no chance of the smouldering match causing a premature discharge.

At Nagashino the presence of the fence and the spearmen ashigaru, with their 5.6-metre-long spears, would have provided the protection that the arquebusiers needed, and it is probable that any such combats at this time in the battle only occurred against Takeda cavalrymen who had passed through the gaps in the fence. This allowed the creation of a 'killing-ground' for separated horsemen, who became the prey for both samurai swords and ashigaru spears. To add to the defence from palisade and spear, dense clouds of smoke would also have been expected, a factor that this writer saw illustrated dramatically when observing arquebuses being fired at Nagashino in the annual festival.

Hand-to-hand fighting

The *Zōhyō Monogatari* also recognized that once the enemy had reached one's line, an unloaded arquebus was useless, so the author thoughtfully includes advice on when and how the arquebusiers themselves should engage in hand-to-hand fighting under the protection of the spearmen:

> If the enemy come close, because you will be replaced by men with spears, divide up to right and left. Remove the ramrod, sheathe the arquebus in the arquebus bag, and cross swords with them. Aim at the helmet, but if because the loan swords have dull blades you can only chop, aim at the enemy's hands and legs and you can cut at them.
>
> If the enemy are a distance away you can swab out the barrel, which is equivalent to cleaning it. At such time it is wise not to put powder and ball into the arquebus for about half a minute. While the enemy are out of sight carry the arquebus on your shoulder.

One of the longest and most useful accounts of ashigaru on the battlefield is a passage in the chronicles of the Kuroda family describing the battle of Kimhae in 1592. It contains an excellent description of the deployment of arquebusiers and confirms the reliance placed on such men. The background is as follows. The first two divisions of the Japanese army of invasion landed in Korea at the port of Pusan. The third division was under the command of Kuroda Nagamasa, who was loathe simply to disembark in a port now occupied by Japan. Accordingly he sailed to the west to land at Kimhae, where there was more prospect of samurai glory.

The overall commanders of the vanguard ashigaru, Yoshida Nagatori and Uehara Shinza'emon, went as the vanguard for the entire army and captured the boats at the shore side. Then, having seen from on board that all was well, they landed half the ashigaru, led by the kashira. This first unit quickly ran up to a low piece of raised ground, and when it was seen to have taken up a

ABOVE LEFT

The yumi ko gashira was the officer in charge, and one of his responsibilities, shown in this illustration from *Zōhyō Monogatari*, was to keep the archers supplied with arrows.

ABOVE RIGHT

An ashigaru archer bends his bow against a support so that he can fit the string. He has a spare bowstring on a reel at his left side, and his quiver is covered with black bear fur.

position with its arquebuses, the remaining ashigaru under Nagatori and Shinza'emon also disembarked:

They [the commanders] landed the horses and mounted them, and galloped off to nearby high ground, while in addition positions were taken with arquebuses among the bamboo and wooded areas. After this the five ranks of the whole army successively disembarked without difficulty. Subsequently the 100 arquebus ashigaru divided into two. The advance unit reformed their original ranks and turned against the enemy, and attacked the left flank of the enemy who were withdrawing from the second unit, firing arquebuses. Seeing the signs that the Korean soldiers were shaken by this, those who remained advanced as one, and many arquebuses were fired. Because the enemy were arranged in close ranks no bullets were wasted, and they fell in rapid succession. Nagamasa saw this and ordered the conch to be blown, brandished his saihai and gave the signal to advance.

An account which is much briefer, but very useful because it quantifies the effects of arquebus fire, is found in the *Kirin Gunki*:

There was a dreadful noise in the castle as over 100 shooters attacked, accompanied by about 60 horsemen. The arquebuses of the ashigaru were continually replaced and their firing produced 600 or 700 dead or wounded.

The use of the word 'replaced' suggests rotating volley fire, but a very different use of the ashigaru arquebus is contained in the following amusing extract, which is concerned with the preliminaries to the siege of Ulsan in 1597. As the actual fortress of Ulsan was still being built, many of the Japanese troops were quartered outside the walls, which is where the following incident occurred:

Over halfway through the night of the 13th day of the 12th month a furious sound of gunfire broke out in the Nabeshima camp. Near the camp was a large swamp to which many swans came every night. When flying away at dawn they passed over the Nabeshima camp. The ashigaru had been told about this by Nabeshima, and they would fire their arquebuses at the flying birds, bringing down one or two. This happened every night. When the sound of gunfire happened that night Yasumasa thought they were shooting swans again.

The gunfire, however, was not the ashigaru taking pot-shots at the swans, but a full-scale Chinese attack. The passage continues:

However, many troops from the Nabeshima and Chugoku contingents then came fleeing into Yasumasa's camp. Yasumasa quickly put on his armour, seized his spear and galloped off. Eleven of his samurai were there to protect him.

Archery squads

As the Japanese troops were not within the secure walls of a castle but in a temporary camp outside, they were quickly overrun, and were eventually saved by the next group dealt with in the *Zōhyō Monogatari*: the ashigaru archery squads.

On the matter of the disposition of the archery corps, stand one archer in the space between two matchlock men, to cover the arquebuses reloading. An arrow can be loosed in between the two matchlockmen firing, thus covering the reloading interval.

Just as in the case of the arquebuses, the yumi ko gashira [lieutenant of the archer squad] takes charge of the archers.

The rapid fire of the ashigaru archers required a constant replenishment of arrows, so the arrow bearer carried a box with a load of 100 arrows on his back.

ABOVE RIGHT

To be a weapon bearer to the daimyō was a tremendous responsibility. In this illustration from *Zōhyō Monogatari* we see the bearer of the lord's bow and arrows. The weapon and its missiles are fixed into a sturdy wooden frame, which could be positioned on a flat surface on its own.

When the enemy are a distance away it is important not to fire arrows from the quiver. The ko gashira who is in command will take charge of the matter, and will order the firing of arrows when the enemy are closer. The decision about the effective firing distance is a difficult one to make.

Target priorities are again the horses, because 'when the enemy advance in a dense mass divide up into right and left sections and fire. In the case of a mounted enemy fire at the horses.' Like the arquebusiers, the archers also had to be prepared for hand-to-hand fighting:

When the arrows in the quiver are running low, do not use up the last arrow, but make a line to permit firing to continue, and engage in hand to hand fighting. When forced to withdraw defend from a spear's length away, and then fire into the space. This should be completely successful. If you are forced to fire while looking up at their faces you cannot ward off an enemy. These are the secrets of bow fighting… The bowstring must be folded up so that it is not cut through when this is done.

The surprise attack by the Chinese army on the Japanese encampment outside the 'building site' of Ulsan castle in 1597 was repulsed by well-trained ashigaru archers under the firm leadership of a young samurai hero:

The enemy attacked the encampment of Mōri's samurai Reizei Minbu, and in the end killed Minbu. The troops who saw this stayed in the castle, but one man among them, Yoshimi Taizō, in spite of being a youth of 18 years old, excelled in the Way of Bow and Arrow. He stood the troops under his command in a circle and, having ordered the ashigaru, 'Draw the enemy near, and shoot in such a way that the arrows are not ineffective,' charged into the midst of many thousands of the enemy.

Spearmen

The final weapon group discussed in the *Zōhyō Monogatari* are the spearmen ashigaru, who had to be particularly well drilled and well disciplined, because their enormous nagae yari pikes had the potential to cause as much trouble for friend as foe if not used correctly. Some of the most vivid lines in the *Zōhyō Monogatari* concern spear fighting. The length of the nagae yari, and the need for the ashigaru spearmen to keep the blades even, implies the existence of some form of 'pike drill'. Using the *Zōhyō Monogatari* and other accounts, it is possible to work out what this accepted system may have consisted of:

The arquebus and bow rounds having finished, the spears are under orders. Before the fighting starts place the sheaths inside the mune ita [the top of the armour breastplate]. Long scabbard-like spear sheaths must be thrust into the belt at the side.

Unlike samurai spearmen, where spears are thought of as only for thrusting with, here many are of one mind, with spear points moving together, keeping a rhythm. When one or two meet it is fine to fight individually, but when spears are used en masse there must be coordination and timing, with no exception. As for spear techniques, it is believed to be a good thing to be able to knock down an enemy sashimono [literally a flag, but indicating the horseman himself]. When the enemy are mounted a quick thrust at the horse's belly will make it buck and the man will fall off.

Line up in one rank three shaku apart, not thrusting but at the ready in a large row to hit the enemy. When facing an attack by horsemen line up in one rank kneeling, lie the spear down and wait. When contact is imminent lift up the spear head into the area of the horse's breast. When the point pierces the skin hold on to it! Whether you are cutting at men and horses, it may be that you will feel you are being forced to pull out

PREVIOUS PAGES

This double page spread from *Ehon Taikō ki* is an excellent depiction of ashigaru warfare. On the left, ashigaru under the command of a samurai ashigaru-taishō (identified by his flag bearer) are making a sally out of a defended castle past fences of brushwood. The besiegers have let the vanguard group pass by, and have then caught the following group in a volley of arrows fired through the openings of wooden shields. We can also see groups of spearmen with spears of differing lengths, and a unit of arquebusiers at the ready. All are wearing typical ashigaru armour with conical jingasa.

the spear, and it is a general rule to stand fast to the bitter end and not throw into disorder the collaborative actions. After you have driven the enemy back, to pursue for about one chō is sufficient.

The section concludes with advice on how far to stick the spear into an enemy, and a comment that the successful employment of many spears requires skill, perseverance and constant readiness. A good illustration of controlled spear work occurs in the *Ōu Eikei Gunki*, the great chronicle of the wars in the north of Japan at the time of Sekigahara. In the section on the attack on Yuzawa castle, a frontal and a flank attack are delivered simultaneously, and naginata are also used:

Iyo Choza'emonjo Sadahira and Ichikuri Heibu Shorin with 300 men, plus the forces under Yoshida Magoichi and Nishino Shuri Ryōshun and Magosaburō of the same family with 500 men, arranged their spear blades in an even line and went to fight against the Yuzawa side. From the flank at the same time eighteen nagae yari men acquired a name for themselves by advancing in one rank holding spears and naginata. They cut into all sides of the dense crowd as they surrounded the unfortunates…

RIGHT

In one of the most interesting illustrations from *Zōhyō Monogatari* an ashigaru offers water to a horse, using his jingasa as a bowl. The horse, which is clearly troublesome, is tethered by a rope and also has a band tied around its front legs. At the rear of the saddle are two bags containing rice and soy beans. The lord's matchlock pistol is in a holster at the right front of the saddle.

Spear carriers and standard bearers

Most of the ashigaru who were not attached to the disciplined weapons units would be in close attendance upon the daimyō, and here the opportunities for individual glory, and, for that matter, death, were that much greater. It was the sandal bearers and spear carriers who would willingly receive the arrows and bullets meant for their masters. One of the most dramatic scenes in the film *Kagemusha* shows the ranks of Takeda Shingen's bodyguard, among whom are many ashigaru, closing in around him to give protection during a surprise night attack.

The most vulnerable position for an ashigaru to occupy was standard bearer in a daimyō's army. To kill an ashigaru standard bearer could be a feat akin to taking the head of a worthy samurai. In the Momii Nikki account of the battle of Awataguchi a certain Yata Genji earns a commendation this way:

> The general Sanshichi was jammed tight and was attacked. Over 700 of his followers were crowded together. While some recovered and went back others were killed. The Flag Commissioner Tobe Shirō was cornered by the kashira Eta Heiko and the retainer Yata Kotairō and was

In this drawing by Hokusai, one ashigaru blows a conch trumpet while another beats the war drum.

This illustration from *Zōhyō Monogatari* shows an ashigaru wearing no armour except for a jingasa. He is likely to have been in charge of a pack-horse unit. He has two swords of simple design, as shown by the single coil of braid on the hilt. His provision bags are tied around his body.

killed in the press, and Yata Genji also slew the standard bearer. To a loud yell from those present he snatched away Nobuo's uma jirushi, which was in the form of a golden pestle…

In the *Banshō Sayo Gunki* we read of another desperate attempt to 'keep the flag flying':

One of the great drawbacks of the arquebus was its inability to fire in wet weather. Several ideas were tried to overcome this difficulty, such as weather-proofing the fuse by boiling it in a chemical mixture. One later innovation is shown here in a picture from *Geijutsu Hiden Zue*. A small box is fitted over the touch hole, allowing the whole operation of firing to take place under cover.

The swift current separated those who had the flags and the uma jirushi of Ukita… then the flag carrier too was killed by a galloping horse as he walked along, the uma jirushi fell to the ground many times and finally had to be abandoned.

Not surprisingly, service in the particularly dangerous role of standard bearer was likely to ensure promotion to samurai. In the *Komatsu Gunki*:

A groom checks a horse's shoes, while two others control two horses, from a section in *Ehon Taikō-ki*. An attendant helps fit a sashimono to a samurai's back, while an ashigaru unpacks a huge armour chest. In the centre, an ashigaru threads the pole through the tags on a banner. Everywhere the ashigaru are busy preparing that which a samurai may need.

A certain Deguchi, a retainer of Eguchi's, held Motokura Nagahide's hata jirushi, and while he had it performed feats against the rebels on many occasions… Eguchi recommended promotion for this and gave him a 200 koku fief…

Another account is found in the *Kiyomasa-ki*:

As the defeated army flooded out and it was realized that they were scattering in all directions, the men accompanying Kiyomasa were Shoba-yashi Shunjin, Morimoto Gidayu, Kashihara Tōgorō, Ikeda Jinshirō,

ASHIGARU IN A DAIMYŌ'S ARMY *c.*1600
This plate shows three ashigaru of the time after Hideyoshi's Separation Edict when ashigaru had effectively become the lower ranks of the samurai – a status made legal and binding by the Tokugawa. This distinguished them from labourers impressed into an army such as happened during the Korean campaign. The ashigaru on the right wears a tatami-gusoku (literally straw-mat armour) that folded up to be carried or stored. It consisted of metal plates sewn on to a cloth backing and joined with chain mail. The central fellow tying his hachimaki wears an unusual okegawa-dō that has separate side plates. It could therefore be worn as a hara-ate, an armour that consisted of only the breastplate. The figure on the left, who is an arquebusier, has a hotoke-dō (literally Buddha armour) with a smooth lacquered surface. In his hand is a reinforced headband.

An interesting page from *Geijutsu Hiden Zue* showing how to fire in the dark on pre-selected targets using cords to gauge the elevation. A similar scene occurs in the film *Kagemusha*.

Wada Takemaru, the bow carrier Mizutani Yasu no jō, the uma-jirushi carrier Yokichi, the sandal bearers Itsuho, Oyoshi, Hike and Ōe Jinshichi.

It may first be noticed how many of these close attendants on Kato Kiyomasa have no surnames. These include the ashigaru who held Kato Kiyomasa's great standard that bore the motto of the Nichiren sect of Buddhism, 'Namu Myōho Renge Kyō' ('Hail to the Lotus of the Divine Law'). Because of his conduct at this battle the uma jirushi carrier Yokichi was promoted to the status of samurai, and in the *Zokusen Kiyomasa-ki* (the second series of the *Kiyomasa-ki*) we can read more about him:

[at the time of the above battle] …present with Kiyomasa. Kashihara Tōgorō, Katō Hiraza'emon are recorded, a certain Wada Takemaru was among them… As for the uma-jirushi carrier Yokichi at the time he received from Shobayashi Yo'emon a fief of 300 koku.

Accounts of individual ashigaru glory outside the ranks of a daimyō's attendants are very rare indeed. One of the few in existence concerns how an ashigaru was inspired by the sight of a dead samurai's sashimono banner lying on the battlefield, and went on to earn great glory:

One of their common soldiers had lost heart and retreated, but when he was about to drink water from a stream by the roadside, he saw the great sashimono where it had fallen into the water. He saw the characters on it, and regretted that he had retreated. This mere ashigaru hurried back

This excellent modern depiction of the stages of firing an arquebus volley by artist Colin Upton shows the different roles of the men in the arquebus squads. The ko gashira directs the operation, the bullet carrier gives out the supply, and the arquebusiers load and fire. Spare fuses are kept on a frame at the front, and to save time in reloading the ramrod is stuck into the ground. (Reproduced from the *Taikō Wargames Rules*, by Flagship Games Ltd)

and charged into the midst of the great army of the enemy. He fought with great desperation and took three helmeted heads… He ended his career with 200 koku.

The above accounts show how the successful general on the battlefield achieved loyalty and efficiency at all levels of those under his command. Every ashigaru had his place, his function and his value. The *Zōhyō Monogatari* is eloquent testimony to this, but Matsudaira notes throughout that discipline is essential, and reserves his strongest language for ashigaru who are careless with equipment:

It is the rule that on the battlefield no equipment must be abandoned. Small spear scabbards must be placed within the mune ita of the armour. Long scabbards must be kept at the side. Ramrods should be placed in the side like a quiver and not mislaid. It is also the rule that horses must not be allowed to wander freely. This is strictly forbidden.

Nevertheless, the whole tone of the *Zōhyō Monogatari* is one of positive acceptance, recognizing that by 1649 ashigaru were a vital part of any army, and that the resources devoted to their welfare, training and support were never wasted. By dint of edict, definition and achievement they had long since achieved the ultimate accolade that Japan's traditional warrior class could bestow. Ashigaru, who had once been no more than a peasant rabble, had become samurai.

忍者

Part 3
Ninja

Japan's secret warriors

For any military historian the ninja remains one of the most fascinating mysteries of Japanese samurai warfare. The word ninja or its alternative reading *shinobi* crops up again and again in historical accounts in the context of secret intelligence gathering or assassinations carried out by martial-arts experts. Many opportune deaths may possibly be credited to ninja activities, but as they were so secret it is impossible to prove either way. The ways of the ninja were therefore an unavoidable part of samurai warfare, and no samurai could ignore the secret threat they posed, which could ruin all his carefully laid plans. As a result ninja were both used and feared, although they were almost invariably despised because of the contrast their ways presented to the samurai code of behaviour. This may be partly due to the fact that many ninja had their origins in the lower social classes, and that their secretive and underhand methods were the exact opposite of the ideals of the noble samurai facing squarely on to his enemy.

This paradox, that ninja were beneath contempt and yet indispensable, is a theme running through the whole history of ninja warfare. It is also fascinating to note that the popular extension of the image of the ninja to a superhuman who could fly and perform magic also has a surprisingly long history in Japan. Such stories were being told as early as the beginning of the 17th century, when many of the historical accounts became mixed up with other legends.

The origins of the ninja

Secret operations, from guerrilla warfare to the murder of prominent rivals, are topics that may be found throughout Japanese history, but it is only from about

the mid-15th century onwards that we find references to such activities being carried out by specially trained individuals who belonged to organizations dedicated to this type of warfare. Much of the activity is focused around the Iga and Koga areas of central Japan, so this location and time period will provide the major setting for this part of the book.

The traditional view of the ninja as a secret, superlative, black-coated spy and assassin derives from two different roots. The first is the area of undercover work, of espionage and intelligence gathering (and even assassination) that is indispensable to the waging of war. The second is the use of mercenaries, whereby the leaders of military operations pay outsiders to fight for them. In Japan these two elements came together to produce the ninja and, curiously enough, the ninja provide almost the only example of mercenaries being used in Japanese warfare. Part of the reason for this was that secret operations were the antithesis of the samurai ideal. A daimyō would not wish to have his brave and noble samurai's reputations soiled by carrying out such despicable acts. Instead he paid others to do them. It was an unusual but highly valued service, and the Japanese historian Watatani sums up the situation as follows:

> So-called ninjutsu techniques, in short are the skills of shinobi-no-jutsu and shinobi-jutsu, which have the aims of ensuring that one's opponent does not know of one's existence, and for which there was special training. During the Sengoku Period such techniques were used on campaign, and included sekko [spy] and kancho [espionage] techniques and skills.

The term shinobi is merely the alternative reading of the character *nin*; hence *shinobi no mono* rather than ninja. But ninja trips more readily off a Western tongue, and has therefore become the popular term.

As undercover operations are fundamental to the conduct of war in any culture, it is not surprising to read of such techniques being used throughout Japan's own turbulent history, but the first written account confirms that even at that early stage such activities were somehow questionable, even when they produced results. In *Shomonki*, the gunkimono that deals with the life of Taira Masakado and was probably completed shortly after his death in AD 940, we read:

> Over forty of the enemy were killed on that day, and only a handful managed to escape with their lives. Those who were able to survive the fighting fled in all directions, blessed by Heaven's good fortune. As for Yoshikane's spy Koharumaru, Heaven soon visited its punishment upon him; his misdeeds were found out, and he was captured and killed.

Spying was the classic ninja role, so we may note here the first written confirmation that such activities were perceived as contrary to samurai behaviour.

Like *Shomonki*, the two greatest gunkimono, *Hogen Monogatari* and *Heike Monogatari*, were written for an aristocratic audience who wished to hear of the glorious deeds of their ancestors. The activities of the common foot soldiers, who outnumbered the mounted samurai by 20 to one in the armies of the time, are almost totally ignored, so it is not surprising that stories of ignoble undercover acts are conspicuous by their absence. The one exception is the story that begins *Heike Monogatari*, when Taira Tadamori thwarts an attempt to assassinate him by using the sort of trick later attributed to skilled ninja. Being warned beforehand that rivals in the Court intended his death,

> …he provided himself with a long dagger which he put on under his long court dress, and turning aside to a dimly lit place, slowly drew the blade, and passed it through the hair of his head so that it gleamed afar with an icy sheen, causing all to stare open-eyed.

The bringing of weapons within the presence of the emperor was a serious offence, and Tadamori was ordered to give an account of himself, whereupon he showed that the knife was a dummy, but it had frightened off the assassin.

We hear nothing more of ninja-like activities during the decisive Gempei War of 1180–85. Instead it was conventional samurai warfare that established Japan's first shogunate. During the 14th century a war broke out when Emperor Go-Daigo tried to regain the power that had been taken away from the imperial line by the shōgun. The result was that Japan ended up with two rival emperors, and *Taiheiki* tells how ninja were involved in the destruction by fire of a fortress called Hachiman-yama:

> …the fall of this castle would benefit the enemies of the Southern Court, and in Kyōto there were enemies from the northern provinces who remembered the approach through the valley. One night, under the cover of rain and wind, Hachiman-yama was approached by a highly skilled shinobi who set fire to the temple.

Elsewhere we read another account of a similar secret raid on a fortified place, a speciality that the ninja were to make their own: 'In 1367…on the 11th day of the same month Tadaoka Rokugoro Saemon cut down a shinobi who had entered Ototsu castle.'

The *Taiheiki* also contains the earliest account of a ninja-like assassination. The assassin was not a professional ninja, but young Kumawaka, the 13-year-old son of a certain Lord Suketomo, who had been sent into exile for his part in the conspiracy of Go-Daigo. Suketomo had been placed in the custody of the lay monk Homma Saburo, who had him executed. Kumawaka swore revenge on Homma Saburo, and for someone who was not a professional assassin his

新撰太閤記

阿能の局の兄 丹波の住人

真鍋六郎太夫

節義を後の紫を顕はし

真鍋の信長の為に亡ぶる丹波の豪家波多野の族福井主水の頼受安土城て父信長の寝処を恐の忍を貫し信長の用心深く雪との終お自殺し市に晒さる妹を哀と義死と訴ふ其義を賞て妾と之阿能局と

Warriors of Medieval Japan

Two ninja on the wall of Iga Ueno castle.

but others made it to nearby Mikawa, where they were well treated by Tokugawa Ieyasu, who was destined to become the last of the three unifiers and who revived the shogunate in 1603. Back in 1581 he was just another daimyō, but from 1603 onwards all the activities of the ninja of Iga and Koga were conducted on behalf of the Tokugawa family, and their mercenary days were over. Tokugawa Ieyasu was an astute politician, and surely nothing illustrates his foresight better than the fact that he took Japan's finest ninja into his service.

In 1582 Oda Nobunaga was murdered by Akechi Mitsuhide, who then set himself up as shōgun and began to hunt down any rivals. Tokugawa Ieyasu was visiting Sakai when the coup occurred. Having only a handful of personal retainers with him, he was faced with the difficult prospect of getting back to Mikawa by sea or land without being intercepted by the Akechi samurai. The

overland route lay via Iga, so with the help of local supporters Ieyasu set off. The *Mikawa Go Fudoki* continues the story:

> From here on it was mountain roads and precipices as far as Shigaraki, with many mountain bandits. Yamaoka and Hattori accompanied them, defying mountain bandits and yamabushi alike…Hattori Sadanobu was praised for the great extent of his loyalty, and on leaving he was presented with a wakizashi forged by Kunitsugu… Yamaoka, father and son, took their leave beyond the Tomi pass on the Iga border.

Thus, by a combination of friendly guides they made it to the Iga border. Here more allies took over:

> Hattori Hanzo Masashige was an Iga man. Sent on by Tadakatsu, he went ahead as guide to the roads of Iga. The previous year, when Lord Oda had persecuted Iga, he had ordered, 'The samurai of the province must all be killed.' Because of this people fled to the Tokugawa territories

ABOVE LEFT
Ninja with sword. A member of the Iga Ueno ninja re-enactment society poses for the camera during the 2002 Ninja Festival.

ABOVE RIGHT
Ninja with a shinobigama (kusari-gama). Combination weapons involving sickles were a popular choice for ninja.

of Mikawa and Totomi, where it was ordered that they be shown kindness and consideration. Consequently their relatives were able to pay them back for this kindness. Beginning with Tsuge Sannojo Kiyohiro and his son, two or three hundred men of Tsuge village, and over 100 Koga samurai under Shima Okashi no suke and others…came to serve him…and they passed through the middle of the mountains that were the dens of mountain bandits.

The serious nature of the perils Ieyasu faced is illustrated by the fate of his retainer Anayama Baisetsu, who took a different route back to Mikawa and was murdered along the way. There is also a story in connection with Ieyasu's escape that is almost too good a ninja tale to be false! Akechi's men, who had been ordered to be on the lookout for him, searched the ship in which Ieyasu fled from Ise. Ieyasu was hidden under the cargo in the hold. The soldiers began thrusting their long-bladed spears into the cargo to find anyone concealed therein. One of the spear blades cut his leg, but Ieyasu responded coolly by taking the head towel from his forehead and quickly wiping the blade clean of blood before it was withdrawn.

Serving the shōgun

Oda Nobunaga's murder was avenged by the second of the unifiers, Toyotomi Hideyoshi, who marched his army against Kyōto and destroyed Akechi Mitsuhide at the battle of Yamazaki. From this time on Hideyoshi went from strength to strength, and over the next 20 years conquered the whole of Japan. When he defeated the Hōjō in 1590 he gave Tokugawa Ieyasu their territories as a reward. Ieyasu chose not to base himself at the Hōjō's main fortress of Odawara but further east in the small town of Edo. It was a successful move, as Edo is now called Tokyo, and what is now the palace of the emperor of Japan was Ieyasu's own Edo castle, guarded by the men of Iga and Koga.

The Iga detachment at Edo was under the command of the man who appears in popular works as the most famous ninja of all, Hattori Hanzo Masashige, who had acted as a guide through Iga. Hanzo was born in 1541, the son of Hattori Yasunaga, a hereditary retainer of the Tokugawa. He fought his first battle at the age of 16 in the form of a night attack on the castle of Udo in 1557, and went on to serve with distinction at the battles of Anegawa (1570) and Mikata ga Hara (1572). His nickname was 'Devil Hanzo'. He died in 1596, aged 55, and was succeeded by his son, Hattori Masanari.

The later wars in which ninja were involved on behalf of the Tokugawa will be described later. From 1638 onwards Japan was at peace, and military skills declined, yet during this time the myth of the ninja as we know it today began to grow, until a mixture of historical accounts and legends produced the 'superman' ninja who could fly in the air.

Recruitment and training

Ninja recruitment

From the mid-15th century onwards, certain samurai families began to develop particular skills in intelligence gathering, undercover warfare and assassination. These were the ninja families. Like so many other martial-arts traditions in Japan, their skills and traditions were passed on from father to son, or more usually from sensei to chosen pupil, who may not always have been a relative. In a real sense, therefore, ninja were born, not made, and the expression 'recruitment' refers only to the negotiations made between daimyō and the ninja leader for the use of his men's services.

However, when Tokugawa Ieyasu took the men of Iga and Koga under his personal wing in 1581, the source of supply dried up, and we begin to see other daimyō training and using their own home-grown ninja. Strangely enough, this was not officially forbidden, and in 1649, in the shogunate's laws for military service, we read that only those daimyō with incomes of 10,000 koku and above were allowed to have shinobi in their armies.

The school of *ninjutsu* called the Nakagawa-ryu, which served the daimyō Tsugaru in Mutsu Province in the mid-17th century, provides a good example of the recruitment and training process. The founder of the school was a samurai called Nakagawa Shoshunjin, an expert in ninjutsu. The most fascinating account of his life is the *Okufuji Monogatari*, which says that 'he could change into a rat or a spider, and transform himself into birds and animals' – an early illustration of the magical powers traditionally attributed to ninja. In reality Shoshunjin had the command of a group of ten young samurai whom he trained to practise ninjutsu, and forbade anyone else from coming near the place where they exercised, which was at the southern corner of the castle and called Ishibayashi. Shoshunjin called the group the Hayamichi no mono ('the short-cut people') and its numbers soon increased to 20. Since the duties of the group members were to act as spies or secret agents, they were put into operation entirely on the word of the daimyō, and their training was kept strictly secret.

Ninja selection

There is a splendid story about Nakagawa Shoshunjin's first visit to the Tsugaru mansion to be interviewed by Tsugaru Gemban, a *karo* (senior retainer) of the Tsugaru. Tsugaru Gemban challenged Shoshunjin to prove his ninja abilities by stealing the pillow from under his head while he lay sleeping. That night Gemban lay down on his futon, and as time passed he heard the pitter-patter of a passing shower beginning to fall outside the house. He carefully avoided letting his head move from the pillow, until he suddenly felt rain falling on to

Hattori Hanzo, the leader of the ninja of Iga and a samurai general in his own right under Tokugawa Ieyasu, is buried in this grave in the grounds of the Seinenji temple in Tokyo. Hanzo's spear is preserved inside the temple.

his face. He raised his eyes, and quickly noticed that the ceiling was leaking. In spite of himself his head moved off the pillow at an angle. When he lowered his head once again the pillow was missing, and as he turned his head in surprise he saw Shoshunjin standing beside him, grinning broadly, and with the pillow in his hands!

Unfortunately, the story is probably not authentic, as similar versions are told of ninja employed by other daimyō. For example, Mōri Motonari's general Sugiwara Harima no kami used a ninja, who, according to legend, was asked to steal a sword from his master's bedside, and a certain Kato Dansai was asked to steal a naginata from beside the bed of Naoe Yamashiro no kami of the Uesugi family. Nevertheless, it illustrates the respect that the daimyō had for ninja skills, and the need to hire someone who could be trusted.

Ninja training

We may certainly envisage the ninja of Iga and Koga being trained for their future roles as soon as they could walk. The ninja leaders of the province were minor landowners and, in common with all daimyō of any size, great emphasis was laid on family connections and hereditary loyalty. Any boy born into a conventional samurai family would grow up expecting to be a warrior, and many hours of his childhood would be spent learning the martial arts. Skills with the famous samurai sword, the spear, bow and, later in ninja history, guns would be most important. A young samurai would also be expected to ride well and to swim.

For a young ninja, of course, the curriculum would be more extensive. He would also have to learn about such matters as explosives and the blending of poisons, and become an expert in fieldcraft and survival. This would include such 'ninja lore' as how to purify water and how to cook rice in camp by wrapping it in a wet cloth and burying it underneath a campfire.

He would have to be superbly physically fit to enable him to scale the walls of castles and become an expert in martial arts, including unarmed grappling techniques. We may therefore envisage the fledgling ninja being trained from an early age in all these skills. He would also have to know how to draw a map and would have a great advantage if he could read and write. If he was to adopt the disguises of other professions, he would need an in-depth knowledge of them to be convincing.

Models of ninja equipment, most of which are described somewhere in this book, on show in the Ninja Museum at Iga Ueno.

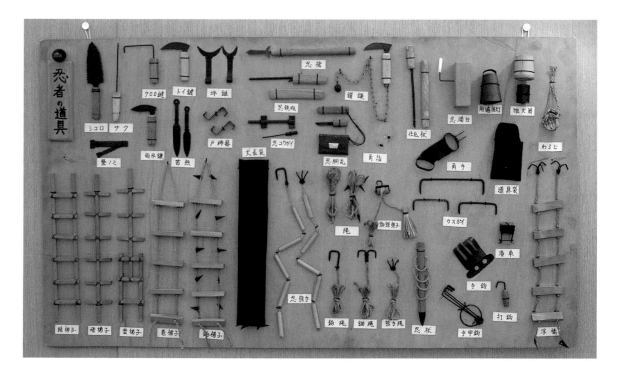

Belief and belonging

At a psychological level the young ninja would need to develop a detachment from death and the fear of dying that was even more complete than that customarily expected of ordinary samurai, who were presented with the ideal of serving their masters with unflinching zeal to the very end. 'The way of the samurai,' wrote a famous warrior, 'is found in death,' and how much more it was in the way of the ninja. There was also the chilling samurai tradition of ritual suicide, whereby, in situations of certain defeat, any disgrace could be wiped away by the act of hara kiri that released one's spirit.

The ninja's concept of his own fate was therefore a more intense version of the samurai worldview. The major difference in attitude that would be inculcated in the ninja, as distinct from the samurai, was the complete acceptance of the knife in the dark as a legitimate activity. This was contrary to so much of the samurai tradition that relied on stories of noble warriors who fought in an ideal and often idealized way. The accepted samurai code involved first of all being very visible, so that both friends and enemies recognized who it was that won the supreme distinction of being the first to go into battle or the first to scale a castle wall during an assault. How different it was for a ninja! Dressed in black and with no flag to identify him, his role in a siege would be to enter the castle days before the assault and lie low until emerging to cause mayhem by setting fire to towers, killing guards or even assassinating the commander. His job done, the ninja would withdraw into anonymity and let the first samurai in the assault party receive all the glory. It was an attitude totally different from the rest of samurai warfare, and carried the additional opprobrium that the noble samurai, who depended upon the ninja's activities for his own achievements, officially despised the ninja for behaving in such an underhand way.

Ninja appearance and equipment

Men in black

The traditional ninja garb of a full black costume is so well known that it is usually taken for granted, but there are in fact no authentic written accounts where ninja are actually described as being dressed in black. Usually they appear to have disguised themselves to blend in with the enemy. As the *Buke Meimokushō* relates:

> They travelled in disguise to other territories to judge the situation of the enemy, they would inveigle their way into the midst of the enemy to discover gaps, and enter enemy castles to set them on fire, and carried out assassinations, arriving in secret.

The earliest pictorial reference to a ninja in black is a book illustration of 1801, which shows a ninja climbing into a castle wearing what everyone would immediately recognize as a ninja costume. However, it could simply be that it is pictures like these that have given us our image of the ninja rather than vice versa. It is a long-standing artistic convention in Japan, seen today in the *Bunraku* puppet theatre, that to dress a character in black is to indicate to the viewer that he cannot see that person. To depict a silent assassin in an identical way in a picture would therefore be perfectly natural and understandable to the contemporary Japanese viewer, and need not imply that the resulting illustration is in any way an actual portrait of a ninja.

Nevertheless, it is obvious that if a ninja was to perform the role most often noted for him, that of entering a castle in secret by night, then a head-to-foot costume of black would be the most sensible thing to wear. We may therefore safely conclude that in this situation at least the traditional black costume was authentic, although some authorities maintain that the black was tinged with a little red so that bloodstains would not show.

ABOVE LEFT

Ninja mail armour. This ensemble from the Arashiyama Historical Museum in Kyōto shows a simple suit of armour that could have been worn under a ninja's costume.

ABOVE RIGHT

An actor in the familiar black costume climbs the wall of Iga Ueno castle.

The ninja costume

The ninja costume was simple but very well designed for its purpose. The jacket was not unlike the jacket worn for judo or karate, having no ties. So that nothing would catch on any protrusions when climbing a wall, the 'tails' of the jacket were tucked inside the trousers. These were like the kobakama, the trousers commonly worn by samurai when riding a horse. They were quite narrow and tied below the knee. Over the calves would be worn cloth *kiahan* (gaiters), again very similar to standard samurai equipment in which small weapons could be concealed, while on the feet would be black *tabi*, the classic Japanese socks with a separate compartment for the big toe, and reinforced soles. *Waraji* (straw sandals) would complete the ninja's footwear. A shirt with close-fitting arms also seems to have been worn according to most illustrations, and the whole ensemble was pulled tightly together round the waist by a long black belt. The biggest difference from a samurai's costume, however, was to be found above the neck, because the ninja's head was wrapped in an all-enveloping cowl, with only the face above the mouth, or even only the eye slits, visible. This was created from two separate pieces of black cloth.

Several museums in Japan have examples of lightweight body armour that could be worn under the ninja costume. The construction was that of a heavy cloth backing on to which were sewn small lacquered metal plates joined by thin sections of ring mail. Reinforced hoods, not unlike the ninja cowl, were made of similar material. As the ashigaru in a samurai army wore very different types of armour, it is not unreasonable to associate these simple body armours with ninja. Standard samurai kote and suneate would also have provided extra protection for very little additional weight.

OPPOSITE PAGE

NINJA IN TRADITIONAL COSTUME WITH ESSENTIAL PERSONAL EQUIPMENT

This ninja wears the traditional black ninja costume. The ninja suit was a simple but very well-designed item based around trousers and a jacket with no ties. So that nothing would catch on any protrusions when climbing a wall the 'tails' of the jacket were tucked inside the trousers, which were tapered. Over the calves would be worn cloth gaiters, again very similar to standard samurai equipment, while on the feet would be black tabi (**1**). Waraji would complete the ninja's footwear. A shirt with close-fitting arms was worn, and the whole ensemble was pulled tightly together round the waist by a long black belt (**2**). The ninja's head was wrapped in an all-enveloping cowl. His utility bag hangs from his belt.

Tetsu bishi (caltrops) could also be carried (**3**). These consisted of sharp iron spikes arranged in the shape of a tetrahedron so that one spike was always protruding upwards. As samurai wore thin-soled footwear, tetsu bishi could be very effective in slowing down pursuers. A ninja might carry a selection of different shaped shuriken, the 'ninja throwing stars' that were projected with a spinning motion (**4**). Also illustrated are the so-called 'ninja's essential six items': The Kaginawa (hooked rope) (**5**). This was the most important climbing device and would be carried from the ninja's belt when not in use. An amegasa (sedge hat) (**6**). A straw rain hat would have been very useful for concealing one's identity as well as during the rainy season. A folded towel three shaku (foot) long, known as a sanjaku tenugui (**7**). This was the ninja equivalent

of the samurai item that could be used as a bandage and a sling as well as a towel. An uchitake, a waterproof gunpowder container inside a bamboo tube (**8**). This was a simple powder flask doubly sealed against the weather. A tinderbox would be used for ignition. The purpose was more one of setting fire to something rather than creating an actual explosion. An Inro (medicine carrier) (**9**). The inro was standard wear for any Japanese samurai, and consisted of a small lacquered box with several interlocking compartments, pulled tight by a draw cord. It could contain pills, potions and antidotes to poison. A lacquered, water-proof writing box with slate pencil called seki hitsu, literally 'stone brush' (**10**). Literacy was expected of a ninja so that he could draw a map of enemy installations and write messages.

Ninja disguises

The use of disguise is frequently mentioned in the chronicles, and different disguises suited different situations. If the ninja was required to travel widely round an enemy's territory observing the layout of his troops and the defensive features of his castles, what better cover could there be but to assume the role of a *komuso*, the sect of Zen monks who played the flute and wore enormous baskets over their heads? They would be seen on the highways and byways, playing music and begging. The itinerant *yamabushi* (the mountain monks) were also frequently seen on Japanese roads, and this was a better disguise to adopt when the mission was to deliver a message in private to a friendly ally, because yamabushi were invited into people's homes to say prayers and give blessings. Even a simple Buddhist monk sent out begging, his face partly concealed by a large sedge hat, might be a ninja. Strolling players such as *sarugaku* dancers and puppeteers might provide cover for spying activities in a daimyō's castle town. They would no doubt be searched for weapons if they were invited to give a performance inside a castle, but the mere act of entering a castle and making one's way through the maze of interlocking walls and gates to the daimyō's private apartments would yield much valuable intelligence for a rival.

Yamabushi. The disguise of one of these mountain ascetics was a popular one for a ninja.

Standard ninja equipment

The most important ninja weapon was his sword. This was the standard Japanese fighting sword or katana, renowned for its strength and sharpness. Both the length and curve of katana blades varied considerably, and for convenience the ninja would choose a blade that was shorter and straighter than usual. One unusual way of carrying a sword must be mentioned. This arose from the ninja technique of exploring a potentially dangerous dark place such as a castle's corridors. The ninja would balance the sword's scabbard out in front on the tip of the sword blade, with the scabbard's suspensory cords gripped firmly between his teeth. This extended the ninja's range of feel by a good six feet, and if the scabbard end encountered an enemy, the ninja would let it fall and lunge forward in the precise direction of the assailant. A sword could also be used in climbing a wall, because the strong iron tsuba (sword-guard) could provide a step if the sword was leant against the wall. The ninja would loop the end of the suspensory cord round his foot so that he could pull his sword up when he had climbed the wall.

Needless to say, the ninja would have had an array of weapons secreted about his person. A simple-looking Japanese folding fan might well conceal a

The komuso, flute-playing Zen mendicants, provided a useful disguise for a ninja as they were able to roam the country at will, their identity disguised beneath the curious 'wastepaper basket' hat. These komuso, however, are the genuine article, photographed in Yura (Wakayama Prefecture) during the midnight Bon Festival in August 1997.

knife blade. Heavy iron knuckle-dusters called *tekken* are also known. Another fairly standard piece of ninja equipment was a hooked rope for climbing. This consisted of a three- or four-pronged grapnel attached to a coil of thin but very strong rope. It was most conveniently carried hanging from the belt. A utility bag might also be suspended from the belt, and this could contain small throwing weapons such as knives or the well-known *shuriken* (ninja stars) that were flung with a spinning motion.

Maki bishi (caltrops) could also be carried. The iron version (*tetsu bishi*) consisted of iron spikes arranged in the shape of a tetrahedron so that one spike was always protruding upwards. As samurai wore thin-soled footwear, tetsu bishi could be very effective in slowing down pursuers. There was also a simple but very effective alternative in the *tennen bishi*, the dried seed pod of the water chestnut. The dessicated pod dried naturally into a shape of a caltrop with sharp spikes at four vertices. Poisons and their antidotes and emergency food supplies might also find their way into the utility bag when appropriate.

Specialized ninja equipment

There was also a weird and wonderful array of specialized weapons and devices that ninja could use in appropriate circumstances. Many of these are drawn and described in *Bansen Shukai*, the 17th century ninja manual. We will deal first with devices to assist climbing into a castle – a very common ninja activity.

OPPOSITE PAGE
NINJA SPECIALIZED EQUIPMENT AND ITS USE
This plate shows various items of ninja specialized equipment in use.
Uchikagi (a metal climbing device)(**1**). This consisted of a strong iron hook mounted on a wooden handle. Its purpose was to aid climbing, but as well as acting like an extension to the hand as shown here, it would probably also be very useful in providing a step for a descent. The insert diagram shows another climbing aid. Saoto hikigane (listening device) (**2**). They acted like an ear trumpet, so the ninja could listen in to conversations and ascertain the movements of guards. Details are shown in the insert diagram. They were essentially no more than simple tapered metal cylinders. Tsubogiri

(breaking and entering tool) (**3**). Two devices in succession could open small gaps between the planking. The first was the tsubogiri, which looks like a two-pronged iron fork, which would enlarge the gap slightly by twisting, making a space just large enough for a thin leaf-shaped saw with small teeth to be inserted. Shikoro (thin saw) (**4**). Using this broad-bladed thin saw a ninja could cut through wooden joints at the side of a window or an outside screen. The insert diagram shows a long-handled version. Kunai (gouger) (**5**). As Japanese castle walls were made on a wattle and daub core and plastered over, so a ninja would use a kunai, which looked like a cross between a broad-bladed knife and a paint scraper. By gouging and cutting, the

ninja could rapidly carve out a hole large enough for him to climb through. Shinobi gama (**6**). The sickle and chain combination was a well-known martial-arts weapon that was derived from agricultural implements, and in its ordinary form was known as the kusari-gama. The chain had a weight on the end and could be flung to halt a pursuer. The attacker would then drag him off his feet and kill him with the sickle blade. The ninja version had a smaller but very sharp blade kept scabbarded when not in use. Tekken (claws or 'knuckle dusters') (**7**). These were made of iron and originated as wall-climbing devices. They could also be used for fighting. Hokode (hand claws) (**8**). These would help a ninja climb a wall and also act as an anti-personnel weapon in a fist fight.

Let us consider the typical ninja attacking a castle in secret by night. First, he has to cross the ditch or moat. He could always swim, and even ordinary samurai were expected to be so skilled at swimming that they could use their weapons while treading water. But if explosives were involved in the ninja's plans then he could not risk getting the powder wet. He might therefore use his hooked rope to cross the moat hand-over-hand. Alternatively, if the ninja were operating as a group, one man could swim the moat and then help his comrades rig up a simple rope ladder, but if the moat was wide a safer alternative might

be to cross using some form of flotation device. *Bansen Shukai* also shows a prefabricated boat, and the Togakure-ryu school of ninjutsu used a number of floats tied together. The best known flotation device was the *mizugumo*, the so-called 'water-spider'. These wooden water shoes were illustrated in *Bansen Shukai*, and look very unstable. In fact they were not intended for use in crossing water, merely to aid stability on swampy ground.

The castle wall now had to be climbed, and in many cases the deeply curved stone walls with many gaps allowed the ninja to climb up without difficulty, but mechanical devices would sometimes be used. The standard hooked rope has already been mentioned, but for more difficult ascents some form of portable ladder was needed. The simplest was a straightforward rope ladder with strong wooden rungs and a stout hook at the top. An ingenious version of this consisted of a series of short bamboo sections. A rope was threaded through each section, alternating between pieces threaded across the middle and through their whole length. A hook was attached to the top, and when the whole length of the rope was pulled tight and secured the result was a lightweight if flimsy ladder. Other help might be provided for the feet by means of spiked climbing devices called *tekkokagi*, which acted like crampons.

Having surmounted the stone base the ninja was faced with the white plaster walls that lay on top. Some were simple outer walls pierced by arrow and gun ports, others were made up of elaborate superstructures and towers. As there would be a considerable overhang because of the tiled protective surface on top of the white wall, the ninja might decide to cut his way into the defended position. Here the construction of the walls came most admirably to his assistance. They were made on a wattle and daub core and plastered over, so a ninja would use a *kunai*, which looked like a cross between a broad bladed knife and a paint scraper. By gouging and cutting, the ninja could rapidly carve out a hole large enough for him to climb through.

Many of the buildings within the walls of a Japanese castle were made of wood. Climbing these could be made easier by using an *uchikagi*, a metal hook on a wooden handle, or a *kasugai* (cramp), which was an iron bracket rammed into the surface to give an extra foothold. In most cases the target inside the castle would be the daimyō's yashiki, which was often a palatial structure built in addition to the keep and used for entertaining visitors. It would be heavily guarded. Portable listening devices called *saoto hikigane*, which acted like ear trumpets, enabled the ninja to listen in to conversations and ascertain the movements of guards. For a ninja to enter such a wooden building unseen he would have had to use some form of saw. Several types are illustrated in the ninja manuals. The *hamagari*, for example, was a long thin saw with many very sharp teeth mounted on a folding iron shaft like a penknife. Alternatively, using two devices in succession, the ninja could open small gaps between the planking. The first was the *tsubogiri*, which looked like a two-pronged iron

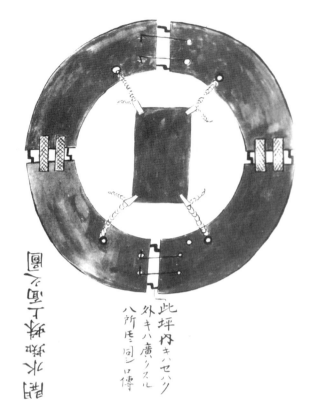

ナシテ外ハ名ヶケテ雲梯ト云ス口傳

高クメ及ハサル所ニ八結梯ノ上ニ飛梯ヲ結付此コトヶ

此製作ハ別ニ作ルニ非ス結梯ニテモ又飛梯ニテモ

雲梯圖説

此製作ハ大竹ヲ割合セ結梯如ノ作ル此上下シクレー

圖ヲ畫テ模水ヲ開

此坪丹キハセハノ外キハ廣クスル八所モニ同シ口傳

fork. Its use would enlarge the gap slightly by twisting, making a space just large enough for a *shikoro*, a thin leaf-shaped saw with small teeth, to be inserted. The tsubogiri could even be used to crack the wood, but this would create a sound that might give the ninja away. Alternatively locks could be picked using an array of burglar's tools.

Ninja also had to be fully conversant with firearms and explosives technology. The matchlock arquebus, introduced to Japan in 1543, was too clumsy to be considered a ninja weapon except when it was used as a sniper's firearm. Matchlock pistols could more easily be carried by a ninja, but the ideally suited wheel-lock pistol arrived too late in Japan for it to be used in war. In addition the ninja had a huge range of mainly Chinese explosive devices at his disposal. There were two main types. The first were soft-cased bombs built round a paper or wicker carton and designed to release smoke or poison gas, or to alarm an enemy by their thunderclap explosion. Fragments of iron, broken pottery or dried human faeces could be included to make them into anti-personnel devices. The second type were hard-cased bombs, either of pottery or iron. The latter could produce fearful wounds like a fragmentation bomb, and large models would have had sufficient force to blow a hole in a castle's plaster walls. Small versions could be thrown by hand, making them

ABOVE LEFT
This illustration from *Bansen Shukai*, the manual of ninja lore published in 1683, shows a ladder with a hinged section. The ladder is light in weight.

ABOVE RIGHT
This illustration from *Bansen Shukai* is of the famous (and notorious!) water spider. One was supposed to have been worn on each foot to allow the ninja to cross swampy ground – not water.

effectively hand grenades. Ignition was provided from a tinderbox or a smouldering cord kept in a weather-proof lacquered container. An ingenious device was the *hyakuraiju*, a number of small cases of gunpowder strung together on a short rope. They were timed to explode in series, so that an enemy might think that they were under attack from a number of assailants.

A ninja would also be expected to be a sharpshooter with a bow and arrow, and there were small versions of ninja bows that could be carried more easily. Ninja also made good use of the martial-arts weapons that were derived from agricultural implements, such as the well-known *kusari-gama*, the combination of a sickle and a chain. The chain had a weight on the end and could be flung to halt a pursuer. The attacker would then drag him off his feet and kill him with the sickle blade. The ninja version had a smaller but very sharp blade kept in a scabbard when not in use. It was called a *shinobi gama*.

The famous Myoryuji or Ninjadera (ninja temple) in Kanazawa (Ishikawa Prefecture) is one of the best of the very few authentic 'ninja-proofed' buildings to have survived. This is a view of the shoji staircase. The vertical sections of the tread are of translucent paper, enabling a spear thrust to be delivered against any unwelcome caller.

Ninja techniques

Ninja relied on more than just clever gadgets for entering defended places. Teamwork and co-operation were also essential, and well-practised acrobatic skills may well have given rise to the myths of ninja being able to fly. For example, there were two, three and four-man techniques for climbing over a wall. In the first type one ninja would run forward with his comrade on his shoulders. He would then leap from this elevated position. Two men could assist a third to 'fly' over a wall by giving him a powerful leg up. Four might construct a human pyramid.

Other ninja might use one of the foot soldier's pike-like long spears and pole-vault over a gap. It may even be the case that ninja were lifted off the ground using kites to spy on an enemy castle or drop bombs. The technology for this certainly existed, but the extension of it to 'human gliders' or even 'human cannonballs' belongs to the realms of ninja fantasy.

The daily life of a ninja

The ninja homelands

Two places are indelibly associated in the popular mind with ninja and ninjutsu. These are the Iga Province and the southern area of Omi Province known as Koga, and the bulk of historical evidence suggests that the popular view of Iga and Koga as the most important cradles of ninja is broadly correct. In the chronicle *Go Kagami Furoku* we read: 'There was a retainer of the family of Kawai Aki no kami of Iga, of pre-eminent skill in shinobi, and consequently for generations the name of people from Iga became established. Another tradition grew in Koga.' In other words, the inhabitants of the Iga/Koga area (they share a common border) developed a certain expertise in the skills and techniques that were to become known as ninjutsu, and, more importantly, they hired themselves out as mercenaries until their province was sacked by Oda Nobunaga in 1581.

A brief glance at a map of medieval Japan gives one a clue as to why the Iga/Koga area could have the potential to produce a number of independent-minded families who by their military skills were sufficiently secure to be able to place these talents at the disposal of others. Iga Province (now the north-western part of Mie Prefecture) was entirely landlocked, and almost the whole length of its borders followed the tops of several ranges of mountains. Thus the villages in the flatlands within nestled inside a ring of natural defences, pierced only by steep mountain passes. The one side of Iga that is not entirely protected by mountains is the north, where it borders Koga, the southern portion of Omi Province. It was a situation somewhat analogous to that of contemporary Switzerland, though on a much smaller scale, where mountains provided such a good natural defence that its equally formidable inhabitants could become the mercenary soldiers of Europe.

A more detailed look at the topography also reveals that this was politically a very sensitive region. It lies just to the south of the 'neck' of medieval Japan, the narrow strip of land between Lake Biwa and the Bay of Owari that divides the country neatly in two. At the mouth of Lake Biwa lay the then capital, Kyōto, and from it ran the two main highways to the east: the Tokaido and the Nakasendo. The two roads were in fact one and the same as far as Kusatsu. The Tokaido then headed for the sea on the coast of Ise Province, just skirting north of Iga/Koga by the Suzuka Pass, then followed the Pacific coast. The Nakasendo turned north-east along the edge of Lake Biwa and threaded through the vast mountains of the 'Japan Alps' to join the Tokaido in the vicinity of modern Tokyo.

The Iga/Koga area thus formed a bridge between the main trade routes from the capital and the vast and wild mountains of the Kii Peninsula to the south. These mountains amaze one even today by the solitude they present for a region so close to the urban sprawl of Osaka and Kyōto. Within these mountains were villagers who lived their entire lives in one tiny valley community shut off from the rest of Japan until comparatively recent times, and visited only by the wandering yamabushi who traversed this wild country on their pilgrimages. Several accounts refer to these mountains as the haunt of bandits who acted as highwaymen along the Tokaido or as pirates on the sea coast of nearby Ise Province. Many of the ninja myths, such as that of the legendary outlaw Ishikawa Goemon who was supposed to be adept in ninjutsu, no doubt have their origin in the elaboration of the exploits of very un-magical gangs of robbers. The historian Sasama sums up the Iga situation at the beginning of the Age of Warring States as follows:

> In Iga Province at about the time of Ōnin, Jinki Iga no kami was provincial shugo, but thereafter for generations they declined and in Iga there were few who lived there to rule the jizamurai (country samurai). The jizamurai…were affiliated to families on the mountains and beaches of neighbouring provinces and were brigands and pirates, and lived by hunting and fishing. In later years the so-called Iga-shū began to be recruited to various provinces such as Odawara in groups of 50 men or 30 men and were used for ambushes.

What Sasama is describing is nothing less than the formation of an ikki, the associations created by low-ranking samurai families for mutual protection. The archaeological evidence presented by the numerous fortifications of Koga is also very revealing. Of 21 yamashiro sites identified, many date from early in the Age of Warring States, evidence of extensive but small-scale military activity at the time. The various families were joined together in the classic ikki model of a complex hierarchy of mutual support, thereby providing the ideal conditions for mercenary activity to flourish. The Wada family, for example, controlled a series of mountain-top fortresses along a river valley, and Wada Koremasa (1536–83) was sufficiently strong in Koga to give refuge there to the future Shōgun Ashikaga Yoshiaki after the suicide of his brother Ashikaga Yoshiteru in 1565.

Daily life in the ninja village

Although the Iga ikki came together for mutual protection on an equal basis, the social structure within an individual ninja community was based on a rigid hierarchy. At the top of the tree were the jonin, who were the distinguished heads of families. Depending on his wealth, a jonin resembled either a minor daimyō or a village headman of the jizamurai class. Examples of jonin are the famous Hattori Hanzo, Momochi Sandayu and Fujibayashi Nagato no kami. Below the jonin were the *chunin*, who acted as the family's executive officers and leaders. The chunin would make arrangements for the hiring of ninja on a mercenary basis. Below them were the lowly genin, the ninja actually sent into action against an enemy.

The typical ninja village would be very different from a daimyō's bustling castle town, and at first sight would be virtually indistinguishable from any prosperous agricultural centre in a typical daimyō's territory. The big difference would be in the means employed for the village's defence, but these would be very subtle. So on the hills around there would be a chain of smoke beacons to give advance notice of any attack. Within the village itself the houses of the genin would be found on the outskirts, while the home of the jonin would be the village's central focus. This might consist of nothing more than a wooden farmhouse, but it would be located within a maze of rice fields which acted as a moat when flooded, as they would be for much of the year. Steep earthen banks and a bamboo fence or prickly hedge provided other defences. The paths between the rice fields were narrow, and a bell tower housed the means of alerting the villagers when danger threatened.

The ninja house

In several places in Japan today it is possible to visit so-called ninja houses that have been moved from their original locations and re-erected as tourist attractions. They inevitably contain various trap doors and hiding places, but how authentic are they? It seems reasonable to conclude that a powerful and well-patronized jonin should turn his own techniques to his own advantage, and make his home as secure as possible against the surprise attacks that he himself performed so well. As will be discussed below, the genuine fear of

A NINJA DISGUISED AS A YAMABUSHI RETURNS HOME TO HIS VILLAGE IN IGA PROVINCE
This plate shows a ninja returning home to his village in Iga Province after an undercover operation where he has been disguised as a yamabushi.

In the distance is a simple Buddhist temple with a graveyard and a Shintō shrine (**1**). The big difference is in the means employed for the village's defence, but these are very subtle. On the hills around there are a series of smoke beacons to give advance notice of any attack, and a simple watchtower on the edge of the village (**2**).Within the village itself the houses of the genin are located on the outskirts among the rice fields (**3**). The home of the jonin is the village's central focus. This might look like nothing more than a wooden farmhouse such as would be occupied by any ordinary village headman, but it is located within a maze of rice fields which act as a moat when flooded, as they would be for much of the year. Steep earthen banks and a bamboo fence or prickly hedge provide other defences. The paths between the rice fields are narrow, and there are designated places where valuables may be buried (**4**).

assassination made many powerful daimyō introduce well-authenticated features into their own mansions or castles. The most straightforward were features of building design that allowed a visitor to be monitored in secret by the jonin's guards, who could overpower an assassin in seconds. A loose floorboard, situated just to the side of where the jonin's arm would be when he held an audience, could conceal a sword ready for use. Sliding panels, so common in Japanese houses, could be redesigned to pivot around a central axis,

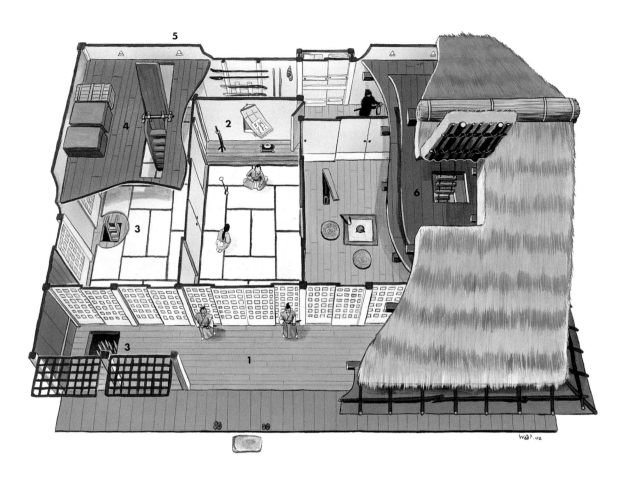

A NINJA HOUSE

In this illustration we are looking inside the jonin's house in the ninja village. It is every bit as well defended as the village. The house is a thatched farmhouse, but it is very cunningly designed. Many 'ninja' features have been added on to the basic-style Japanese farmhouse. These are intended as a defence against attack.

Typical polished wooden corridors give access to rooms floored with tatami (straw mats) (**1**). The jonin's main reception room is well guarded (**2**). There is a secret bolt hole behind the hanging scroll through which a guard can listen to the conversation and enter if required. There is a secret underground passage (**3**) and also a very nasty booby trap in the

corridor with spikes beneath – an assailant would not know which was which. The upper floor is accessed by means of a 'rotating' staircase (**4**), pivoted so that it can snap shut. The upstairs plaster walls are pierced with windows that can act as gunports (**5**). The top storey is almost invisible and has a trap door through the thatch leading to the roof (**6**).

so that a man could virtually disappear in the blinking of an eye. Staircases could be made to fold away, confusing any attacker. A trap door in a dark corridor could drop an assailant on to a row of poisoned spikes. A disappearing staircase that could be instantly retracted by standing on the protruding end after climbing it would also fool any pursuing ninja.

The most interesting example of a ninja-proofed house to have survived, and undoubtedly the most authentic, is the well-known Nijo jinya in Kyōto. This house situated quite near to Nijo castle was the house of Ogawa Nagatsuka, a former samurai who had become a rice merchant, and many of the so-called anti-ninja devices were in fact very sensible fire precautions, which is why it has survived for so long. Nevertheless, there are also several crime prevention features that were designed specifically to protect the owner from entry by unauthorized persons. These will be described in the later section on assassination.

The ninja on campaign

Interior view of the Ninjadera in Kanazawa, which formed part of the outer defence works for Kanazawa castle, the seat of the Maeda daimyō.

For the ninja, 'campaign life' had a totally different meaning from that of the conventional samurai or ashigaru. Ninja could be hired for specific, short-term operations or might be taken along with an army for campaigns of an unspecified or unknown duration. A siege, for example, could take months, during which ninja would be used for intelligence gathering or to cause confusion inside the castle.

Spying and espionage

The *Buke Meimokushō* illustrates the use of ninja for intelligence gathering and spying prior to a military campaign:

> Shinobi-monomi were people used in secret ways, and their duties were to go into the mountains and disguise themselves as firewood gatherers to discover and acquire the news about an enemy's territory…they were particularly expert at travelling in disguise.

These were the occasions when the disguise of a komuso might be appropriate. The earliest written reference to ninja from Iga or Koga in action in this way occurs in the supplement to the *Nochi Kagami*, the annals of the Ashikaga shogunate. In one particular section we read: 'Concerning ninja, they were said to be from Iga and Koga, and went freely into enemy castles in secret. They observed hidden things, and were taken as being friends.'

The section goes on to mention a specific campaign in which Iga men were involved:

> Inside the camp at Magari of the Shōgun Yoshihisa there were shinobi whose names were famous throughout the land. When Yoshihisa attacked Rokkaku Takayori, the family of Kawai Aki no kami of Iga, who served him at Magari earned considerable merit as shinobi in front of the great army of the shōgun. Since then successive generations of Iga men have been admired. This is the origin of the fame of the men of Iga.

A view of the successive roofs of the Ninjadera in Kanazawa.

The ninja girl attendant at the ninja house in Iga Ueno demonstrates how a low trapdoor can give access to the garden.

The reference to the names of Rokkaku Takayori and the Shōgun Ashikaga Yoshihisa enables us to identify this action as one fought in the year 1487. Yoshihisa, who had been raised to the position of shōgun at the age of nine by his father Yoshimasa, took steps to restore his family's military prowess as soon as he was of an age to do so. His chance came in 1487, when some 46 of the landowners of Omi Province, including a number from Koga, appealed to the shōgun against the excesses of the shugo of Omi, Rokkaku Takayori, who was in the process of seizing everyone else's lands for himself. This in itself was nothing remarkable. The shugo were the provincial governors appointed by the Ashikaga, and the disorder of the Ōnin War had enabled many a shugo to disregard his obligation to the shōgun and treat the territory entrusted to him as his own. But a proud young shōgun, the most warlike of his family for a century, did not see such presumption as inevitable, and would not tolerate it. He therefore took personal charge of an expedition against Rokkaku Takayori and besieged him in his castle of Kannonji in Omi Province.

Young Yoshihisa set up camp at the nearby village of Magari. He was joined by several allies sympathetic to the cause of the shogunate and made good progress, but unfortunately Yoshihisa's physical health was not the equal of his mental condition. He was taken ill in camp and succumbed to a sickness from which he was eventually to die. His army therefore struck camp and returned to Kyōto. So by about 1487 the use as mercenaries of shinobi from Iga was well established. Unfortunately we do not know exactly how the ninja were used against Kannonji castle, but intelligence gathering was probably deployed.

Arson

Moving on 60 years from the *Nochi Kagami* account, there is good evidence of the use of ninja from Iga to set fire to buildings. The story is found in a reliable chronicle called the *Tamon-In nikki*, a diary kept by the Abbot Eishun of Tamon-In, a priory of the great Kōfukuji monastery of Nara. The entry for the 6th day of the 11th month of the 10th Year of Tembun (1541) reads as follows:

> This morning, the sixth day of the 11th month of Tembun 10, the Iga-shū entered Kasagi castle in secret and set fire to a few of the priests' quarters. They also set fire to outbuildings in various places inside the San no maru. They captured the Ichi no maru and the Ni no maru.

The word 'maru' refers to the successive baileys of the castle. The chronicle goes on to identify the defender of Kasagi castle as a certain Kizawa Nagamasa, which allows us to sketch in some more details about the circumstances surrounding the action. In 1540 Kizawa Nagamasa's territory was invaded by the ambitious 17-year-old Miyoshi Chokei. The Kizawa army took up a position at Kasagi, where they were attacked by Miyoshi's ally, Tsutsui Junsho,

Girl ninja from the Iga Ueno ninja house pose for the camera.

A ninja jumping off a castle wall in a shot kindly arranged by the Iga Ueno City Department of Tourism. This is the classic image of the acrobatic ninja superman.

so it is presumably Tsutsui Junsho who used the Iga ninja against the defenders. The men of Iga were worthy of their hire, for in the assault that followed the arson attack Kizawa Nagamasa was mortally wounded and the castle soon fell.

It is also interesting to note the presence inside Kasagi castle of a very famous family from the locality – the Yagyū. They were represented in the person of Yagyū Ieyoshi, father of Muneyoshi, who was later to found one of the most celebrated schools of swordsmanship in Japan. Yagyū village lay at the foot of Mount Kasagi, and when Kasagi fell the Yagyū continued the struggle, young Muneyoshi fighting the first battle of his life against the Tsutsui in 1544. A century later Muneyoshi's grandson, Jubei Mitsuyoshi, was to have tales told about his exploits as a ninja, so it is fascinating to see the family on the receiving end of ninjutsu in 1541.

These men from Iga clearly owed no vassal allegiance to any of the daimyō they served on campaign. Their service must therefore have been that of paid mercenaries, which is supported by the use of such words as 'hired', 'employed' and so on, although the nature of the payment remains a mystery. The whole topic of money was, however, regarded by samurai in general as unspeakably vulgar, so this is perhaps not so surprising.

Assassination

The best-known of all ninja campaign activities, and the one most exaggerated by fiction and romance, was the ninja's role as the silent and deadly assassin. This is the image of the ninja par excellence, dressed in black, sneaking into the castle at the dead of night, and then polishing off his sleeping victim with knife or poison. During the Sengoku Period, assassination by silent, expert, professional killers was often the only chance that rivals had of extinguishing the great daimyō who were customarily surrounded by bodyguards. Even though the fear of ninja assassination may have been exaggerated out of all proportion to the actual risk, there was no sense in taking any chances.

The measures taken to protect against assassinations can be seen in various locations in Japan to this day. Castles were of course very well defended. The private quarters at Inuyama castle, for example, have wooden sliding doors at the rear, behind which armed guards would always be at the ready. The design of the approach to a castle could be arranged so that a visitor was under observation from the moment he entered the outermost gate. Blind spots and dark shadowy areas could also be 'designed out', and the ultimate example must be Himeji castle, where the approach to the keep is made via a labyrinth of passages and paths.

In fact an entire building could theoretically be 'ninja-proofed', as shown by the famous and extraordinary 'nightingale floor' built in Nijo castle in Kyōto. As thousands of tourists discover every year, it is impossible to walk along the highly polished corridors without raising the tuneful squeaking from the carefully counterbalanced floorboards that was likened to the sound of a nightingale singing and gave warning of an approaching assassin. The clothes that were required to be worn at the shōgun's court also helped the Tokugawa family. The long *naga-bakama*, the wide trousers that actually covered the feet and had to be dragged behind as one walked, made an assassination attempt on the shōgun almost a physical impossibility.

Outside his castle or his mansion, a daimyō would be at his most vulnerable when recovering from wounds, for which purpose a number of 'secret springs' would be maintained. The Japanese have appreciated from very early days the

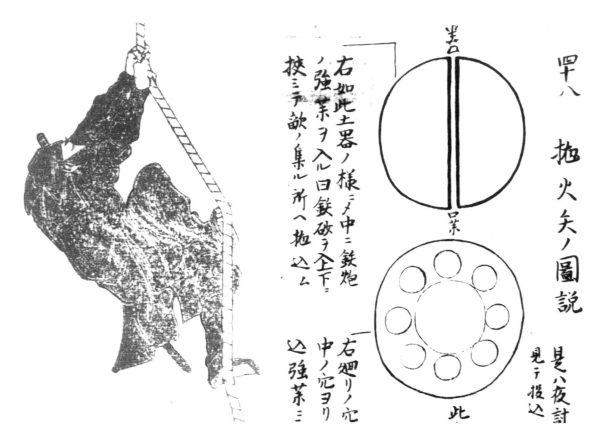

ABOVE LEFT

It is not generally known that Japan's great artist Hokusai included a picture of a ninja in his voluminous *Manga* (sketchbooks). Here he is, climbing a rope in classic ninja style.

ABOVE RIGHT

A ninja fragmentation bomb in the form of the Chinese thunder crash bomb is shown in this picture from *Bansen Shukai*. The bombs had a metal case and worked by sending shards of the iron case far and wide. The illustration also shows how arquebus balls could be arranged inside the bomb. Noxious substances and jagged fragments of pottery could also be included to add to the mayhem.

healing power of natural springs. Japan is thus dotted with hot-spring resorts, and a daimyō would have had his own in distant locations deep in the mountains which ninja could not find. The confusion of the battlefield might also allow the opportunity for an assassination to take place. The daimyō's battlefield headquarters consisted of an area screened off by a curtain called a *maku*, and he would be heavily guarded. The most loyal samurai would form an impenetrable ring round their lord if danger threatened. Nevertheless several examples exist of assassination attempts being made.

In spite of all precautions there were few daimyō who were not subject to some form of assassination attempt. They therefore lived their lives surrounded by loyal bodyguards who kept their lord under constant protection, never separated from him by more than a thin wood and paper screen. Matsuura Shigenobu, the daimyō of Hirado island, kept a heavy club in his bathroom. Mōri Motonari reckoned that a daimyō should trust no one, particularly relatives – a wise precept illustrated by the case of Saito Toshimasa, who had made an early career change from Buddhist priest to oil merchant and became a daimyō in his own right by murdering his adoptive father. Hōjō Sōun acquired his future base of Odawara castle by arranging for the young owner

to be murdered while out hunting. Even the powerful Oda Nobunaga was eventually to meet his end from a night attack on his sleeping quarters by a rival, though it took a small army rather than one ninja to do it.

Takeda Shingen, who apparently had two doors on his lavatory, is recorded as recommending that even when alone with his wife a daimyō should keep his dagger close at hand. One unsuccessful attempt on his life was made by a ninja called Hachisuka Tenzo, sent by Oda Nobunaga. Tenzo was forced to flee, and the Takeda samurai pursued him into a wood, where he concealed himself from the moonlight among the shadows of the trees. A spear thrust from his pursuers caught only his costume, and he subsequently evaded capture by hiding in a hole in the ground, which he had already prepared. Nobunaga's chosen assassin may well have been an Iga man, for we know that he had some on his payroll.

Oda Nobunaga's ruthless ways of waging war made him the target of several assassination attempts. Rokkaku Yoshisuke, who had seen his territory in Omi Province invaded by Nobunaga in 1571, hired a Koga ninja called Sugitani Zenjubo, whose particular speciality was sharpshooting with the long-barrelled arquebus. Zenjubo lay in wait for Nobunaga as he was crossing the Chigusa Pass between Omi and Mino Provinces, and fired twice, presumably with two

The mysterious mountains of Iga Province – heartland of the ninja.

separate guns. Both bullets struck home, but were absorbed by Nobunaga's armour and the padded shoulder protectors beneath. Zenjubo escaped to the mountains, but was apprehended four years later and tortured to death.

The year 1573 witnessed an attempt on Nobunaga's life by a certain Manabe Rokuro, the chief steward of a vassal of the daimyō Hatano Hideharu. Oda Nobunaga destroyed the Hatano in 1573, and Manabe Rokuro was instructed to take revenge. He tried to sneak into Nobunaga's castle of Azuchi and to stab Nobunaga while he was asleep in his bedroom, but was discovered and captured by two of the guards. He then committed suicide, and his body was displayed in the local market place to discourage any other would-be killers.

The semi-legendary ninja Ishikawa Goemon is credited with another attempt on Nobunaga's life. He hid in the ceiling above the victim's bedroom and tried to drip poison down a thread into Nobunaga's mouth. But the most remarkable assassination attempt on Nobunaga is recorded in the *Iranki*. Three ninja each took aim at Nobunaga with large-calibre firearms when he was inspecting the ruinous state of Iga Province that his invasion had brought about. The shots missed their target, but killed seven of Nobunaga's companions.

Other examples of assassinations that failed include Tokugawa Ieyasu's sending of a ninja called Kirigakure Saizo to murder his rival Toyotomi Hideyoshi. Saizo hid beneath the floor of Hideyoshi's dwelling, but a guard managed to pin him through the arm with the blade of his spear, which he had thrust at random through the floorboards. Another ninja, presumably in the service of Hideyoshi, then 'smoked him out' using a primitive flamethrower.

Who killed Kenshin?

The most famous ninja assassination story is of how Uesugi Kenshin was murdered in his lavatory by a ninja who had concealed himself in the sewage pit, and who thrust a spear or sword up Kenshin's anus at the crucial moment. Kenshin died a few days later, and it was suspected that Oda Nobunaga had sent the assassin. The succeeding months only served to emphasize the benefits to Nobunaga, because Kenshin's nephew and adopted heir fought each other for the inheritance, thus weakening the Uesugi immeasurably.

The actual circumstances surrounding Kenshin's death are quite well recorded, and do not necessarily contradict the ninja theory, because he appears to have suffered some form of crisis, probably a stroke, while in his lavatory. The *Kenshin Gunki* states that 'on the 9th day of the 3rd month he had a stomach ache in his toilet. This unfortunately persisted until the 13th day when he died.'

The strongest evidence against death from anything other than natural causes comes from accounts of the months leading up to Kenshin's death, when he composed a poem concerned with his apprehension that his life was coming to an end. In other words, in the days leading up to the catastrophe in his toilet he was already anticipating death, and it was no surprise to him when it came. Kenshin was also a very heavy drinker, and sometime during the ninth month of 1577 held state with several of his closest retainers, to whom Naoe Kanetsugu later confided his fears for their daimyō's condition. Naoe observed that Kenshin had seemed to get sicker as every day went by. So what was wrong with him? An important clue is given in another diary that noted that in the middle of that winter Uesugi Kenshin was getting very thin, with a pain in his chest 'like an iron ball'. He often vomited his food, and soon was forced to take only cold water. All the symptoms point to cancer of the stomach or oesophagus, with the 'iron ball' being the actual tumour. Stomach cancer is still a very common cause of death in Japan, and is also associated with heavy drinking. The knowledge of his illness would of course have been kept a closely guarded secret lest Nobunaga found out, so if a ninja had been despatched it would have been without the knowledge that his victim had only months or perhaps weeks to live. Kenshin's close retainers knew of the tumour in his stomach, so a sudden crisis may have been recognized by them as a distinct possibility. If this were so, then Nobunaga's ninja may well have unwittingly committed the perfect crime.

A hypothetical assassination attempt

Reference was made earlier to the house in Kyōto called Nijo jinya that exhibits several protective measures against ninja assassinations. Let us examine these using a hypothetical attempt on the life of its owner, Ogawa Nagatsuka.

The group of three ninja sent to kill him are operating as a team, and even if only one of their number survives to land the final blow, their task will have been accomplished. Ogawa is presently sitting in the *o-zashiki*, the main hall of the house, and is having a conversation with a trusted ninja whom Ogawa sent to spy on a rival disguised as a yamabushi. He arrived as expected at the front porch, where he removed his footwear and was escorted along the corridor by a guard. In keeping with tradition, he placed his sword in a rack at the entrance to the o-zashiki. Ogawa, however, suspects that the man might be a double agent, and this is confirmed when he suddenly kicks aside the low table dividing them and lunges at Ogawa with a concealed dagger. Ogawa is ready. He was apparently cooling himself with an ordinary fan, but the fan has iron staves and these are sufficient to parry the blow just long enough for the assassin to be tackled from an unexpected direction. From where the ninja is sitting the skylight in the ceiling above them looks just like a window, but he does not know that it hides a secret room where Ogawa's bodyguard has been watching every move and listening to every sound. Almost as the assassin moves the guard drops on to his back.

This gives Ogawa the opportunity to retrieve the sword hidden in a secret compartment at his side. His bodyguard has dealt with the assassin, who now lies dead before him, but Ogawa knows that there are probably others lurking. He pulls back the sliding door and enters the narrow hallway. He can hear the squeaking of the nightingale floor as someone runs from the front door. Whoever it is has not called out to him, so it probably isn't one of his own men. Ogawa takes no chances, and where the corridor turns there is an apparent blind corner. But the artistic-looking timbers provide a staircase to a concealed room above, entered by an innocuous-looking opening. Ogawa scrambles in. He is not a moment too

This illustration shows a team of ninja engaged gaining access to a heavily defended castle to carry out espionage or assassination. Here they are crossing the castle moat, which is too deep to wade through, and climbing up the stone walls. The castle's walls are in the typical Japanese style of sloping surfaces made from stone. There are plenty of hand holds, but rope ladders are still useful, particularly for the uppermost sections. The ninja are using three types of equipment to cross the moat. The first uses ukidaru, two very clumsy bucket-like floats, which must have been unstable (**1**). The second ninja is using a more credible swimming aid, a series of floats tied together (**2**). The third ninja uses the famous wooden water spider that appears in *Banzen Shukai* (**3**), actually used for swampy ground. Other equipment includes a shinobi kumade (**4**), a collapsible sectioned bamboo pole that enables a hooked rope to be lifted over the branch of a tree with the minimum of sound. A ninja shows how a sword could also be of use in climbing a wall, because the strong iron tsuba could provide a step if the sword was leant against the wall (**5**). The ninja would loop the end of the suspensory cord round his foot so that he could pull his sword up when he had climbed the wall. The ninja in the top left employs a rope ladder with a stout hook at the top (**6**). The rungs consist of a series of short bamboo sections threaded onto ropes. A hook was attached to the top, and when the whole length of the rope was pulled tight and secured the result was a lightweight if flimsy ladder. (**7**) is the oar for a boat made from split bamboo.

soon, because two ninja come flying down the hallway. They run straight past his hiding place and come to the end of the corridor where the entrance to Ogawa's bathroom is. On the wall beside it is a shelf. They do not know that it is in fact a hidden staircase that could be dropped down and as easily pulled up again. Ogawa could have used it had he not employed the other device earlier.

The guard has now arrived behind the two ninja. One goes into the bathroom to search for Ogawa. The other turns and slashes at the guard, but his sword catches on a low beam. This allows the guard to leap into the small tea room as a shuriken whizzes over his shoulder. He jumps into a closet, which the ninja slashes at furiously with his sword, only to reveal a back door through which the guard has slipped into an adjacent room and then out into the garden. In the garden are hiding places for valuables. The ornamental rocks could also be used as weapons, but for now it will be the scene of a sword fight to the death.

Meanwhile the other ninja, having found no signs of Ogawa on the ground floor, has run back along the corridor and up the fixed staircase to the first floor. However, as a precaution some time before the guest arrived, Ogawa's guard removed two floor panels as ankle breakers. In the dark the ninja stumbles into the first of these holes and is momentarily off guard. Ogawa's man lunges at him, and even though it only produces a slight flesh wound the ninja is knocked down the cul-de-sac stairway into the room below.

However, his companion has killed the other guard in the garden and on returning to the hallway has guessed the real nature of the shelf. He swings his sword at it and when it falls he runs upstairs. This has taken him into a room immediately adjacent to the one in which Ogawa was concealed, but Ogawa has already left his first hiding place and climbed up into the top storey of the building via a retractable rope ladder. In the dark it looks as though it is a solid ceiling. The ninja hears a noise from along the corridor and runs along to where his companion has disappeared down the stairs. He realizes that his comrade is dead when two guards come running up the stairs towards him. Running back

Nijo jinya's courtyard and entrance. Unfortunately no photography is permitted inside this fascinating building.

into the room above which Ogawa is now concealed, the ninja swings his sword at the lattice window and breaks it to pieces. He crashes through and lands in the courtyard outside. He has no companions now to help him scale the wall, so he rips out the suspensory cord from his sword as he leans it against the wall and jumps up using the sword-guard as a step. The last the Ogawa guards see of the ninja is his sword winging its way over the wall behind him. Their master is safe and two ninja are dead. It was a successful night's work for them.

The ninja's experience of battle

For a ninja, the distinction between peacetime and wartime operations was blurred, but when a daimyō was engaged in a major military campaign a ninja's role could be greatly enhanced. Ninja could be employed for intelligence gathering prior to an attack, or used on a battlefield to cause confusion in the enemy ranks. Ninja were also very useful in longer-term siege warfare, either as spies, arsonists or assassins or in other roles. All the examples that follow are taken from authentic and reliable historical accounts.

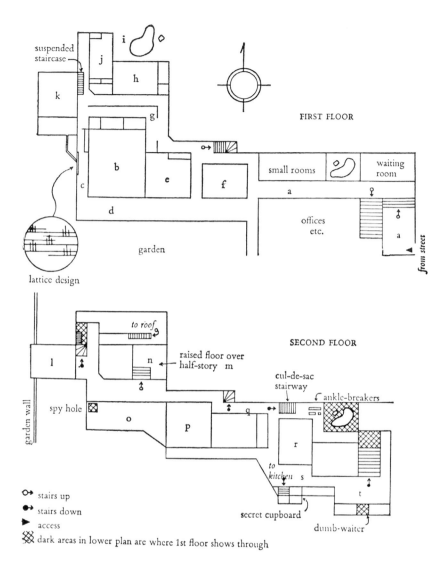

FIRST FLOOR

suspended staircase

lattice design

SECOND FLOOR

garden wall

spy hole

to roof

raised floor over half-story m

cul-de-sac stairway

ankle-breakers

to kitchen

secret cupboard

dumb-waiter

stairs up
stairs down
access
dark areas in lower plan are where 1st floor shows through

Plan of Nijo jinya in Kyōto. The plan is keyed as follows to enable the reader to follow the hypothetical assassination attempt described in the text: a) the street entrance (see separate photograph); b) o-zashiki, the 15-mat reception room; c) and d) the corridor; e) eight-mat room; f) six-mat room; g) hallway giving access to the concealed half-storey above; h) six-mat room looking out on the garden; i) garden, with places for hiding valuables; j) small tea room, its closet has a secret door; k) the daimyō's bath house, outside in the corridor is a stairway that looks like a shelf but can be lowered; l) upstairs room allowing emergency escape (see separate photograph of windows viewed from outside); m) concealed room; n) tea room on raised floor over concealed room; o) concealed guard room above reception room; p) eight-mat room; q) narrow landing with low ceiling to limit swordplay and ankle-breaking exposed beams; r) small tea room; s) dark hallway with modern staircase at front; t) modern hallway. (Plan reproduced from *Kyōto: a contemplative guide* by G. Mosher, by kind permission of Tuttle and Co.)

Ninja at Sawayama, 1558

The first example concerns the Rokkaku family of Omi Province. A member of the Rokkaku family, Rokkaku Takayori, was mentioned earlier for having had ninja used against him by the Shōgun Yoshihisa in 1487. In 1558 or thereabouts his grandson, Rokkaku Yoshikata, fought a campaign against a treacherous retainer called Dodo, who fortified himself within Sawayama castle, the site of which is near the present town of Hikone. In spite of a siege that lasted many days Yoshikata could not budge him, and he decided to employ a ninja from Iga called Tateoka Doshun.

The upstairs window of Nijo jinya in Kyōto. The glazing is a modern addition.

Doshun must have been of chunin rank, because we read of him leading into action in person his team of 48 ninja, of whom 44 were from Iga and four from Koga. He proposed using a ninja technique called *bakemono-jutsu* ('ghost technique') which was a very dramatic title for an absurdly simple operation. Doshun stole one of the paper lanterns that bore Dodo's family mon. Several replicas were constructed, and Doshun and his men calmly walked straight in through the front gate! Once safely inside they started to set fire to the castle, and so secret were their activities that Dodo's garrison concluded that traitors had emerged from within their own midst. In spite of heroic efforts to extinguish the fire, panic began to spread as quickly as the flames. At this point Rokkaku Yoshikata ordered his main army into a victorious final assault.

Ninja at Maibara, 1561

The next example from 1561 illustrates the mercenary nature of the ninja very well: first, because they refuse to move into action other than on their own terms, and second, because we see a certain Kizawa Nagamasa using Iga ninja against the same Rokkaku Yoshikata who had employed them in 1558! In 1561 Kizawa Nagamasa tried to re-take the castle of Maibara (then called Futo) to the east of Lake Biwa, which had recently fallen to the Rokkaku. Nagamasa placed matters in the capable hands of two commanders called Imai Kenroku and Isono Tamba no kami. They in turn engaged the assistance of three genin

A straw sandal in which a dried seed pod of the water chestnut has embedded itself. These were nature's caltrops and were used by ninja.

from Iga to mount a night attack as a prelude to a more conventional assault. In the *Shima Kiroku* we read that 'the Iga-shū entered in secret, started fires in the castle, and at this signal the keep and second bailey were conquered', and in the *Asai Sandaiki* we read that 'we employed shinobi no mono of Iga… They were contracted to set fire to the castle.'

Such are the bare bones of the action, but things did not go quite according to plan. On the night of the 1st day of the 7th month the Iga ninja were in position and the 'conventional' forces had begun to move forward. But it soon became clear to Imai Kenroku, stationed on a nearby hill, that the ninja had not moved into action. When he complained about their hesitation he received the reply that a samurai from north of Lake Biwa could not possibly understand ninja tactics, and that he would have to wait for a propitious moment. But by now the 'conventional' army was on the move. The fire attack was late and the ninja, in the manner of mercenaries the world over, implied by their refusal to attack until ready that unless allowed to conduct warfare in their own way they would all go home. The ninja leader suggested that Imai Kenroku should regroup his forces. If he withdrew for about an hour, the ninja would raid the castle, and the signal to move forward would be fire appearing from it.

This Imai Kenroku agreed to do, but the results were almost disastrous. His army blundered across the front of his comrade Isono Tamba no kami, who appears not to have been informed about the manoeuvre, and the samurai of the latter army drew the conclusion that a dawn attack had been made on them from the castle. A horseman in the front line called Kishizawa Yoichi sprang into action in an attempt to be first into the battle. He also observed, just ahead of him, the 'enemy' commander, so he galloped forward, and the unfortunate Imai Kenroku, trying desperately to control the night march of his army, received Yoichi's spear thrust in his back. Being totally unprepared for any assault, as he knew there were only friendly troops behind him, Imai was too shocked to give any resistance and fell dead from his horse. The two armies began fighting each other, and 20 were killed before order was restored. By then the ninja had set fire to the castle, and the two shattered allies joined forces to attack it. Futo eventually fell, to everyone's relief, but at quite a price.

Ninja at Kaminojo, 1562

The example that follows shows ninja in a much better light. The complicated background is as follows. When Imagawa Yoshimoto was killed at the battle of Okehazama in 1560, his followers rushed to abandon the cause of his doomed family and join the victorious Oda Nobunaga. The future Shōgun Tokugawa Ieyasu wanted to change sides, but the late Imagawa Yoshimoto had a son, Ujizane, who held a number of hostages from Ieyasu's own family, including his wife and son, whose throats would surely be cut at the least indication of a change of allegiance. Ieyasu's problem was solved by one dramatic stroke in the year 1562.

The Imagawa's western outpost was a castle called Kaminojo, held for them by a certain Udono Nagamochi. It promised to be a useful prize for the Oda, and if Ieyasu was able to capture it quickly on Nobunaga's behalf any hostages taken from Kaminojo could be exchanged for Ieyasu's own family. It would of course have to be done quickly before the news got out and Imagawa had a chance to murder them. The source for the action, the *Mikawa Go Fudoki*, takes the story on:

> Mitsuhara Sanza'emon said, 'As this castle is built upon a formidable precipice we will be condemning many of our allies to suffer great losses. But by good fortune there are among the go-hatamoto some men associated with the Koga-shū of Omi Province. Summon the Koga-shū through their compatriots and then they can sneak into the castle.'

The leader of the men of Koga was a certain Tomo Sukesada. He engaged over 80 ninja and:

> This group were ordered to lie down and hide in several places, and on the night of the fifteenth day of the third month sneaked inside the castle. Before long they were setting fire to towers inside the fortress.

In other words, they carried out a classic ninja raid under cover of darkness. The *Mikawa Go Fudoki* account, however, adds some interesting points of detail. First, the raiding party deliberately made as little sound as possible while they ran around killing, so that the defenders thought they were traitors from within the garrison. The ninja were also dressed like the defenders, thereby causing confusion, and as they spread out they communicated with one another using a password:

> …the garrison were utterly defeated and fled. The keeper of the castle, Nagamochi, fled to beside the Hall of Prayers on the north side of the castle, where Tomo Sukesada discovered his whereabouts, came running up, thrust his spear at him, and took his head as he lay prostrate. His sons Fujitaro Nagateru and Katsusaburo Nagatada were captured alive by Tomo Suketsuna.

Two hundred of the Udono garrison were burned to death in the conflagration that followed, but this was of less importance to Ieyasu than the priceless reward of Udono's two sons as hostages. Following the battle Ieyasu sent a *kanshajo* (letter of commendation) to Tomo Sukesada praising the service he had rendered at Kaminojo. It is preserved in the archives of the Iwane, a prominent family of Koga:

> This is concerning the time when Udono Fujitaro Nagateru was defeated. Such renown has not been equalled in recent times. Since that time I have been occupied with one thing and another and have neglected to write for some years. [I wish you] good health, and have the honour to congratulate you. I have been pleased to listen to the particulars of the matter despatched by both my retainers Matsui Sakon Tadatsugu and Sakai Masachika.

As the only kanshajo in history addressed to a leader of ninja, the letter provides unique written proof of the value Ieyasu placed on their particular abilities. However, the affair of the two sons of Udono was not quite over. As part of the hostage agreement, Ieyasu allowed Imagawa Ujizane to keep what was left of Kaminojo castle, and after its repair Ujizane reappointed the Udono brothers as its defenders. Having already suffered one defeat at the hands of Ieyasu the pair began a rather unwise policy of outwardly supporting the raids into Mikawa Province by the Ikkō-ikki. The raids particularly infuriated a certain Matsudaira Kiyoyoshi, whose relatives had been held hostage but had not been part of the deal struck over the fall of Kaminojo. They had subsequently been put to death by impaling them on sharp stakes, so Kiyoyoshi took his revenge by launching a furious attack on Kaminojo castle:

Two members of the Iga Ueno ninja re-enactment group are about to enter the castle through its 'stone-dropping hole', the Japanese equivalent of machicolations. These holes would have a door across, secured from the inside, so the ninja would have to use cutting devices.

But, as might be expected, the Udono brothers defended it vigorously, and the attackers were thoroughly beaten, many being either wounded or killed in action. On hearing that the attacking force were on the point of being defeated His Lordship set out in great haste, set up his army in camp on Natoriyama, and sent men of Koga who attacked the castle. Taking advantage of an unguarded point they made a commotion in the castle as Ieyasu had ordered them to. The Udono brothers had run out of defensive techniques. Fujitaro gathered seven samurai about him, but when they were all killed the castle fell.

That was the end of the Udono brothers, who had earned their place in history by being the only samurai to have been defeated by the same ninja twice.

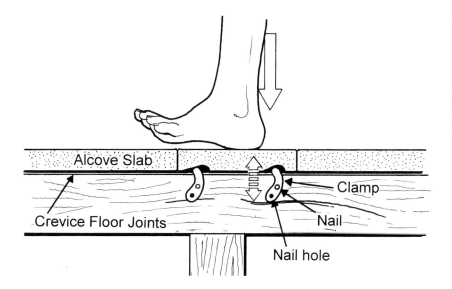

The mode of operation of the famous nightingale floor in Nijo castle in Kyōto. Contrary to popular belief, the squeaking sound is not produced directly by the floorboards themselves, but by the offset metal hinges triggered by the pressure of a foot.

Ninja at Sekigahara, 1600

When the second unifier of Japan, Toyotomi Hideyoshi, died in 1598 his son Toyotomi Hideyori was only five years old, and a coterie of jealous daimyō began to intrigue among themselves, all eager to be seen as the infant Hideyori's protector. Tokugawa Ieyasu played off one rival against another, until all the daimyō were divided into two armed camps. Matters were resolved in the autumn of 1600 with the cataclysmic battle of Sekigahara, the largest battle ever fought on Japanese soil. The ninja of Iga and Koga, who were now retainers of the Tokugawa, played their part in the campaign.

The preliminary moves of the battle of Sekigahara consisted of a spate of attacks and sieges on castles, including the castle of Fushimi to the south-east of Kyōto. It was held for Ieyasu's 'Eastern Army' by the Torii family, who held off the 'Western Army' for as long as they could manage, thus giving Ieyasu's forces time to move into position from the east. The Torii were helped in their defence by the actions of several hundred warriors from Koga, some of whom were inside the castle, while others harassed the besiegers from outside. About 100 were killed in the fighting, and after the successful conclusion of the Sekigahara campaign Ieyasu held a memorial service for their spirits.

The actual battle of Sekigahara began at dawn on a foggy autumn morning, and was fought for the best part of the day on a restricted front between large mountains. There is only one account of undercover operations of any sort at Sekigahara, yet this one is unique and was in fact carried out by the Shimazu clan of Satsuma against the Tokugawa. The Shimazu appear to have developed an extraordinary gunnery tactic whereby sharpshooters were deliberately left behind when an army retreated to act, in effect, as 'human booby traps'.

A prefabricated collapsible ninja boat from *Bansen Shukai*. The sections are fastened together using clamps, and surrounded by waterproofed cloth.

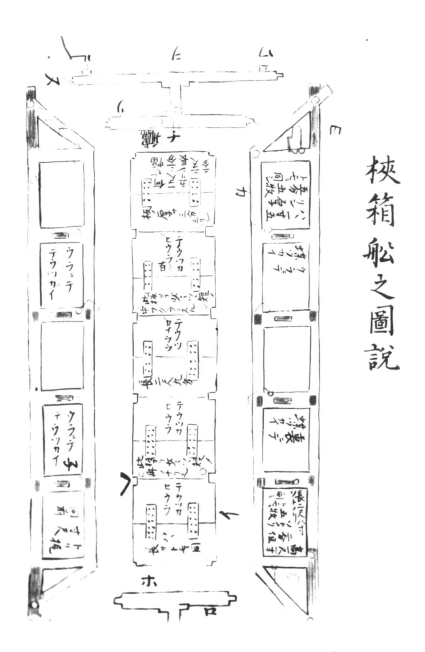

Towards the end of the fighting the Satsuma samurai were forced to retreat before the fierce charge of the 'Red Devils' of Ii Naomasa, who dressed all his followers in brilliant red-lacquered armour. On came the Ii samurai to where a number of 'human booby traps' were lying in wait. One spotted Ii Naomasa coming towards him and fired a bullet which went through the horse's belly and shattered Naomasa's right elbow. Both man and horse collapsed, and Naomasa had to be carried from the field.

There is an interesting addition to the story, because the wounded Ii Naomasa received first aid from a ninja in his own service, Miura Yo'emon, who was the *joshin* (chief vassal) of the Ii. He was an Iga man, and Ieyasu had presented him to Ii Naomasa in 1583. When Naomasa was shot, Yo'emon gave him some black medicine to drink which was designed to help stop the bleeding. The Miura's residential quarter in Hikone is remembered today as Iga-machi.

Ninja at Osaka, 1615

The victory of Sekigahara was almost totally decisive. Tokugawa Ieyasu was proclaimed shōgun in 1603, and reigned from Edo castle where his Iga and Koga men provided a secure guard. The Iga men's duties included guarding the innermost parts of the palace, which were known as the O-oku. Here were the quarters of the shōgun's concubines. The Koga group, who were half the number of their Iga comrades, guarded the great outer gate of the castle called the Ote mon.

In 1614 the ninja were back in action again on the battlefield, when Toyotomi Hideyori, now grown to manhood, gathered into his late father's massive fortress of Osaka tens of thousands of disaffected samurai who had suffered from the Tokugawa seizure of power. The challenge was too great for Ieyasu to ignore, and in the winter of 1614 he laid siege to Osaka's walls, which measured almost 12 miles in perimeter. The Tokugawa side used ninja from both Iga and Koga under Hattori Masanari and Yamaoka Kagetsuge respectively. One of Ieyasu's leading commanders at the siege of Osaka was Ii Naotaka, who had inherited his father's territories and his red-clad samurai army, so it is not surprising to note the name of Miura Yo'emon in his service. Miura went to the Nabari area of Iga to recruit ninja for use in the siege; they fought in the army as well as carrying out individual operations.

The Osaka garrison had strengthened the outer defences by constructing a barbican out into the moat called the Sanada-maru. An attack was carried out on the fourth day of the 12th month, and was led by Ii Naotaka, who crossed the dry moat beneath the barbican's walls. Because there was a dense morning fog the attackers found it difficult to advance, and a hail of bullets came from within the castle. Casualties were mounting as the Ii's comrades galloped forwards and called for a retreat, but because of the noisy mêlée the order was scarcely heard. Miura Yo'emon, who was currently removing arrowheads from the wounded, ordered his ninja into action in a move that showed a subtle understanding of the samurai mind. They approached the mass of men in the moat and fired on them at random. Their comrades, surprised by the arrows that came flying at them from behind, turned towards them and thus 'attacked to safety', the need for an actual 'retreat' having been avoided. On another occasion a ten-man ninja unit entered the castle with the

Warriors of Medieval Japan

aim of creating discord between the commanders. We know that one of the commanders did in fact commit suicide around this time, so ninja may have been involved.

This first half of the Osaka siege, known as the Winter Campaign of Osaka, came to an end with a spurious peace treaty that led to the flattening of the outer defence works. In the summer of 1615 Ieyasu returned to the fray and laid siege again to the now weakened castle. The ninja of the Winter Campaign had returned to Iga somewhat dissatisfied with their rewards and had to be summoned once again by Miura – evidence that even at this late stage those not in the direct service of the Tokugawa were still behaving like mercenaries. Here they lent a form of service similar in vein to that of the winter operation when there was an incident at the headquarters of the general Okayama Kansuke. So many camp followers and local people had swarmed into Okayama's camp that observation of the enemy had become impossible and military operations were severely restricted. Miura applied his ninja version of crowd control by firing randomly into the multitude, who quickly dispersed.

There were apparently two or three wounded persons in the unit of Todo Takatora, who was nonplussed and in fact praised the ninja for their action. It is not surprising that Todo understood ninja, for he had taken part in Nobunaga's Iga invasion of 1581 and had subsequently been granted part of Iga as his fief. Following Tokugawa Ieyasu's recommendation, he fortified his territory by erecting the present-day Ueno castle on the site of the temple where the Iga warriors had assembled during the Iga Revolt.

The 'Summer Campaign' of Osaka was finally settled by a fierce pitched battle at Tennōji to the south of the castle. The Ii ninja unit fought alongside the regular troops, and as evidence of their success a record states:

Item, one head: Miura Yo'emon
In the same unit:
Item, two heads: Shimotani Sanzo
Item, one head: Okuda Kasa'emon
Item, one head: Saga Kita'emon.

As the defenders retreated back into the castle, Ii Naotaka opened up on the keep with a number of very heavy cannon and the castle fell. Toyotomi Hideyori committed suicide as Osaka blazed around him.

Ninja at Shimabara, 1638

The fall of Osaka castle meant the disappearance of the last major threat to the Tokugawa shogunate that was to arise for the next two and a half centuries. The one serious outbreak of armed strife that occurred during the Tokugawa rule

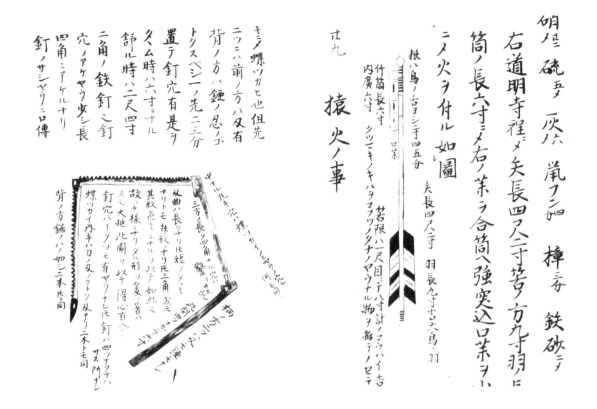

happened in 1638 at Shimabara in Kyūshū, where what began as a peasant farmers' protest developed into a full-scale revolt. The Shimabara Rebellion has always attracted the attention of Western historians because of the overtly Christian nature of much of its motivation. Christianity had been banned in Japan in 1637, after much sporadic persecution. No foreigner was allowed to land in Japan, and no Japanese was allowed to leave. Shimabara thus provided a focus for persecuted Christians as well as rebellious farmers, although the latter had grievance enough. The local daimyō, Matsukura Shigemasa, was an oppressive tyrant given to punishing those of the lower orders who offended him by dressing them in straw raincoats and setting fire to the straw.

Matters came to a head when the insurgents fortified themselves in the dilapidated old castle of Hara on the Shimabara Peninsula and defied all local attempts to defeat them. Eventually the shōgun, Tokugawa Iemitsu, mounted a full-scale expeditionary force from Edo, and the Tokugawa samurai were plunged into a world they thought had gone for ever. It is not surprising to see the ninja of Koga returned to their earlier roles of siege warfare, and the records of their activities, which are quite well detailed, contain some of the best accounts of ninja in action at any time. A good summary comes from a diary kept by a descendant of Ukai Kan'emon:

ABOVE LEFT

This clever folding saw, the ninja equivalent of a Swiss army knife, appears in *Bansen Shukai*.

ABOVE RIGHT

A ninja rocket, matching exactly contemporary Chinese descriptions, appears in this illustration from *Bansen Shukai*.

1st month 6th day. They were ordered to reconnoitre the plan of construction of Hara castle, and surveyed the distance from the defensive moat to the ni no maru, the depth of the moat, the conditions of roads, the height of the wall, and the shape of the loopholes. The results were put on a detailed plan by the guard Kanematsu Tadanao, and sent to Edo and presented for inspection by the shōgun, Tokugawa Iemitsu.

A further account of the fighting, the *Amakusa Gunki*, the journal of Matsudaira Kai no kami Kagetsuna, tells us:

15th day. Men from Koga in Omi Province who concealed their appearance would steal up to the castle every night and go inside as they pleased.

The Ukai diary describes a particular raid by the Koga men to deprive the garrison of provisions:

1st month 21st day
The so-called Hara castle raid was a provisions raid, by the orders of the Commander-in-Chief Matsudaira Nobutsuna. They raided from the Kuroda camp near the western beach and cooperated in the capture of

BELOW LEFT
The ninja girl attendant at the ninja house in Iga Ueno demonstrates how a rotating door works.

BELOW RIGHT
A ninja picks the lock on the gate of the ninja house in Koga.

thirteen bags of provisions which the enemy depended on as a lifeline. This night also they infiltrated the enemy castle and obtained secret passwords.

In his account of the provisions raid in his book *The Nobility of Failure*, Ivan Morris mentions the ninja action, but adds the strange detail that they had ropes attached to their legs so that their dead bodies could be pulled back. This seems such an unlikely course of action that it may be assumed that Morris has mistranslated the idiomatic expression 'life-line' which appears in the account.

The most exciting raid happened six days later, and is recorded in the Ukai diary. The commander of the Tokugawa force, Matsudaira Nobutsuna, was unsure about the condition of the enemy garrison inside the castle. He suspected that provisions would be running low, so he despatched the ninja inside to gather information. The Koga men were advised that only two or three out of their number could expect to return alive. Volunteers were found in the persons of Mochizuki Yo'emon, Arakawa Shichirobei, Natsume Shika no suke, Yamanaka Judaiyu and Tomo Gohei, whose surname appears in a list of those involved in the attack on Kaminojo in 1562 – a nice illustration of the continuity of the ninja tradition:

> 1st month 27th day
> We dispersed spies who were prepared to die inside Hara castle. Then we raided at midnight from the Hosokawa camp, and those who went on the reconnaissance in force captured an enemy flag; both Arakawa Shichirobei and Mochizuki Yo'emon met extreme resistance and suffered from their serious wounds for forty days.

The ninja attacked under cover of darkness, causing confusion by the use of hyakuraiju, the set of timed explosives. No sooner had they erupted than the defenders immediately doused all the lights, which were customarily provided from pine torches round the perimeter and within the castle. The garrison sentries were of course on full alert, but the ninja concealed themselves in some brushwood and waited until the defenders relaxed their guard later in the night. When it was quiet they scaled the walls using the ninja climbing equipment described earlier. Arakawa and Mochizuki were first into the castle, but in an act of carelessness uncharacteristic of ninja but no doubt helped by the pitch darkness, Arakawa fell into a pit. The moon had risen by the time Mochizuki pulled him to safety. Both men were dressed the same as the men of the garrison, and when the pine torches were rekindled they raced off through the middle of the enemy. To prove to their commander that they had got so far with their mission, they tore down one of the many banners bearing a Christian cross that fluttered everywhere in the castle, and took it back as a souvenir. As they descended the walls they were subjected to a hail of bullets,

The ninja house at Iga Ueno, brought from a nearby village. This is one of the most popular sites on the ninja tourist trail.

arrows and stones, which caused injuries from which they suffered for many days. The long and patient blockade of the castle soon paid dividends. By the last few days of the siege, provisions were low, as the *Amakusa Gunki* records:

White rice	10 koku
Soy beans	3 koku
Miso	10 casks

As one koku was the theoretical amount needed to feed one man for one year, it can be seen how desperate their plight was becoming, and the garrison was reduced to eating the seaweed they were able to scrape off the rocks at low tide:

2nd month 20th day
A final counterattack that the enemy had planned was obstinately given back, but now the enemy army that attacked them had only seaweed and grass to eat.
2nd month 24th day
More and more general raids were begun, the Koga ninja band under the

ENTERING A DAIMYŌ'S MANSION FOR AN ASSASSINATION

The ninja has now entered the daimyō's private apartments in the castle to assassinate him. These could be located inside the keep, which would make the ninja's task more difficult, but in many cases the yashiki was a separate building within the inner bailey. The wall of the room is cut away so we can see the corridor and rooms. The interior design is typical of a daimyō's mansion. Within the heavy outside sliding doors there is a polished wooden corridor that leads to a succession of rooms divided from each other by paper screens. The floor of the corridor is a nightingale floor, and this may well have saved the daimyō's life. A ninja is throwing shuriken at the guards approaching down the corridor. While his companion is dealing with the guards, a second ninja is killing the daimyō. The intended victim was asleep, but the sound of the nightingale floor awoke him, and he is now struggling with his assailant.

The insert diagram shows the ninja technique for exploring a potentially dangerous dark place such as a castle's corridors. The ninja would balance the sword's scabbard on the tip of the sword blade, with the scabbard's suspensory cords gripped between his teeth. This extended the ninja's range of feel by six feet, and if the scabbard encountered an enemy, the ninja would let it fall and lunge forward in the direction of the assailant.

direct control of Matsudaira Nobutsuna captured the ni no maru and the san no maru, and after this, until the fall of the castle, they were under the command of Suzuki Sankuro Shigenari and his small ten-man unit, and Nakafusa Mino no kami, the head of the ninja 'office' sent from the shogunate. They had a duty to communicate with the battle lines of each daimyō as they went into action.

Ninja in a narrow corridor. This posed shot, kindly supplied by the Department of Tourism of Iga Ueno City, depicts perfectly the classic image of the ninja approaching his prey.

The commander of Hara castle, Amakusa Shiro, tried a diversionary raid that, though brave, had little effect. It consisted of a disjointed charge into the besieging camps, and served largely to confirm in the Tokugawa soldiers' minds that the garrison were becoming very desperate indeed. When the final attack on Hara was launched, the Koga ninja acted in a liaison capacity between the various units assaulting the castle, as well as taking part in the actual fighting.

When Hara castle fell, it took with it the hopes of those who had led the Christian rebellion, and marked the last time that ninja would be used in battle. From this time on the operation of ninja would be theoretical rather than practical, with the myth growing stronger the further it diverged from reality.

Aftermath – the ninja myth

The tradition of making the ninja considerably larger than life has a very long history indeed. The first trend one can discern is that of associating ninja and ninjutsu with famous warriors who are historical personages, but who at some time in their careers led a mysterious or fugitive life. The two great heroes Minamoto Yoshitsune (1159–89) and Kusunoki Masashige (1294–1336) are the ones most often mentioned, to the extent that they are sometimes credited in popular works with the foundation of two separate 'schools of ninjutsu', the Yoshitsune-ryu and the Kusunoki-ryu, but there is no historical evidence whatsoever for either claim. In the case of Yoshitsune, identification is often made of his retainer, Ise Saburo Yoshimori, a samurai who accompanied him on his wanderings, as a skilled ninja, but in works such as the *Gikeiki* he is simply a loyal samurai warrior.

The second identifiable trend is to link the ninja with the followers of Shugendo, the colourful yamabushi. On the face of things, ninja and yamabushi seem to have little in common apart from their inherent mystery. Perhaps one reason may be that the guise of a wandering yamabushi was the ideal cover for a ninja in a role that involved espionage and travel. One of the greatest legends of Japan, that of Benkei and Yoshitsune's flight from Yoritomo, has ninja disguised as yamabushi, and there is a famous story about the barrier of Ataka, where the fugitives are challenged about their real identity. It is possible that yamabushi themselves acted as spies for rival daimyō, thereby abusing their right of free travel.

The final development of the ninja myth involved the transformation of these undoubtedly authentic assassins and spies into superheroes. What is remarkable in this trend is that the process began while real ninja still had the potential to carry out their craft. Perhaps some of the operations they undertook, such as the murder of Uesugi Kenshin, seemed so inexplicable that the use of magic or invisibility was the only reasonable conclusion to draw. However, there are parallels with another transformation that was taking place at the same time: the creation of the myth of the invincible samurai swordsman. Just as the hardened battlefield warrior acquired a new image of the supreme individual samurai, so his unglamorous and deadly mirror image that was the ninja acquired his own mysterious powers that transcended reality. Ninja fought in ways that samurai would not entertain and in situations and conditions where even the bravest samurai might hesitate to enter. With the authentic historical operations noted above to consider, the greatest wonder is that anyone should feel it was necessary to create fiction out of ninja, when the facts concerning these most remarkable warriors of feudal Japan are themselves so extraordinary.

僧兵

Part 4
Warrior monks

Introduction

Buddhism at war

Buddhism is popularly regarded in the West as being a very peaceful religion, but this was by no means the image presented by the famous warrior monks of medieval Japan. From the 10th century onwards the great monastic foundations of Nara and Mount Hiei maintained private armies that terrified the courtiers and citizens of the capital with their religious and military power. Armed with long naginata in addition to bows and swords, they became involved in numerous conflicts from the 10th to the 14th century, cursing emperors and fighting samurai with equal enthusiasm.

The Age of Warring States was to see several developments in Japanese monk warfare. The monks of Mount Hiei continued to be involved in fighting along with the monks of the Shingon sect located at Negoroji in Kii Province. But the most important trend was the reduction in their influence compared to the younger populist sects of Buddhism such as Nichiren-shū and Jōdo Shinshū. The latter formed Japan's greatest ikki – the Ikkō-ikki (the 'single-minded league'). They became so powerful in Kaga Province that they even overthrew the local daimyō and ruled the province for a century. Their 'fortified cathedrals' at Nagashima and Ishiyama Honganji rivalled any samurai castle, and Ishiyama Honganji withstood the longest siege in Japanese history. They were also at the forefront of technological development, and the monks of Negoroji were renowned for their skills with firearms.

Who were the warrior monks?

Before describing the origins and development of the Japanese warrior monks it is necessary to examine the nomenclature. The word that is usually translated

A modern woodblock print showing the classic image of the warrior monk of the Heian Period. We note his suit of armour poking out from under his robes, his headcowl, and of course his vicious looking naginata.

Saicho had been born in 767 and had left the unsettling politics of Nara behind him to find spiritual peace on a mountain, so when the capital was transferred to Kyōto a Buddhist temple was already waiting to protect the city from its most dangerous quarter. Enryakuji soon became involved in the performance of numerous sacred rituals connected with the imperial court, and it was not long before it achieved recognition as *chingo kokka no dojo* (the temple for the pacification and protection of the state).

Enryakuji therefore became one of Japan's most privileged foundations, and Saicho and his disciples received aristocratic support to establish their own Tendai sect of Buddhism. The new sect was intended to operate outside the influence of the Office of Monastic Affairs, which was dominated at the time

A SŌHEI OF ENRYAKUJI 1100–1571
The warrior monk costume changed little throughout their history. He is wearing a kimono and pair of trousers. The undergarments would be white, with the outer robe being white, tan or saffron. A jacket would be worn over the outer kimono, usually black, and often of a stiff gauzy 'see-through' material. The example here has no sleeves. Footwear consisted of waraji worn over white tabi and often long kiahan. Parts of the warrior monk's armour are just visible under his robes. We see the

kote and the kusazuri. He carries the traditional naginata. His other weapon is a tachi. This white headcowl is tied in a different way, having been folded and tied around the head to cover the mouth and leave only the upper part of the face exposed (**1**). Instead of a cowl, a warrior monk might wear a white hachimaki tied round his shaven head (**2**). A monk would carry Buddhist prayer beads (**3**). These were of wood, and could be of very different sizes. Warriors monks are often depicted wearing a pair of geta (wooden

'clogs') (**4**). Each geta was carved out of one piece of wood to produce a raised platform for the foot. They could be lacquered or were left as bare wood. A sword of tachi form, carried with the cutting edge pointing down (**5**) is slung from the belt using the attachments shown. Different types of naginata (**6**) are shown. From left to right: a wide bladed one, very Chinese in appearance; a shobuzuri naginata with blade and shaft of almost equal length, favoured during the 12th century; a short-bladed variety with a heavy iron butt.

by Nara. Enryakuji also catered for the personal needs of the Kyōto nobility, who showered wealth upon it. The administration of these assets and the organization of Enryakuji itself were entirely the private domain of its leaders, and by the 11th century the monastery complex on Mount Hiei consisted of about 3,000 buildings. Enryakuji owned much property elsewhere in Japan, making it a very wealthy place indeed.

Although the imperial government had no direct control over Enryakuji, there were two ways in which the monastery might be influenced. First, the emperor retained the right to appoint the *zasu* (head abbot), although this was not a privilege that he could exercise in an arbitrary fashion. As we shall see, most of the inter-temple battles and armed demonstrations by warrior monks in the streets of Kyōto concerned appointments of which they did not approve. Secondly, abbots born to the most prominent courtly families usually headed the branches of Enryakuji, known as the *monzeki* (noble cloisters).

The first temple feuds

There was no reason why political disagreements over the affairs of an important religious institution should necessarily lead to armed conflict, but by the middle of the 10th century bitter disputes over the imperial control of senior appointments led to brawling between rival monks and eventually to the use of weapons. These inter-temple or inter-faction disputes were not 'religious wars' as we know them in the West. They did not involve points of doctrine or dogma, just politics, and the campaigns and battles of the warrior monks that occurred from the 10th to the 14th century were almost exclusively concerned with rivalries between and within the temples of Nara and Mount Hiei. The monastic involvement in the 12th-century civil wars was a very different situation, because at that time samurai leaders, eager to recruit as many fighting men as possible to their banners, enlisted the support of the sōhei armies that had learned their trade by fighting each other.

The first major incident involving violence by monks against monks occurred in 949, when 56 monks from Nara's Tōdaiji gathered at the residence of an official in Kyōto to protest against an appointment that had displeased them. In 969 a dispute over conflicting claims to temple lands resulted in the death of several Kōfukuji monks at the hands of monks from Tōdaiji. It is almost certain that weapons were used in the fight, so the days of the warrior monk may be said to have arrived. It was also around this time, probably during 970, that we read of Enryakuji being involved in a dispute with the Gion shrine in Kyōto and using force to settle the matter. Subsequently Ryogen, the chief abbot of Enryakuji, made the decision to maintain a permanent fighting force at Mount Hiei. This was the first of the warrior monk armies. Strange to relate, this dramatic decision was contrary to both the letter

The Shaka-do of the Enryakuji on Mount Hiei. This particular building was formerly at Midera.

and the spirit of the pronouncements Ryogen had previously made regarding monastic discipline, because in 970 he had issued a code of 26 articles that were intended to curb widespread abuses by the clergy of Mount Hiei. This included rules that monks should not leave Mount Hiei during their 12-year period of training and that they should not cover their faces. But it also forbade monks from carrying weapons, inflicting corporal punishment or violently disrupting religious services. This is a curious contradiction, which may indicate that Ryogen's army was an entirely separate entity from the actual monks. The newcomers may simply have been mercenaries and not monks at all – the sources are by no means clear on this point. We may therefore possibly regard Ryogen's initial recruitment of warriors as a 10th-century version of an institution hiring a specialist firm of security guards.

In spite of their intense rivalries and frequent conflicts, there were occasions when Enryakuji and Miidera were willing to join forces to attack a third party. Thus we hear of them united against Nara's Kōfukuji in 1081. During this incident, Kōfukuji burned Miidera and carried off much loot, but later that same year the alliance seems to have been forgotten when Enryakuji burned Miidera following the shrine festival incident noted above. In 1113 Enryakuji burned the Kiyomizudera in Kyōto over a rival appointment of an abbot.

The Tokondo or Eastern Golden Hall of Kōfukuji in Nara. The original structure was built in 726 and was burned during the Gempei War. The present building was erected in 1415.

Enryakuji and Miidera united against Nara again in 1117 in an incident described in *Heike Monogatari*, the great epic of the 12th-century wars, which quotes the sad words of the ex-emperor Go Shirakawa-In: 'There are three things that are beyond my control: the rapids on the Kamo river, the dice at gambling, and the monks of the mountain.'

The warrior monks in the Gempei War

From about 1180 onwards the activities of the warrior monks became submerged in the Gempei civil war, which was fought between the rival samurai clans of Taira and Minamoto. Both sides courted the monastic armies to augment their own military forces, and there was considerable warrior monk involvement in one of the first major conflicts of the war, the battle of Uji. In spite of the bravery shown both by monks and by samurai the rebellion failed. After the battle Taira Kiyomori decided that the warrior monks of Miidera should not be allowed to forget their unfortunate alliance. Tomomori, one of Kiyomori's sons, led an attack that was highly destructive, but much worse was in store for the temples of Nara. They may not have had time to go to war in support of the rebellion, but neither had they opposed it. At first Kiyomori behaved with caution, and sent a force of 500 men with orders to use no violence unless absolutely necessary. The monks attacked the deputation. Sixty samurai were killed and had their heads displayed around the pool of Sarusawa opposite the southern gate of Kōfukuji. Furious at this reaction, Kiyomori immediately sent his son Shigehira with orders to subdue the whole city of Nara.

WARRIOR MONKS OF KŌFUKUJI AT THE DEFENCE OF NARA 1181
Here we see the last desperate charge of the warrior monks of Nara during the attack on their city by samurai of the Taira clan following the battle of Uji. Wielding their traditional naginata, the sōhei charge out of the courtyard of the burning Tōdaiji through the Nandaimon (great southern gate). The monks are shown here in full 'battle dress'. They wear an assortment of simple dō maru and yoroi armours and have heavy suneate.

The subsequent burning of Nara sent a chill through Mount Hiei. Enryakuji was now the only warrior monk institution that had not been burned down, and when in 1183 the Minamoto leader Kiso Yoshinaka entered Enryakuji the monks sheltered him for a while, but they did not dare take an active part in his military campaigns.

Mount Hiei remained quiet during the Shōkyū War of the 13th century, but during the Nanbokuchō Wars of the 14th century it provided a refuge for the son of Emperor Go-Daigo. Go-Daigo attempted to restore the old imperial power that the shōgun had supplanted. His son is known to history as the 'Prince of the Great Pagoda', and the warrior monks were his first allies. Accounts of his operations show that monk armies were as well armed and confident as their predecessors, and almost as unsuccessful. There was some brief but savage fighting (see below) before Go-Daigo's rebellion was crushed. The war went on for many years more, led by loyalist samurai from the Kusunoki clan, but they appear to have made little or no use of warrior monk armies.

Monks and monto in the Age of Warring States

For the next 100 years the warrior monks of Mount Hiei continued to play at politics until the major convulsion in Japanese society called the Ōnin War changed Japan for ever. At first Enryakuji stood aloof from the conflict around it, but it was eventually drawn into an alliance with the Asai and Asakura families against Oda Nobunaga, a move that was to lead to its destruction. The main impetus for warrior monk activity in the Age of Warring States came from Negoroji, which owes its fame to the Buddhist priest Kakuban, known to posterity as Kogyo Daishi (1095–1143). He was regarded by his followers as a reformer and restorer of Shingon, much in the same way as Rennyo was viewed within Jōdo Shinshū. Kogyo Daishi was given the estate containing Negoroji by ex-emperor Go Toba in 1132, and grew to exercise great influence within Shingon. His views met with opposition from rivals on Kōyasan, so that he was eventually driven out and retired to Negoroji. Kogyo Daishi's faction became known as the Shingi (new meaning) branch of the Shingon sect, but there was never the tragic split that other sects were to experience. Instead the monks of Negoroji channelled their energies against samurai.

The greatest religious-based armies of all, however, had nothing to do with the old Buddhist sects of Tendai or Shingon, but drew their support from the Buddhism of the mass-movement populist sects, who recruited chiefly among the peasantry. Further details of their beliefs are given below, but for now we may note that instead of scholars they produced highly motivated but very ordinary working men who were caricatured by their enemies as simple fanatics. These faith-based communities of priests, farmers, families and children had no

Rennyo, the great reformer of Jōdo Shinshū and the inspiration for the formation of the Ikkō-ikki, from a scroll in Yoshizaki.

need to recruit mercenaries as Enryakuji had once done. To be a believer was to be a warrior, so although the vast majority of their armies were not monks in any conventional sense, their meticulously observed ritual behaviour, their enthusiastic military training and their devotion to the cause made them Japan's new holy warriors.

The original meaning of the word 'ikki' was not a league but a riot, and it was as rioting mobs that the Ikkō-ikki first became known to their samurai betters. The other word, Ikkō, provides a clue to their religious affiliation. It means 'single-minded' or 'devoted', and the monto (disciples or adherents of the Jōdo Shinshū) were indeed completely single-minded in their devotion and determination.

Their great reformer of Jōdo Shinshū, Rennyo (1415–99), had fled north to Echizen Province to escape the influence of Mount Hiei, whose monks saw him as a threat to their control of the religious life of the capital. Here he re-established his headquarters at Yoshizaki, and very soon his followers became enmeshed in the struggle for supremacy that was going on in adjacent Kaga Province between various samurai clans in the confusion following the Ōnin War. In 1488 Rennyo's Ikkō-ikki revolted against samurai rule by the Togashi family, and after a series of fierce skirmishes the control of Kaga passed into

their hands. For the first time in Japanese history, a group that were neither courtiers nor samurai ruled a province. These were heady days for the Ikkō-ikki, and as the 15th century drew to a close the sect spread out from Kaga and established itself in a series of key locations including Nagashima and Ishiyama Honganji, built where Osaka castle now stands. The latter provided a refuge when the sect's Kyōto headquarters were destroyed. Ishiyama Honganji's strength was tested in 1533. To the great relief of the Ikkō-ikki,

A woodblock print depicting the fight for the broken bridge during the battle of Uji in 1180. We are looking from the northern bank, and see the Taira samurai making an attack. In the upper left-hand corner may be seen the naginata of the warrior monks of Miidera.

their massive temple complex set within a natural moat of rivers and sea withstood the assault and indeed appeared to be impregnable. This welcome demonstration of its strength and safety encouraged further commercial settlement, and the surrounding merchant community experienced a considerable growth over the next few years. It soon became the nucleus for an army that was to occupy the time and stretch the resources of many samurai generals for the next 50 years.

The Ikkō-ikki of Mikawa Province

Another important centre of Ikkō-ikki activity was Mikawa Province. Several temples, including three in Okazaki – Shomanji, Joguji and Honsoji – possessed Ikkō-ikki armies. Their temple lands impinged upon the territory of the future shōgun, Tokugawa Ieyasu, and it was through his successful campaigns against the Mikawa monto that Ieyasu learnt the military skills that were to stand him in such good stead in the years to come.

Tokugawa Ieyasu's fear was that the Mikawa monto would try to do in his province what Rennyo's men had done in Kaga, and soon the young Ieyasu was engaged with the monk armies at the battle of Azukizaka in 1564. It was to Ieyasu's great advantage that among the Ikkō-ikki supporters were samurai who happened to belong to the Shinshū sect but who had considerably divided loyalties. Some were also vassals of Ieyasu, and at first their religious inclinations had made them choose the Ikkō-ikki side in the battle. But as time wore on the traditional samurai loyalty to the lord proved the stronger force and many who changed sides, such as Ishikawa Ienari, were to become Ieyasu's most trusted companions. Needless to say, such loyalty did not extend down to the peasants who comprised the bulk of the Ikkō-ikki armies. To them all samurai were ultimately enemies, eventually to be swept from power in the province.

Ieyasu also benefited from the support given to him by his own particular sect of Buddhism, the Jōdo-shū, the original Amidist sect from which Shinshū had sprung. Daijuji, the temple where Ieyasu's ancestors were buried, represented Jōdo in Okazaki. In 1564 the Daijuji sent a contingent of Jōdo warrior monks to fight for Ieyasu, and with their help the Ikkō-ikki of Mikawa were finally crushed. A subsequent peace conference established that Ieyasu would restore their temples to their original state. This he did with vigour, by burning each one to the ground, arguing that a green-field site was the original state.

The warriors of the Holy Lotus

We noted earlier how Enryakuji had reacted angrily to the growth in influence of Rennyo's Jōdo Shinshū in Kyōto, but by the year 1500 Enryakuji found its traditional pre-eminence threatened by the emergence of another populist Buddhist sect, the Nichiren-shū, otherwise known as the Hokke-shū or Lotus sect. The Hokke-shū had been particularly successful in the capital, where its teachings found favour among the craftsmen and merchants, but as this was the Sengoku Period the 21 Nichiren temples in Kyōto were surrounded by moats and earthen ramparts for protection. Attached to each were the adherents of Nichiren, who had formed their own self-governing, self-defending organizations analogous to the Ikkō-ikki communities.

It is tempting to see the townsmen's Lotus sect in Kyōto and the Ikkō-ikki of the provinces as two sides of a 'town' versus 'country' divide, identified along sectarian lines. There is indeed some truth in this, and that would certainly have been the impression given when an army of the Ikkō-ikki marched on Kyōto in 1528. The townsmen armies of the Lotus sect, unconcerned at the reasons why they were being attacked, armed themselves and paraded through the streets under the Nichiren banner, chanting verses from the *Lotus Sutra*. When the Ikkō-ikki moved in they were successfully driven off.

Five years later in 1533 the Lotus warriors joined forces with local strong man Hosokawa Harumoto to hit back at the Ikkō-ikki. Their target was Ishiyama Honganji, a place impossible to conquer by assault, but a simple demonstration of power was all that was presently needed. Just as the Lotus warriors had planned, the Ikkō-ikki left Kyōto alone after that, so the shōgun returned to his palace in 1534 secure in the support of his citizens. But although the Ikkō-ikki had been persuaded to back off from Kyōto, the Lotus sect's aggressive religious fundamentalism and their fierce assertion of property rights caused great concern to a religious institution that was much nearer to home. The monks of Enryakuji felt that these upstarts had supplanted them in the very heart of power. So, just as their predecessors had taken direct action against courtiers five centuries earlier, the warrior monks of Mount Hiei descended on Kyōto once again. No longer were they content to parade the *mikoshi* (portable shrines) in front of terrified courtiers. Instead, in true Sengoku fashion, this latest manifestation of mountain power made a surprise attack and burned down all 21 Nichiren temples in Kyōto. The self-governing structure of the townsmen was not totally destroyed but was so weakened that it collapsed when Oda Nobunaga entered the capital in triumph in 1568.

The destruction of Mount Hiei

Having rediscovered their long-dormant military strength, the newly reinvigorated warrior monks of Mount Hiei sought allies among prominent local daimyō. Their location, to the north-east of Kyōto, put them in closest proximity with the territories of the Asai and Asakura families, who were Nobunaga's main rivals to the north of the capital and threatened his communications past Lake Biwa. During 1570 Oda Nobunaga defeated the Asai and Asakura at the battle of the Anegawa. Their destruction was far from complete, and later that same year they took advantage of Nobunaga's temporary absence from the scene to swoop down from the north in revenge. Nobunaga's finest general, Toyotomi Hideyoshi, met them in battle near Sakamoto and drove them back into the snow-covered mountains, where they would probably all have been slaughtered had not the warrior monks of Mount Hiei come to their aid.

The Jōdo monks of the Daijuji temple in Mikawa fight for Tokugawa Ieyasu against the Ikkō-ikki.

By 1571 the Asai and Asakura had recovered from their beating and looked towards Mount Hiei for a formal alliance that would take on Oda Nobunaga once again. The threat was a very real one, so Nobunaga sent messages warning Enryakuji of dire retribution if it decided to help his enemies any further. But, faced with monastic intransigence, Nobunaga decided to make the first move. Unlike the swamps and walls of the Ikkō-ikki headquarters, Mount Hiei was

virtually undefended except by its warrior monks. The attack had the prospect of being a pushover, but the ruthlessness with which it was pursued sent shock waves through Japan.

Oda Nobunaga's stated aim was to burn down the entire Enryakuji temple complex as a precaution and as a warning to any other warrior monk communities that might be watching. The assault began on 29 September 1571.

The monks of Mount Hici feed the troops of Asakura Yoshikaga after their defeat by Hideyoshi, an unwise move that led to their destruction.

Nobunaga first burned the town of Sakamoto at the foot of Mount Hiei, but most of the townspeople had already taken refuge on the mountain. Next he took particular care to destroy the Hiyoshi shrine of the mountain king, and then his 30,000 men were deployed in a vast ring around the mountain. At a signal from a conch trumpet they began to move steadily up the paths, burning and shooting all that stood in their way. By nightfall the main temple buildings of Enryakuji had gone up in flames. Many monks were unable to resist, but faced the situation with the detached frame of mind that their Buddhist training had cultivated:

'Let us concentrate our attention on the Moon of Perfect Enlightenment, and chastise our hearts in the water that flows from the hillside of Shimei. Scalding water and charcoal fire are no worse than the cooling

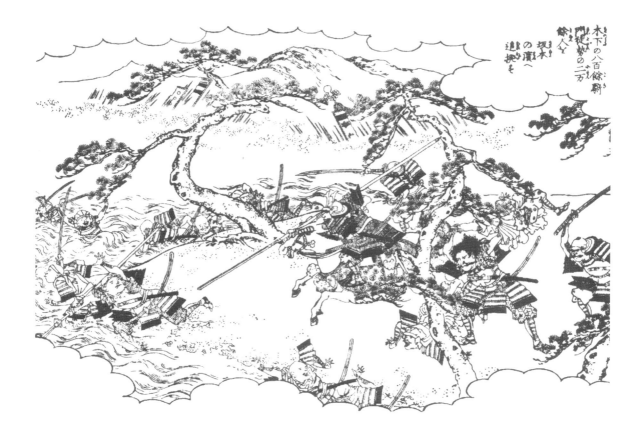

木下の八百餘騎
門徒勢の二万
坂本の嶺へ
追撞を
餘々

breeze.' So saying they threw themselves into the raging flames, and not a few were thus consumed by the flames. The roar of the burning monastery, magnified by the cries of countless numbers of the old and the young, sounded and resounded to the ends of heaven and earth.

An army under Hideyoshi defeats a warrior monk army on the shores of Lake Biwa in 1571.

Next day Nobunaga sent his gunners out on a hunt for any who had escaped, and the final casualty list probably topped 20,000. Even though this was not his largest massacre, it was the most notorious act of Oda Nobunaga's violent career, and marked the end of the long history of the warrior monks of Enryakuji. In time the trees would grow again and the monks would rebuild, but never again would they reappear as warrior monk armies.

Oda Nobunaga and the Ikkō-ikki

The reunification of Japan began with the campaigns of Oda Nobunaga, who shot to prominence following his victory at Okehazama in 1560. The years between 1570 and 1581 were marked by Oda Nobunaga's greatest achievements – the battles of the Anegawa and Nagashino, the invasion of Ise and Iga provinces, and the building of Azuchi castle. Yet all these campaigns and historic advances were carried out against a background of a continuous threat from, and sporadic war with, the Ikkō-ikki. They threatened Oda Nobunaga both militarily and economically, and he was determined to destroy them.

With the pacification of the Ikkō-ikki of Mikawa the focus of Ikkō-ikki activity was in the north, where the self-governing communities of Echizen and Kaga ruled the roost, and west to the great foundations of Nagashima and Ishiyama Honganji. Compared to the isolated temples of Mikawa, these positions were very strong indeed. Both consisted of a complex series of stockaded fortresses built around a castle and set within a river delta. Nagashima's location controlled the route from Owari Province into Ise, and with it the main lines of communication south of Lake Biwa between Nobunaga's secure territories and the capital. Ishiyama Honganji was built on a slope where Osaka castle now stands at the mouth of the Kisogawa at its point of entry to the Inland Sea. For several years the operations against the three centres ran concurrently, but for simplicity each one will be described separately, beginning with the river delta of Nagashima.

The name Nagashima is believed to derive from 'Nana shima', or 'the seven islands', which, with a host of smaller islands, reed plains and swamps, filled the delta. It lay on the border between Owari and Ise provinces to the south-east of the present-day city of Nagoya. Three rivers, the Kisogawa, the Nagaragawa and the Ibigawa, enter Ise Bay. Their direction has continually shifted throughout history, but even today the long, flat island of Nagashima, set among broad rivers and waving reeds, can easily conjure up the appearance it must have presented to the Ikkō-ikki who garrisoned it during the Age of Warring States.

There were effectively two key areas of Nagashima's defences: Nagashima castle, and the fortified monastery of Ganshoji. The castle had been built in 1555 by Itō Shigeharu, who lost it to the Ikkō-ikki when he was swept from power in a manner that was becoming only too familiar to daimyō who had this particular variety of rival on their doorstep. As Owari was Oda Nobunaga's home province his family felt the presence of the Nagashima ikki very acutely, and certain members of the Oda clan engaged them in battle at the northern edge of the Nagashima delta at Ogie castle in November 1569. The Ikkō-ikki were completely victorious, and killed Nobunaga's brother, Nobuoki. The loss of his brother added a personal dimension to Nobunaga's strategic need to overcome Nagashima.

Nobunaga appointed his trusted generals Sakuma Nobumori and Shibata Katsuie as commanders. The Ikkō-ikki made suitable preparations, strengthening their outposts and setting up various defensive measures. Nobunaga's army made camp on 16 May 1571 at Tsushima to the north-east of Nagashima, which was divided from the complex by a particularly shallow yet broad river. An attack was planned on the area immediately to the west of Tsushima against the series of *wajū* (island communities protected by dykes against flooding), from where an attack could be launched on the Ganshoji, but this first operation against Nagashima was an unqualified disaster. Shibata Katsuie was severely wounded, and no impression was made on the defences. As the Oda army withdrew they burned several villages on the outskirts, which probably had no effect other than inclining the sympathies of the local population more towards the cause of their neighbours.

The burning of Mount Hiei took place shortly after the disaster at Nagashima, so it was with renewed confidence that Nobunaga moved against Nagashima once more. He first reduced a minor Ikkō-ikki outpost within Owari Province by leading the defenders out on the basis of a spurious peace

The monument to the Ikkō-ikki in the courtyard of Ganshoji in Nagashima.

treaty and then massacring them where they stood. The attempt at intimidation was clear, but the defenders of Nagashima were discouraged neither by the attack on Mount Hiei nor by the fate of their fellow holy warriors in Owari. The new campaign began in July 1573, and this time Nobunaga took personal charge of the operations. The numbers of his army are not recorded, but it contained a well-drilled arquebus corps. Nevertheless, for the second time in two years the Oda army was forced to withdraw.

Nobunaga returned to the fray for a third time in 1574, but he was now much better armed. His conquest of Ise Province had brought to his side an unusual naval talent in the person of Kuki Yoshitaka (1542–1600), a man who, like many of the Japanese sea captains of his day, had once been a successful pirate. Nobunaga recruited Kuki and his fleet to take the fight close to the Ikkō-ikki fortifications in a way that had never proved possible before. Yoshitaka kept up a rolling bombardment of the Nagashima defences from close range with cannonballs and fire arrows, concentrating on the wooden watchtowers.

The presence of the ships served to cut off the garrison from supplies and from any possible relieving force. It also enabled Nobunaga's land-based troops to take most of the Ikkō-ikki's outlying forts. This allowed Nobunaga to control

The destruction of Enryakuji by the troops of Oda Nobunaga in 1571. This was the blackest deed associated with the name of the great general.

access from the western side for the first time. Supported by Kuki Yoshitaka, a land-based army carried out a three-pronged attack from the north. The defenders were gradually forced back, though with enormous resistance, and were squeezed into the small areas called Nakae and Yanagashima. There was little else in the way of territory and almost no hope of relief. By the end of August 1574 they were slowly starving to death and ready to talk peace, but their overtures fell on deaf ears. Mindful of the death of his brother, and his own humiliation at their hands, Nobunaga resolved to destroy the islands of Nagashima as thoroughly as he had destroyed Mount Hiei.

Instead of accepting surrender, Nobunaga began building a very tall wooden palisade around Nakae and Yanagashima which physically isolated the Ikkō-ikki from the gaze of the outside world. Approximately 30,000 people were now crammed into the inner fortifications. Unseen by them, Nobunaga began to pile a mountain of dry brushwood against the palisade. He waited for the strong winds that heralded the approach of the September typhoons (to which Ise Bay is prone) and set light to the massive pyre. Burning brands jumped the small gaps of water, and soon the whole of the Nagashima complex was ablaze. As at Mount Hiei, no mercy was shown, but at Nagashima none was asked for, because the flatlands provided no resistance to the fierce fires, and all the inhabitants of the Ikkō-ikki fortress were burned to death before any could escape to be cut down.

In 1575, the same year as his great victory at Nagashino, Oda Nobunaga left his base at Tsuruga and swept through Echizen, recapturing the province from Ikkō-ikki forces. It was one of his best-coordinated actions and involved an amphibious attack from hundreds of ships by Akechi Mitsuhide and Toyotomi Hideyoshi as he marched up from the south. Yet by its savagery Echizen was a campaign that put even the destruction of Enryakuji into the shade. Nobunaga was gleeful at the results, which he described in letters. In the eighth lunar month of 1575 Nobunaga attacked Fuchu (now the town of Takefu), and wrote two letters from the site to the Shoshidai Murai Nagata no kami Sadakatsu. One contained the chilling passage, 'As for the town of Fuchu, only dead bodies can be seen without any empty space left between them. I would like to show it to you. Today I will search the mountains and the valleys and kill everybody.' By November he could boast to the daimyō Date Terumune that he had 'wiped out several tens of thousands of the villainous rabble in Echizen and Kaga'. In *Shinchōkoki*, Nobunaga's biographer reports:

From the 15th to the 19th of the eighth month, the lists drawn up for Nobunaga recorded that more than 12,500 people were captured and presented by the various units. Nobunaga gave orders to his pages to execute the prisoners, and Nobunaga's troops took countless men and women with them to their respective home provinces. The number of executed prisoners must have been around 30,000 to 40,000.

The Jōdo Shinshū temple in Takefu (formerly Fuchu in Echizen Province), the site of the worst massacre of the Ikkō-ikki by Oda Nobunaga.

Akechi Mitsuhide and Toyotomi Hideyoshi then continued the advance into Kaga, taking in rapid succession the three fortified temples of Daishoji, Hinoya and Sakumi. By the end of 1575 the southern half of Kaga was firmly under Nobunaga's control and the Ikkō-ikki federation was beginning to fall apart.

The fall of Ishiyama Honganji

Nobunaga's first move against Ishiyama Honganji had been launched in August 1570. He left Gifu castle at the head of 30,000 troops and ordered the building of a series of forts around the perimeter. On 12 September the bells rang out at midnight from within Ishiyama Honganji, and Nobunaga's fortresses at Kawaguchi and Takadono were attacked, resulting in the withdrawal of the Oda main body, leaving only a handful of forts to attempt the task of monitoring, if not controlling, the mighty fortress. It was a process that would take 11 years and much of Nobunaga's military resources in a long-term campaign that sucked other daimyō into the conflict like a black hole.

By 1576 the main building of Ishiyama Honganji had grown to become the centre of a complex ring of 51 outposts well supported by organized arquebus squads. In April Nobunaga made a land-based attack on Ishiyama Honganji with a force of 3,000 men under the command of Araki Muneshige and Akechi Mitsuhide. This may have been more of an exercise in testing the defenders' mettle, because 15,000 were pitted against Nobunaga and he was forced to withdraw.

The ferocity of the defence forced Nobunaga to revise his tactics, and he changed his immediate aim to that of reducing the outposts of Ishiyama Honganji's supporters, thus isolating the centre. He attacked the Ikkō-ikki outpost of Saiga in Kii Province to the south and sent Toyotomi Hideyoshi against the other nest of warrior monks at Negoroji. Negoroji was not defeated in this attack but was sufficiently contained so as not to present much of a threat to Nobunaga's immediate plans.

With outside forces reduced to a minimum, Nobunaga tried to starve out the defenders of Ishiyama Honganji, but the fortress island opened on to the narrow Inland Sea. This area was largely controlled by the fleet of Nobunaga's deadly enemies, the Mōri clan, who kept Ishiyama Honganji well supplied, so Nobunaga once again enlisted the services of Kuki Yoshitaka to enforce a blockade. The plans did not work, and in August 1576 Mōri demonstrated his naval superiority by breaking Nobunaga's fleet at the first battle of Kizugawaguchi.

Yet in spite of Mōri's gun-running and provision of food supplies, it soon became clear to the defenders that there were very few Ikkō sympathizers left to come and join them anyway. The evident loss of this support alarmed the Ishiyama Honganji commanders, so Abbot Kosa sent desperate requests for help throughout the country. Many Ikkō-ikki branches were already represented within the castle, and no others came to join them, so by 1578 the tide of the siege was beginning to move Nobunaga's way. At the second battle of Kizugawaguchi in 1578 Nobunaga's huge newly built battleships cut Mōri's supply line for good. The defenders of the Ishiyama Honganji prepared to face Nobunaga's final assault, but astonishingly the siege still had two years left to run. The garrison was under the spirited command of a certain Shimotsuma Nakayuki (1551–1616). In more confident days it had been the intention of Ishiyama Honganji to march on the capital and make Shimotsuma the new shōgun, but it had become clear that support was now coming only from within their own sectarian ranks. No samurai clan had responded to their call to arms, and Uesugi Kenshin, who had threatened Nobunaga from the north and supported the Honganji, died in 1578. The Mōri clan were also unwilling to engage in a full-scale struggle with Nobunaga once they had lost their strategic castle of Miki in 1580. This deprived them of their most convenient base, so the fortress cathedral became completely isolated, just as Nobunaga had planned.

Samurai attacking villagers. This was the fate that the Ikkō-ikki expected to receive at the hands of Oda Nobunaga, hence their dogged defiance.

Dressed in a sombre suit of armour, and under a red banner with an enormous golden sun's disc, Shimotsuma directed his operations as Nobunaga's armies whittled away at the outer lines of his defences. Every day the attacks continued, using up the cathedral's precious ammunition supply. Very soon Shimotsuma's food supplies also began to dry up, and Mōri's fleet could not move from port to aid them. A conference was held between the Abbot Kosa and his colleagues, and in April 1580 an imperial messenger was sent with a letter from no less a person than the emperor of Japan, suggesting an honourable surrender. Oda Nobunaga had of course prompted the letter, but it did the trick, and the fortress surrendered a few weeks later. The actual surrender terms were bloodless, and 11 years of bitter fighting eventually came to an end in August 1580. In spite of the precedents he had set on Mount Hiei and at Nagashima, Nobunaga acted with uncharacteristic generosity towards the sect that had caused him so much trouble. The castle complex was burned down, but Shimotsuma Nakayuki, who had signed a written oath in his own blood, was spared his life, and in a remarkable gesture was presented by his colleagues with a small statue of Amida Buddha in recognition of his services.

The last warrior monks

The long story of the warrior monks was almost over. Kaga Province was finally pacified shortly before Nobunaga's death. The last remnants of the Kaga Ikkō-ikki held out for months in two tiny yamashiro called Torigoe and Futoge until they were overcome and suffered a massacre similar to their brethren in Echizen.

Following Nobunaga's death in 1582 Kennyo, the former leader of Ishiyama Honganji, actively courted the new ruler, Toyotomi Hideyoshi, and sent some of his few remaining Ikkō-ikki warriors to harass Shibata Katsuie's rear during Hideyoshi's Shizugatake campaign in 1583. This endeared him to Hideyoshi and rewards were eventually forthcoming, in contrast to the subsequent experience of the warrior monks of Negoroji, who supported Hideyoshi's rival, Tokugawa Ieyasu, during the Komaki campaign of 1584.

This folly brought terrible retribution upon them in 1585 when Hideyoshi attacked Negoroji and the neighbouring temples that also maintained warrior monk armies. One was Kokawadera, a branch temple of Mount Hiei, and therefore the home of the last Tendai warrior monks in Japan, while across the Kii river where Wakayama castle now stands was Ota castle, headquarters of the local Ikkō-ikki known as the Saiga-ikki. Hideyoshi's army of 6,000 men first crushed four minor outposts, and then approached Negoroji from two separate directions. At that time the military strength of the Negoroji was believed to be between 30,000 and 50,000 men, and their skills with firearms were still considerable, but many had already crossed the river and sought shelter in Ota. Beginning with the priests' residences, the investing army systematically set fire to the Negoroji complex and cut down the warrior monks as they escaped from the flames. Several acts of single combat occurred between Hideyoshi's samurai and the Negoroji defenders.

Whereas fire had succeeded at Negoroji, Toyotomi Hideyoshi chose to reduce Ota by flooding it from a dam built along the north, west and south sides of the castle. On the eastern side the dyke was left open to allow the waters in. Heavy rain helped the process along, isolating the garrison more completely from outside help. The defenders were encouraged at one point by the partial collapse of a section of Hideyoshi's dyke, which caused the deaths of several besiegers as water poured out. Yet soon hunger began to take its toll and the garrison surrendered, led by 50 leading warrior monks, who committed a defiant act of hara kiri. The remaining soldiers, peasants, women and children who were found in the castle were disarmed of all swords and guns. Those found to be from samurai families were beheaded, while the peasants were set free.

The Saiga-ikki of Ota represented the last of the warrior monks, and when Kennyo petitioned Toyotomi Hideyoshi for support to restore the cathedral of the sect, it was only to rebuild it as the religious headquarters of Jōdo Shinshū, and not as an Ikkō-ikki fortress. Hideyoshi made a parcel of land available in Kyōto in 1589, and Nishi Honganji was built in 1591 as a splendid, but completely undefended, Jōdo Shinshū temple. Two of the great sights of modern

The armour worn by Shimotsuma Nakayuki, leader of the Ikkō-ikki armies during the siege of Ishiyama Honganji.

Kyōto illustrate the final settlement of the Ikkō-ikki problem. On leaving the station one is struck by the fact that there are two Shinshū temples: the Nishi Honganji and the Higashi Honganji, both of which appear to be the headquarters of the same organization and which are built almost next to each other. The explanation is that in 1602 Tokugawa Ieyasu, who had himself

WARRIOR MONKS OF NEGOROJI IN TRAINING c.1563
This illustration is based on the eyewitness description by Father Caspar Vilela. In the background we see traditional temple buildings based on those that remain at Negoroji today. On the left some monks are practising target shooting with arquebuses. In the foreground two monks are practising with wooden practice spears. They have wooden spheres at the end to minimize accidents. The 'safety ends' were sometimes covered in leather. Behind them two others practise with bokken, the ancestors of the bamboo swords now used in kendo. The monks are wearing their simplest robes. Like samurai in civilian dress, they have tied their sleeves back with a tasuki, and hitched up the legs of their trousers through their belts to give freedom of movement.

suffered at the hands of the Mikawa monto, took advantage of a succession dispute among Jōdo Shinshū and founded an alternative head temple to rival the existing one built by Hideyoshi in 1591. This weakened the political power of the sect, leaving it as a strong religious organization but never again capable of being revived as the warrior monk army of the Ikkō-ikki.

Ieyasu also revived Kōfukuji as a purely religious foundation, so when he became shōgun in 1603 there were no warrior monks left in Japan, although he did have some ex-warrior monks in his service. These were the survivors of

A battle with the warrior monks of Negoroji, destroyed by Hideyoshi in 1585.

his old allies from Negoroji, who were particularly skilled with firearms. Ieyasu took 16 into his service in 1585, and nine more in 1586, placing them under the command of Naruse Masashige. The Negoro-gumi formed the basis for the Tokugawa firearm squads of the early Edo Period.

Thanks to the generous Toyotomi Hideyoshi, Enryakuji had also come back to life. For over a decade there had been no Enryakuji, just the charred head of Mount Hiei, a black reminder to those who would not obey the rule of Oda Nobunaga. For once it seemed that Miidera, whose monks had supported Nobunaga, had gained the upper hand, but Hideyoshi favoured the reconstruction of Enryakuji, and new buildings began to rise. A wary Hideyoshi limited the number of buildings to 125, not the 3,000 of earlier times, and this is about the number of religious buildings found on its summit today.

Yet Toyotomi Hideyoshi had already given the greatest compliment to the warrior monks that any samurai leader was to pay. He had recognized that the site of the Ikkō-ikki's Ishiyama Honganji was a superb strategic and defensive location. Recalling how it had frustrated his master for so long, he chose it in 1586 as the site for his main castle that was to become the centre of today's great city of Osaka.

Warrior monk recruitment and service

Although most of the warrior monks of the earlier period must have had some genuine loyalty to religious ideals, it is quite clear that the armies of Mount Hiei included more than devout monks within their number. We suggested earlier that Ryogen's original recruits may have been no more than mercenaries, but there was another category of warrior monk: those who joined the communities for some personal reason, such as poverty, glory or the desire to escape from criminal prosecution. This was the stereotype of the akuso ('evil monks') cherished by all their opponents. Recruitment of such men was akin to the haphazard collection of ashigaru early in the Age of Warring States.

At the opposite end of the scale the category of warrior monk also covered some celebrated individuals who possessed a rare military talent. These can be divided into two categories: actual monks who were members of monastic communities, and samurai who had been ordained but who lived a secular life as daimyō.

Benkei

The archetype of the individual warrior monk is of course the legendary Benkei. According to the popular stories about him, Benkei was originally a member of the Enryakuji community but was expelled for bad behaviour. Finding an abandoned shrine somewhere on Mount Hiei, Benkei adopted it as his home and proposed turning it into a one-man monastery. His new temple lacked a bell, so Benkei, who was of large stature and huge physical strength, marched down to Miidera and stole the bell from their courtyard. He carried it back up the hill on his shoulders but, when he tried to ring it, the bell would only give out a plaintive moan that indicated that it wanted to go home. So Benkei gave the bell a good kick, which sent it rolling back down the hill into Miidera. The angry monks then made him replace it in the bell tower.

Benkei's most famous exploits concern his relationship with the great samurai general Minamoto Yoshitsune. They first met on the Goto bridge in Kyōto, where Benkei was currently engaged in stealing valuable swords from passing samurai. He tried the same trick with Yoshitsune, who defeated him in a single combat reminiscent of the legendary one between Robin Hood and Little John. From that day onwards Benkei became Yoshitsune's loyal companion. He fought beside him at Ichi no tani, Yashima and Dan no Ura, and accompanied him on his wanderings when he fled from the wrath of his jealous brother, Minamoto Yoritomo. These exploits, travelling Japan in disguise, have provided the plots for several classic plays of the Japanese theatre.

The temple of Nishi Honganji in Kyōto, symbolic of the solution to the warrior monk problem. It is one of two Jōdo Shinshū headquarters in Kyōto. This is the interior of its huge main hall, built to accommodate thousands of worshippers.

Benkei and Yoshitsune met their deaths at the battle of Koromogawa in 1189. The chronicle *Gikeiki* provides us with an unforgettable image of warrior monk valour when it describes how Benkei, naginata in hand, held the enemy at bay while his master performed hara kiri. There he stood, covered in blood and looking like a porcupine from the scores of arrows that had pierced him. One samurai suggested that Benkei was wearing a horō back to front, but what the man saw was the flow of Benkei's blood. He stood as immovable as the great god Fudo, until the slipstream from a passing horse made him topple over, and everyone realized that he had been dead for some time, but had died standing at his post.

Inei – the monk martial artist

During the 16th century we read of another remarkable individual warrior monk. His name was Inei, and he was the chief priest of the Hozo-In, a

The most famous warrior monk of all was the famous Benkei, shown here with his 'seven weapons'. He is depicted in a scene from a Kabuki play that deals with his wanderings with Yoshitsune.

sub-temple of Kōfukuji. We hear almost nothing of warrior monk armies from Kōfukuji during the Age of Warring States, so Inei's interest in the martial arts is unique.

Inei was a skilled devotee of spear fighting with the yari, the straight-bladed spear that had almost replaced the naginata. One night he was practising with his spear by the pool of Sarusawa. The neck of the spear blade where it joined the shaft was reflected in the waters of the pond and merged with the reflection of the crescent moon. This gave Inei the inspiration to fit a crescent-shaped cross blade to his spear. This weapon became known as the *kamayari* of the Hozo-In. Inei's pupil Shuji fought a famous single combat against the wandering swordsman Miyamoto Musashi, and even though Musashi was victorious the duel gave him quite a respect for the fighting monks.

The samurai monks

As a final example of the individual warrior monk, we must mention the numerous samurai who were also ordained Buddhist priests. Daimyō who had been exiled to temples sometimes returned to warlike activities, while others were moved to have their heads shaved by various personal experiences. Some of the greatest names among the daimyō had taken holy orders, and evidence of their status is noticeable from contemporary paintings. Thus Uesugi Kenshin is usually shown wearing a monk's cowl on his head. Several pictures of Takeda Shingen in armour show him with a *kesa* (ceremonial scarf) across his breastplate. Their names of 'Kenshin' and 'Shingen' are Buddhist appellations, just like the famous Hōjō Sōun. Otherwise there may be small additions to their costume that simply show Buddhist devotion. Honda Tadakatsu, for example, is often depicted with a huge wooden 'rosary', and many used flags with Buddhist motifs. Needless to say, the armies in which these men served, or even led, were not 'warrior monk' armies, but their religious motivation was often a factor in their behaviour, and for Uesugi Kenshin to petition the kami about Shingen's lack of respect for religious institutions was criticism indeed.

Many daimyō who were not monks cherished their Buddhist faith. For example, following the defeat of the Imagawa family, of which he was then a vassal, in 1560, Tokugawa Ieyasu went to his ancestral temple of Daijuji in Okazaki with the intention of committing hara kiri in front of the tombs of his ancestors. Toyo, the chief priest, managed to dissuade him from this course of action, and presented Ieyasu with a white banner on which was written 'Renounce this filthy world, attain the Pure Land', a flag that Ieyasu was to carry with him in all subsequent battles, including ones against the Ikkō-ikki.

Appearance and equipment of the warrior monk

Costume

There is a remarkable consistency among contemporary descriptions and illustrations of the Japanese warrior monks. This enables us to reconstruct the appearance of a sōhei from Enryakuji or Nara with some accuracy. The basis of their costume was the monastic robe, a garment that has hardly changed in style over 12 centuries, so that the Buddhist monks that one encounters today on Mount Hiei or in Nara do not look very different from their predecessors. We may therefore safely conclude that the sōhei of the Enryakuji and Negoroji in the Age of Warring States would have looked similar.

The kimono shares with many other items of traditional Japanese costume a simple style and a long tradition. Over a *fundoshi* or loincloth the warrior monk would wear a succession of kimono, which look like long wide-sleeved dressing gowns. The undergarments would be white, with the outer robe being white, tan or saffron. Over the outer kimono would be worn a jacket, usually

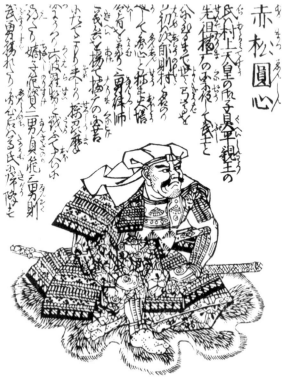

Inei of the Hozo In, the most renowned of the monk martial arts specialists. He is shown at the moment of realization when he saw the reflection of the crescent moon against the shaft of his spear. The artist Yoshitoshi has shown the moon in the sky behind him.

black, and often of a stiff gauzy 'see-through' material that may be noted on monastic costume today. Footwear consisted of waraji worn over white tabi and often long kiahan. *Geta* are often depicted being worn by warrior monks.

Each geta was carved out of one piece of wood to produce a raised platform for the foot. Although geta look clumsy to the Western eye, the Japanese always look very nimble in them.

A warrior monk made the following additions to this priestly garb. Firstly the white headcowl was folded and tied around the head to leave only the face exposed. By contrast, some illustrations show warrior monks without a cowl and with a white hachimaki tied round their foreheads over their shaven pates.

The warrior monk would also wear a suit of armour. Judging from scroll paintings this was usually a simple wrap-around dō maru worn just under the outer robe, rather like a flak jacket. The dō maru was a typical suit of Japanese armour, being made from a series of lacquered metal or leather scales laced together in overlapping rows. A series of these rows would be joined by silk cords to make an armour plate. Otherwise the more elaborate yoroi style with a breastplate was worn, but the yoroi's heavy shoulder guards would not have fitted easily around a monk's robe. In many cases we also see kote under the wide robe sleeves. A kote consisted of a cloth tube to which small armour plates were sewn at vulnerable places. Fuller head protection would of course necessitate the wearing of a helmet instead of the cowl, and in the battle between warrior monks of Nara and the Taira family depicted in the *Kasuga Gongen* scroll, we see many warrior monks who are fully armoured and almost indistinguishable from ordinary samurai.

A monk's weapons

A strong belt around the waist augmented the usual kimono belt and had slung from it a typical Japanese sword. At this time the sword would be of tachi form, and was carried with the cutting edge downwards, so that two hands were needed to draw it. In common with most samurai, a tanto might have been thrust through the belt under the right arm. Tanto are not much in evidence in paintings, but the use of them is confirmed in the famous account reproduced below of the battle of Uji. Bows and arrows were also used, and many monks were skilled archers. The bow was the typical Japanese longbow. The monk's traditional weapon was the fierce-looking cutting weapon called a naginata, which was a form of glaive. The blade was set inside a stout wooden shaft of oval cross section for ease of handling. The pommel was of iron and helped to balance the blade. It could also be used as a weapon in its own right. A naginata blade was similar to a sword blade and forged to an equally high standard, but there were many variations in shape. Some were much wider than sword blades and resembled Chinese halberds. In the 11th and 12th centuries the form called the *shobuzukuri naginata* was preferred, which had a long blade that almost equalled the comparatively shorter shaft. Later models of naginata had a shorter blade and a longer shaft.

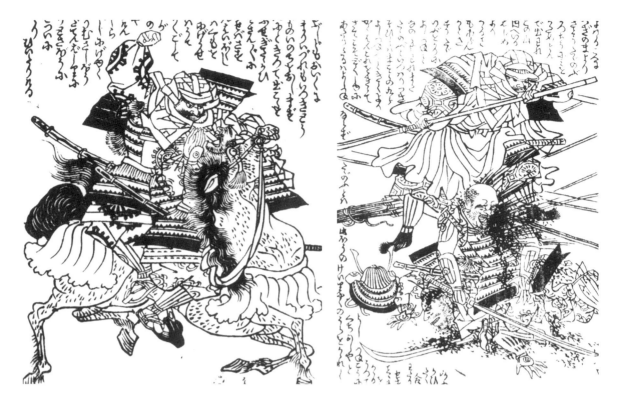

ABOVE LEFT

A warrior monk with headcowl riding a horse. He appears to have pulled a rival warrior monk off the ground and is striking him with his fist.

ABOVE RIGHT

Warrior monks in action. The fellow at the rear has the famous naginata and wears priestly robes and a headcowl.

The warrior monks therefore provided an intimidating sight with their veiled faces, their sharp naginata and their unmistakable priestly garb that proclaimed them as holy warriors. Those represented in scroll paintings or later woodblock-printed books always look very rough and confident characters, and *Heike Monogatari* tells of the warrior monks of Miidera that they were 'all stout men at arms carrying bows and arrows, sword and naginata, every one of them worth a thousand ordinary men, caring not whether they met god or devil'.

Warrior monks on their demonstrations in Kyōto are usually represented dressed in full monastic robes and armour, but the headcowl is frequently absent. Their shaven heads bear a few days' growth of bristles, and headbands are tied across their sweaty foreheads, while in their hands they carry prayer beads. Another fascinating description of the redoubtable warrior monk comes from *Heike Monogatari*'s account of the battle of Nara in 1180:

Now there was among the retiring priests a warrior monk named Saka no shiro Yogaku, who for strength and valour was equal to all the temples of Nara put together. He wore two suits of armour one over the other, a black body armour over another suit with lacings of light green silk, and two helmets likewise, one of five plates over a steel cap, while he brandished a white-handled naginata, curved like a reed in one hand and a huge tachi with black mounts in the other. Gathering some ten of his comrades of the same temple round him, he held the enemy at the Tengai gate for some time and slew very many, but as fast as they fell others came on.

The costume and weapons of the Ikkō-ikki

Contemporary illustrations show the Ikkō-ikki looking less like conventional warrior monks and more like a motley crew, with the bulk of their forces clearly peasants. This is what one would be led to expect because everyone had his (or her) part to play in the defence against the ruthlessness of Oda Nobunaga. In the pictures reproduced here their commander on horseback is dressed in complete samurai armour. He is probably a jizamurai. The ordained priests of Jōdo Shinshū fought alongside their followers, so it is probably they who are depicted in full Buddhist monk's robes and a shaven head. Low-ranking warriors wear a peasant's straw rain cloak and foot soldiers' jingasa. There is finally a mixture of samurai armour and helmets. Many items of military equipment could be obtained very cheaply in the aftermath of a battle.

The Ikkō-ikki sally out from a castle. Their equipment ranges from full samurai armour to peasants' garments.

The armour of the 16th century had developed from the earlier dō maru. Lacing was now spaced into pairs, and smaller shoulder plates were worn. Many suits of armour had solid breastplates, some of which were proudly advertised as being bullet-proof. The older style of dō maru were still worn, particularly by those samurai who were less well off. The okegawa-dō, the simple smooth breastplated armour worn by ashigaru, was quite cheap to produce, so we may imagine hundreds of these suits being available for the Ikkō-ikki armies.

As to weapons, swords and daggers were plentiful, while some still carried naginata. Straight spears (introduced during the 14th century) would also have been much in evidence, and all the 'holy warriors' of the 16th century made very good use of arquebuses, the simple matchlock muskets fired by dropping a lighted match on to the pan. The Jōdo Shinshū temples were among the best customers for the newly established gunsmiths – good evidence of how these monk armies were no peasant rabble but an organized force at the forefront of military technology.

A prominent feature of the Ikkō-ikki armies was the carrying of flags with Buddhist slogans written on them. Most of these were the long vertical nobori-type banners, held on a pole and stiffened by a cross pole at the top. The Ikkō-ikki flags often bore the prayer used by all the Amidist Buddhist sects: 'Namu Amida Butsu' ('Hail to the Buddha Amida'). Another banner stated the conviction that 'He who advances is sure of salvation, but he who retreats will go to hell'. The Lotus warriors of the Nichiren-shū used flags bearing the Nichiren motto 'Namu Myoho Renge Kyo' ('Hail to the Lotus of the Divine Law'). Other Buddhist motifs such as the *sotoba* (a series of shapes indicating the relationship between man and heaven) are also noted. Another contingent that supported Ishiyama Honganji used a flag with a crane design.

Belief and belonging

From tolerance to trouble-making

The religion that underpinned the warrior monks was Buddhism. There is no space here to explore in detail the teachings of the Buddha or the forms that Buddhism took when it came to Japan; suffice to say that the brand of Buddhism espoused by the first warrior monks was that taught by the great temples of Nara and Mount Hiei, whose attitudes and opinions dominated the religious scene. The disputes between them were never about points of doctrine, nor was there any disagreement with Shintō. Kukai (774–835), known posthumously as Kobo Daishi and the founder of the Shingon sect of Buddhism, is one of the holiest and most revered figures in Japanese religion, yet even he revered Shintō so much

The modern temple bell of Miidera. The historic one associated with Benkei is kept inside one of the halls.

that he put his new foundation under the protection of Shintō kami. Saicho did the same at Mount Hiei with his devotion to Sanno the king of the mountain. Among those carrying Sanno's mikoshi into Kyōto during demonstrations would be the *kannushi* (Shintō priests) of the Hiyoshi shrine, while the kannushi of the Kasuga shrine would have been intimately involved with the politics of Kōfukuji.

The big difference in sectarian attitude occurred centuries later with the development of the populist sects. We now see some genuine differences in belief, but how far this was responsible for the violence between the sects is hard to say. One constant factor throughout was the enmity felt by Enryakuji against any new foundation that threatened its traditional predominance in Kyōto. Such was Enryakuji's influence that nearly all the sects described in these pages had founders who had studied on Mount Hiei at some time, but

Enryakuji showed no tolerance to anyone who deviated from their teaching and who went on to found his own sect. For example, the Jōdo-shū, founded by the priest Honen, came in for particularly severe treatment at the hands of Enryakuji. By burning both new editions and printing blocks, Enryakuji's monks suppressed several editions of *Senchakushu*, a major work by Honen, over a period of about 300 years.

The attacks by the Ikkō-ikki and Enryakuji on the Nichiren temples of Kyōto probably had as much to do with politics as with sectarianism. Nevertheless, the destruction was so thorough that the Nichiren sect was for a long time absent from Kyōto and is hardly present in any significant numbers today. By contrast, we noted the firm alliance between Tendai, Shingon and Jōdo Shinshū warrior monks when Hideyoshi attacked Negoroji in 1585. Perhaps by this time a bigger enemy had been recognized. The destruction of Mount Hiei by Nobunaga had certainly sent out strong messages to all the sects.

The religious world of the Ikkō-ikki

The Ikkō-ikki movement derived from a later offshoot of the Jōdo sect, the Shinshū or Jōdo Shinshū ('True Pure Land Sect') founded by Shinran Jonin (1174–1268). It is now Japan's largest Buddhist denomination. The head of Jōdo Shinshū in the 15th century was Rennyo (1415–99), who achieved such fame as a preacher that the warrior monks of Mount Hiei burned his home and forced him to flee to Echizen.

Although poles apart from Enryakuji in its religious, social and political beliefs, the 'single-minded' league of the Ikkō-ikki showed a remarkably similar lack of religious toleration. The basis of the beliefs of both Jōdo and Jōdo Shinshū was a purposeful devotion to the worship of Amida, the Supreme Buddha of the Jōdo (Pure Land) in the West, who will welcome all his followers into the paradise of the Pure Land on their death. This teaching contrasted sharply with the insistence on the attainment of enlightenment through study, work or asceticism stressed by the older sects. To Enryakuji, this was an illusory short cut to salvation.

Jōdo Shinshū promised an even more immediate route to heaven than did Jōdo. 'Call on the name of Amida and you will be saved – now!' was the cry of the sect's founder; hence the practice of *nembutsu* or 'Buddha calling', the prayer sequence noted even on battlefields. This prayer, which could be repeated up to 60,000 times a day by devotees, became the motto of the Ikkō-ikki armies. Shinshū welcomed all into its fold, and did not insist upon meditation or any intellectual path to salvation. As its clergy were not required to be celibate or to withdraw from the world, they were able to evangelize among the peasantry much more freely, and its influence grew rapidly among the common people.

There is no doubting the strong influence that religion had on all aspects of the lives of the members of the Ikkō-ikki, who were Japan's 'holy warriors' par excellence. Its monto welcomed fighting because their faith promised that paradise was the immediate reward for death in battle, and nothing daunted them. In common with the democratic structure of all ikki, oaths were signed on a paper that bore the image of Amida Buddha, and the names were arranged in a circle so that no one took precedence over another. On some occasions these documents were burned, the ashes dissolved in water, and the resulting brew drunk by the confederates as a solemn and binding pledge.

The wide social-class inclusiveness of the Ikkō-ikki communities was a particular irritation to samurai. Prior to the battle of Azukizaka, Ieyasu's retainer, Sakai Tadatsugu, wrote to the Ikkō-ikki temples of Mikawa Province urging them to reflect on the fact that 'shaving the head and wearing priestly robes is only to put on the outward signs of sanctity, like a bat that pretends to be a bird'. Ieyasu clearly did not regard the populist masses of the monto as 'real monks'.

Nichiren-shū was another fundamentalist Buddhist sect with similar social views. It was named after its founder, the monk Nichiren, who was martyred during the 13th century and was famous for having prophesied the Mongol invasions. The sect was otherwise known as the Hokke-shū (Lotus sect), from the importance attached by its believers to the *Lotus Sutra*, expressed through the motto and battle-cry 'Namu myoho renge kyo' ('Hail to the Lotus of the Divine Law').

A samurai who has been ordained as a Buddhist priest wearing the monk's cowl over his robe.

Two scenes of warrior monk life appear in this section from a painted scroll in the Rennyo Kinenkan, Yoshizaki. At the top we see monks in their robes armed with naginata. Below a monk rings the temple bell.

Zen never produced any warrior monks. This was no doubt partly due to its having no dogma as such. As one wag put it, having described the details that differentiated Tendai from Shingon and Jōdo, 'Zen has neither rhyme nor reason'. There were some disputes between the Zen temples of Kyōto and Enryakuji, but there seems to have been no actual fighting between them apart from one isolated incident. Other conflicts were resolved through third parties, and Zen had some very powerful samurai patrons who were willing to take a stand on its behalf. Zen is now the most prominent Buddhist sect in Kyōto.

As a footnote to the discussion of religious belief, we may note that during the 16th century Japan acquired another sect to add to its religious milieu. This was Christianity, which appeared on the scene in 1549, and although many of

The warrior monk Benkei with Minamoto Yoshitsune. They are wearing straw cloaks as a protection against the cold weather. In the background are other warrior monks.

its adherents fought with a devotion otherwise noted among the Ikkō-ikki, there were no Christian warrior monks. The closest parallel is probably the community that led the Shimabara Rebellion in 1638. Their defence of Hara castle against the shōgun's troops is remarkably similar to the story of the defence of Nagashima. Yet there was certainly no fellow feeling across this religious divide, and one of the few comments by a European concerning the Japanese warrior monks is a very caustic one. It comes from the Jesuit missionary Father Luis Frois, who described the destruction of Mount Hiei in less than sympathetic terms. Relating how Nobunaga made 'horrible slaughter of these false priests', he concludes, 'Thus God punished these enemies of his glory on Saint Michael's Day in the year 1571.'

Daily life and training of warrior monks

Daily life at Negoroji

Sources are lacking for any authentic account of how a warrior monk of Nara or Mount Hiei might divide his day between military training and the monastic life of prayer, study and meditation. By contrast a vivid impression of daily life among the warrior monks of the Sengoku Period comes from a report written by the Jesuit missionary Father Caspar Vilela. He visited the monastery of Negoroji, whose warrior monks are particularly interesting because they were renowned for their use of firearms and supplied a contingent of arquebusiers to Ishiyama Honganji.

Vilela described the appearance of the Negoroji warriors as akin to the Knights of Rhodes. This was a perceptive comment, and Vilela clearly had in mind the ferocity of the defence of Rhodes against the Ottomans in 1522. Like the Knights of St John, the Negoroji warrior monks were devoted to their religion and prepared to fight for it. Vilela, however, surmised that most of those he saw had taken no monastic vows, because they wore their hair long and were devoted to the practice of arms, their monastic rule laying less emphasis on prayer than on military preparation.

He also gives a good idea of the training of the warrior monks. Each member was required to make five or seven arrows per day, and to practise competitively with bow and arquebus once a week. Their helmets, armour and spears were of astonishing strength and, to quote Vilela, 'their sharp swords could slice through a man in armour as easily as a butcher carves a tender rump steak!' Their practice combat with each other was fierce, and the death of one of their number in training was accepted without emotion. Fearless on the battlefield, they enjoyed life off it with none of the restrictions normally associated with the ascetic life, indulging freely in wine, women and song.

Daily life of the Ikkō-ikki

Jōdo Shinshū shifted the emphasis of Japanese Buddhism from a monastic-centred organization to the ordinary lives of ordinary people, whose fortified temples housed communities to whom the practice of their religion was a fundamental part of life. Central to the daily life of places like Ishiyama Honganji was the recital of the nembutsu. The devotion associated with the practice only became really apparent when the Ikkō-ikki were about to go into battle and the sound of the mass nembutsu chilled the blood of their enemies, or when a special service was performed and the temple was packed with worshippers. Lamps twinkled on the pure gold surfaces of the altar furnishings. The air was heavy with incense and seemed to throb with the responses from hundreds of voices. Just as Shinran intended, to a believer the scene stood as a promise of the western paradise guaranteed by Amida Buddha.

The warrior monk's diet

It is unlikely that the average warrior monk laid any more stress on the Buddhist prohibition against eating meat than he did on the strictures on the taking of human life. His usual diet would be sparse and simple, although highly nutritious. It consisted mainly of rice, fish, vegetables, seaweed, salt and fruit, augmented occasionally by venison, wild boar and game birds. Rice was boiled in a pan, mixed with vegetables or seaweed, steamed or made into *o-nigiri* (rice balls). *Mochi* were made from rice flour or a mixture of rice and wheat flour. Husked rice could also be made into soup to which was added burdock, aubergines, cucumbers, mushrooms and other vegetables. If the monastery was near the sea, fish, shellfish and seaweed could be added to the diet. Fish was eaten raw (sashimi), grilled, fried or preserved by drying or smoking it. Green tea and sake were a warrior monk's usual drinks.

The warrior monk on campaign

Protest and intimidation

As noted above, the warrior monks would usually go on campaign on their own behalf, but they would sometimes ally themselves to samurai armies. On the occasions when a leader of samurai wished to recruit the services of the warrior monks, delicate discussions would take place, but a dramatic example of how things could go wrong occurred in Nara in 1180. Taira Kiyomori had sent envoys to negotiate an alliance, but the monks most unwisely assaulted the messengers and forcibly shaved their heads, then added insult to injury by making a wooden head, which they called the head of Kiyomori, and kicking it around the temple courtyard!

For the imperial court the greatest threat from the warrior monks occurred whenever they took their grievances into the streets of Kyōto and even to the gates of the imperial palace itself. These monastic 'protest marches' were turbulent affairs, and the monks would reinforce their own intimidating presence by carrying down into Kyōto the sacred mikoshi. *Heike Monogatari* describes several such incidents, one of which resulted from the murder of a Mount Hiei monk by a courtier.

For the imperial family, who otherwise led sheltered and privileged lives, the descent of the warrior monks on Kyōto in a demonstration was as terrifying as

The hondo (main hall) of Negoroji, now located at the Daigoji near Kyōto.

any military campaign, because the unseen weapon that the warrior monks carried was the fear of the gods they represented. By the end of the 11th century the warrior monks had this routine down to a fine art. If the intended victim was a member of the Fujiwara family (a category that included nearly everyone in the imperial court) the monks would march into Kyōto carrying branches of the sakaki tree specially consecrated by the kannushi of the Kasuga shrine, the tutelary shrine of the Fujiwara. To really drive home a point the monks might denounce an offender at the Kasuga shrine – a fate worse than death.

For the Mount Hiei monks the carrying of the mikoshi of Sanno the mountain king was the most dramatic gesture that could be made. Mikoshi may be seen today whenever there is a shrine festival in Japan. They are associated with the Shintō religion rather than with Buddhism, but in the time of the warrior monks Shintō and Buddhism were closely related. Sanno's shrine was the Hiyoshi shrine at the foot of Mount Hiei, and when the monks headed for the capital they would call in and collect the mikoshi, into which the kannushi would ritually transfer the *mitama* (spirit) of Sanno.

About 20 monks carried the mikoshi on poles, exactly as festival shrines are transported nowadays, and any assault on the mikoshi was regarded as an offence to the kami Sanno himself. Every monk also carried Buddhist prayer beads and would readily pronounce a curse upon anyone who offended him. On one occasion the monks chanted the 600 chapters of the *Dai Hannya Kyo* (a Buddhist sutra) as a curse. Sometimes the mikoshi would be left in the streets while the monks returned to the mountain. There it would remain, to the dread of all the citizens, until the monks' desires were satisfied. This subtle form of blackmail was first used in 1082.

Street fighting

The imperial court were particularly vulnerable to such treatment, as their lives were conducted according to strict religious and astrological rules, and Mount Hiei was of course their spiritual guardian. But by the 12th century the newly powerful samurai clans were less easily intimidated, and in 1146 a young samurai called Taira Kiyomori had his first dramatic clash with warrior monks. On the day of the Gion Festival in Kyōto one of Kiyomori's attendants quarrelled with a priest from the Gion shrine. Vowing revenge, Kiyomori led an attack on the Gion shrine while its mikoshi was being paraded. With a haughty samurai disregard for religious scruples Kiyomori deliberately shot an arrow at the mikoshi. It struck the gong on the front and proclaimed the act of sacrilege far and near. Kiyomori had certainly taken a risk. Regardless of the feelings of the offended kannushi, it was widely believed that anyone who assaulted a mikoshi would be struck dead on the spot. But Kiyomori survived, and found that he had stirred up a hornets' nest.

Enraged at the offence to a mikoshi, 7,000 warrior monks from Mount Hiei suddenly descended on the capital, baying for Kiyomori's blood. They expected that he would be banished, but times had changed. The imperial court had become dependent upon samurai armies such as those of Kiyomori's Taira clan for defending them against all incursions, including monastic ones. Kiyomori's continued support was therefore more important than placating the monks, and the court exonerated Kiyomori on payment of a nominal fine.

Few incidents illustrate the rise of samurai power in the land better than Kiyomori's personal defiance. With one arrow a samurai leader had burst the bubble of monastic pretensions. Through this act the power of the Taira family grew and the influence of the monks began to decline, until both were swallowed up in the devastation of the Gempei War.

Heike Monogatari also tells of another occasion when the defiant sōhei advanced on the capital carrying the mikoshi of the mountain king: 'As they entered Ichijo (a street in Kyōto) from the eastern side, people wondered if the sun and moon had not fallen from heaven.' They marched through the city to the imperial palace, where they found an armed guard of samurai and foot soldiers barring their way at the northern gate. The samurai were under the command of Minamoto Yorimasa, who was later to fight shoulder to shoulder

The warrior monks of Mount Hiei descend on Kyōto with their sacred mikoshi. This interesting illustration provides many important points of detail of the warrior monks' appearance. Some have no headcowl, but naginata are much in evidence.

with the warrior monks at the battle of Uji. He showed great respect for the sacred mikoshi: 'Then Yorimasa quickly leapt from his horse, and taking off his helmet and rinsing his mouth with water, made humble obeisance before the sacred emblem, all his three hundred retainers likewise following his example.'

The monks hesitated in their attack, noting the presence of the respected (and respectful) Yorimasa, and his comparatively small army, and decided to attack another gate instead. Here no diplomatic general was waiting for them, but a hail of arrows from mounted samurai:

> A struggle ensued, for the samurai drew their bows and shot at them so that many arrows struck the sacred mikoshi of Juzenji and some of the priests were killed. Many of their followers were wounded, the noise of the shouts and groaning even ascending to the heights of the Bonten paradise, while Kenro-Chijin, the mighty Earth-deity, was struck with consternation. Then the priestly bands, leaving their mikoshi at the gate, fled back lamenting to their temples.

The Ikkō-ikki on campaign

The Ikkō-ikki took control of Kaga Province in 1488, and from then on, in other words for the whole of the Age of Warring States, almost the whole campaign strategy of the Ikkō-ikki was concentrated on their survival in the face of belligerence from daimyō. When the temple was threatened by an attack, the daily life of its community was placed on to a war footing. Just as

every member of Jōdo Shinshū shared fully in its peacetime activities, so did they share in the responsibilities when conflict loomed. Every man, woman and child became involved. All hands were needed, and certainly by the 1570s experience had taught them that if they lost to Oda Nobunaga then a massacre of every member of the community would follow.

The first requirement was to concentrate resources on defending that which was most defensible. So outlying farms and fields might have to be abandoned, with the defensive line probably being drawn at the edge of the *jinaimachi* (temple town). This was likely to be defended already by some form of perimeter fence or wall, or by natural features such as a river, a slope, forest or groves of impenetrable bamboo. There could then be a progressive withdrawal further inside the complex, until a last-ditch stand had to be made within the *hon maru* (inner bailey). Regardless of the strength of any fortified place in Japan, whether it was a castle or a temple, additions could always be made to its defences when there was immediate danger of attack. Archaeological research at the site of Torigoe found large earthenware storage jars buried in the ground. There was also evidence that when the castle changed hands not only repairs but quite considerable alterations were made to the defences in preparation for a counter-attack. The altered features were no doubt based on the experience of the assault. Those sectors that its captors had found easiest now had to be made difficult.

The defence of Hara castle in 1638 by a peasant army that had great similarities to the Ikkō-ikki. The defenders throw rocks and combustible materials on to the attacking samurai.

WARRIOR MONKS INTIMIDATE THE PEOPLE OF KYŌTO *c.*1160

For the warrior monks of Enryakuji the carrying of the mikoshi of Sanno the mountain king was the most dramatic gesture that could be made. The mikoshi is being carried before the cowed citizens by the kannushi from the Hiyoshi shrine of Sanno. This is their prerogative as the spiritual guardians of the shrine. It is carried on poles by about 20 men, and any assault on it was regarded as an offence to the kami Sanno himself. In front march the angry and confident sōhei of Enryakuji. Every monk carries Buddhist prayer beads and would readily pronounce a curse upon anyone who offended him. One presumptuous fellow receives a smack across the buttocks from the pommel end of a monk's naginata. Another monk pronounces a solemn curse using his prayer beads, but his naginata promises a swifter retribution. The monk leader waves his naginata on high. As all they have to fear are terrified courtiers and citizens, the monks wear a minimum of armour.

The warrior monks in battle

Individual weapon skills

The traditional warrior monk weapon, the naginata, had its own style of combat. Slashing strokes were the usual way of fighting and could produce very nasty wounds. A quick upward stroke towards the unprotected groin was a favourite manoeuvre, and a monk on horseback would stand up in his stirrups and whirl the naginata about him. On foot the blade would be switched from one side to another with practised rapidity, or whirled like a waterwheel.

There is a famous account in *Heike Monogatari* of the fighting of three individual warrior monks during the first battle of Uji in 1180. It has often been quoted, but still repays careful analysis as the most complete account in all the Japanese chronicles of how the naginata and other monk weapons were actually used. As noted above, the warrior monks of Miidera and the Minamoto samurai under Minamoto Yorimasa had marched south to join the monks of Kōfukuji, but the night was almost spent by the time they reached the Uji river, which acts as a natural moat to the south of Kyōto. Realizing that the Taira were following them, they tore up the planking on the Uji bridge, and rested for the night in the Byodo-In temple on the southern bank. The story of the warrior monks' involvement begins with the tale of a nimble sōhei who climbed on to the beams of the bridge and, whirling his naginata like a propeller, deflected the arrows that were fired at him:

A modern mikoshi carried in a festival.

Then Gochin no Tajima, throwing away the sheath of his long naginata, strode forth alone on to the bridge, whereupon the Heike straightaway shot at him fast and furious. Tajima, not at all perturbed, ducking to avoid the higher ones and leaping up over those that flew low, cut through those that flew straight with his whirring naginata, so that even the enemy looked on in admiration. Thus it was that he was dubbed 'Tajima the arrow-cutter'.

Later in the same account Tajima is replaced on the bridge by his comrade Tsutsui Jomyo Meishu, who illustrates the individual fighting skills of the warrior monk in no uncertain fashion. Jomyo first leapt on to the beams where they protruded from the riverbank and challenged the Taira to fight him:

And loosing off his twenty-four arrows like lightning flashes he slew twelve of the Heike soldiers and wounded eleven more. One arrow yet remained in his quiver, but flinging away his bow he stripped off his quiver and threw that after it, cast off his footwear and springing barefoot on to the beams of the bridge, he strode across.

From bow and arrow he moved on to his naginata, sword and dagger:

With his naginata he mows down five of the enemy, but with the sixth the naginata snaps asunder in the midst, and flinging it away he draws his tachi, wielding it in the zig-zag style, the interlacing, cross, reversed dragonfly, waterwheel and eight-sides-at-once styles of sword fighting, thus cutting down eight men; but as he brought down the ninth with an exceedingly mighty blow on the helmet the blade snapped at the hilt and fell with a splash into the water beneath. Then, seizing his tanto, which was the only weapon he had left, he plied it as one in a death fury.

Heike Monogatari tells us that when Jomyo eventually retired from the fight he counted 63 arrows sticking out of his armour, which is not unlikely, as other chronicles attest. A direct arrow strike between the eyes that avoided the peak of a samurai helmet would of course be instantly fatal, but it was more common for samurai to die after sustaining multiple arrow hits. This was largely because of the stopping power of their armour, and the popular image

The katana, the standard fighting sword used by all the warriors in this book.

from both woodblock prints and modern movies of the dying samurai crawling along with hundreds of arrows protruding from him is not too much of an exaggeration. The example of Benkei was noted above, and a certain Imagawa Yorikuni, who fought during the Nanbokuchō Wars, needed 20 arrows to kill him, so Jomyo did well to survive. But at first Jomyo was not to be moved from his post:

> Now a retainer…Ichirai Hoshi by name, was fighting behind Jomyo, but as the beams were so narrow he could not come alongside him, so placing a hand on the neckpiece of his helmet he shouted, 'Pardon me, Jomyo, this is no good,' and springing over his shoulder to the front fought mightily until he fell.

The warrior monk army in battle

There was of course more to winning battles than fighting heroic single combats, and the sources are equally rich for the more co-operative aspects of warrior monk warfare. For example, during the Taira attack on Miidera after the battle of Uji:

> At the monastery about a thousand warrior monks, arming themselves, made a shield barrier, threw up a barricade of felled trees, and awaited them. At the Hour of the Hare they began to draw their bows, and the battle continued the whole day, until when evening came three hundred of the monks and their men had fallen. Then the fight went on in the darkness, and the imperial army forced its way into the monastery and set it on fire.

The modern Uji bridge, built on the site of the one that was the focus of the battle of Uji. We are looking north.

The monk hero Ichirai Hoshi vaults over his companion Tsutsui Jomyo to engage the enemy on the broken bridge of Uji during the battle of 1180.

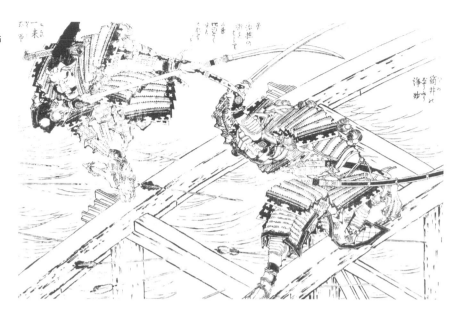

The *Heike Monogatari* account of the defence of Nara in the same year of 1180 is very similar:

> At Nara about seven thousand monks, young and old without distinction, put on their armour and took up their position at Narasaka and Hannyaji, digging ditches across the road and making breastworks and palisades… The monks fought on foot while the imperial army fought on horseback, and as they kept riding up for the attack, the ranks of Nara were thinned and they began to give ground, so that by nightfall, after fighting from early morning, both of their positions were broken through.

Taira Shigehira's mounted samurai bowmen were therefore held off until dark by the determined monks. There were none of the usual niceties of samurai combat because the monkish rabble were thought unworthy of a challenge, but no cavalry charge could break through, so the fateful order was given to use that most deadly of weapons in the samurai armoury: fire. It is probable that Shigehira only intended to burn down a few isolated buildings to break the monks' defensive line, as rival temples had done to each other for two centuries, but a particularly strong wind was blowing. The Kōfukuji temple was reduced to ashes, in spite of all the monks' attempts to save it. The flames then spread to the great Tōdaiji, whose *Daibutsuden* (Great Buddha Hall) housed the enormous statue of Buddha:

> By this time all the warrior monks who had scorned surrender because of fear of dishonour had fallen fighting at Narasaka and Hannyaji, and

The warrior monks of Nara rush to defend their temple against the attack by Taira Shigehira in 1180.

those who remained fled towards Yoshino and Totsugawa. Those who were too old to flee, and the unattached laymen, children and girls, thinking to save themselves, went up into the upper storey of the Daibutsuden or fled into the interior of Yamashinadera in their panic. About a thousand of them crowded into the Daibutsuden and pulled up the ladders behind them so that the enemy could not follow, but the flames reached them first, and such a great crying arose that could not be surpassed even by the sinners amid the flames of Tapana, Pratapana and Avitchi, the fiercest of the Eight Hot Hells.

The author also laments the destruction of Kōfukuji and Tōdaiji, and most of all the loss of the great statue of Buddha:

The colossal statue of Vairochana Buddha of copper and gold, whose domed head towered up into the clouds, from which gleamed the sacred jewel of his lofty forehead, fused with the heat, so that its full moon features fell to the pavement below, while its body melted into a shapeless mass.

In all 3,500 people died in the burning of Nara, and of the original buildings only the imperial repository of the Shoso-In remains to this day. The heads of 1,000 monks were displayed in Nara or carried back to Kyōto.

Warrior monk tactics in the 14th century

The accounts in *Taiheiki*, which deals with the wars of the 14th century, show that warrior monk fighting has changed not at all. There is a vivid account of a single combat between a monk armed with a naginata and a mounted samurai during the Mount Hiei attack on Kyōto. Once again we see the image of a naginata being spun like a waterwheel, just as in the case of 'Tajima the arrow-cutter':

> Just then a monk kicked over the shield in front of him and sprang forward, whirling his naginata like a waterwheel. It was Kajitsu of Harima. Kaito received him with his right arm, meaning to cut down into his helmet bowl, but the glancing sword struck down lightly from Kajitsu's shoulder-plate to the cross stitching at the bottom of his armour. Again Kaito struck forcefully, but his left foot broke through its stirrup, and he was likely to fall from his horse. As he straightened his body, Kajitsu thrust up his naginata, and two or three times drove its point quickly into his helmet. Kaito fell off his horse, pierced cleanly through the throat. Swiftly Kajitsu put down his foot on Kaito's armour, seized his side hair, and cut off his head, that he might fix it to his naginata. Rejoicing, he mocked the enemy.

Battles involving warrior monks were, however, few and far between during the Nanbokuchō Wars. During an incursion into Kyōto by the monks

The Daibutsuden of the Tōdaiji at Nara, built to hold a colossal image of Buddha. It is the largest wooden building in the world under one roof.

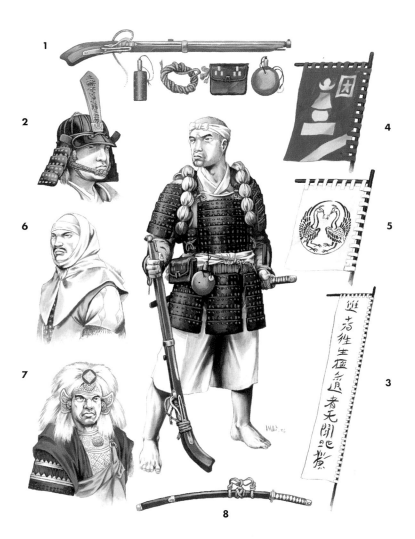

A MONTO OF THE IKKŌ-IKKI AT NAGASHIMA c.1574

Here we see an adherent of the Ikkō-ikki of Nagashima, the island complex that defied Oda Nobunaga for four years. The Ishiyama Honganji troops would have looked very similar. This monto is very different from the warrior monks of Mount Hiei. We note his shaven head with a growth of bristles and his simple trousers and bare feet. He is, however, wearing a well-designed modern suit of armour with strong horizontal plates. He carries an arquebus as well as a sword, and his ration bags of rice are tied round his body. Above him is shown an arquebus (**1**) with its

accessories: a priming powder flask; a fuse reel; a bullet pouch; and a muzzle powder flask. Below is a katana-type sword (**8**), shown with tachi-like suspensory mounts fitted on the reverse side so that the sword is carried with the cutting edge uppermost. (**2**) The head of a warrior monk of the Mikawa Ikkō-ikki, who fought Tokugawa Ieyasu in his younger days. He bears in his helmet a tablet with the slogan 'He who advances is sure of heaven, but he who retreats will go to hell.' (**3**) An Ikkō-ikki flag bearing the same slogan. (**4**) The red and gold sotoba flag of the Ikkō-ikki carried during Oda Nobunaga's siege of Ishiyama Honganji. (**5**) The two cranes flag, carried

during Oda Nobunaga's siege of Ishiyama Honganji by a contingent of Ikkō-ikki from Kaga Province, one of the Ikkō-ikki heartlands. (**6**) At the opposite extreme on the social scale we find the daimyō who were also Buddhist monks. They wore certain items to show their affiliations. Here Uesugi Kenshin (1530–78) is wearing a modified form of the monk's cowl, as shown in nearly all pictures of him. (**7**) Kenshin's rival Takeda Shingen (1521–73) was another 'samurai monk'. In place of a cowl he has an elaborate helmet with Chinese-style fukigayeshi (turnbacks) and with a horse hair plume. His Buddhist item is the kesa, a sort of scarf, worn over his armour.

Two monks of Mount Hiei today. The monks' robes of the Heian Period would not have looked very different.

of Mount Hiei, the samurai defenders used their skills as mounted archers to harass the monks, most of whom were on foot. Arrows were fired as horsemen galloped up and retired, until the resolve of the sōhei was worn away:

> The monks went out before the west gate of the temple, a mere thousand men, unsheathing their weapons and battling against the enemy drawing near. But these pulled back their horses and retreated nimbly when the monks attacked, and galloped round to the rear when the monks stood in their places, as it was planned from the beginning. Thus they galloped and harassed them six or seven times, until at length the bodies of the monks grew weary, by reason that they fought on foot and wore heavy armour. Seizing the advantage, the warriors sent forward archers to shoot them mercilessly.

As the samurai closed in on them the naginata finally came into their own for a last-ditch struggle.

> So they spoke, whirling their great four-shaku-long naginata like waterwheels. Again and again they leaped and attacked with flying sparks of fire. Many were the warriors whose horses' legs were cut when they sought to smite these two. Many were those who fell to the ground and perished with smashed helmets!

The warrior monks had more success when their enemies attacked Mount Hiei and the sōhei were 'playing at home':

A Buddhist priest at prayer in the Fudoji near Kurikara. This gives a good idea of the interior of a typical Buddhist temple in Japan.

Being well acquainted with the land, the monks gathered together in suitable places, from where to let fly arrows in very great numbers. Nor might the warriors retreat easily, but being strangers to the land they galloped into ditches and over cliffs, and fell down together with their horses.

The Ikkō-ikki in battle

The accounts from the Age of Warring States of the Ikkō-ikki in battle are very different from the isolated heroics emphasized by *Heike Monogatari* and *Taiheiki*. Instead there is far more stress laid on the common endeavours of these mass-movement armies. One notable feature, particularly in the accounts of the Ikkō-ikki's wars against their hated enemy Oda Nobunaga, is the use of mass nembutsu chanting as a means of raising their own fighting spirits and intimidating 'the enemies of Buddha'. Thus in 1571 we read of Nobunaga's samurai at Nagashima hearing on the wind the sound of a mass chanting of 'Namu Amida Butsu' as the Ikko-ikki gave thanks for their latest salvation from the 'Devil Nobunaga'. In May 1576 Nobunaga carried out an attack on Ishiyama Honganji known as the battle of Mitsuji, a fierce skirmish provoked by the mass chanting from the defenders.

The Ikkō-ikki army at Nagashima was also brilliant at defensive tactics, and there is a fascinating parallel between them and the contemporary Dutch defenders of their republic against imperial Spain. Any of the citizens of Leiden in 1574, where dykes and ramparts shielded a community sharing a passionate religious conviction, would have felt very much at home at Nagashima that same year!

The first attack by Nobunaga on the island community was a disaster. His mounted samurai began to ford towards the first wajū, only to find that the river bottom was a deep sea of mud. The horses' legs quickly mired, and as the

SAMURAI, SŌHEI AND TOWNSPEOPLE DEFEND KYŌTO AGAINST THE IKKŌ-IKKI 1532
When the Ikkō-ikki moved against Kyōto in 1532 the townsmen armies of the Hokke-shū (Lotus Sect, otherwise the Nichiren-shū after its founder) armed themselves and paraded through the streets under the Nichiren banner, chanting verses from the *Lotus Sutra*. The Ikkō-ikki troops attacked but were successfully driven off by an alliance of samurai, monks and townsmen. In this plate we see the Hokke-shū warriors defending from behind a barricade of straw rice bales, accompanied by the sympathetic samurai general Hosokawa Harumoto. Behind them in the courtyard we see a statue of Nichiren, the founder of the sect. The Nichiren flags with 'Namu Myoho Renge Kyo' ('Hail to the Lotus of the Divine Law') are much in evidence. The Hokke-shū troops are wearing armour typical of the early 16th century prior to the introduction of firearms. To show the often confusing pattern of alliances at the time we have included some warrior monks from Mount Hiei behind the barricades, but in a few years' time they would return to attack the Lotus Sect warriors in Kyōto. The Ikkō-ikki warriors attacking the line are dressed very similarly to samurai.

animals struggled many threw off their heavily armoured riders, who were met by a hail of arrows and bullets, causing severe casualties. As the survivors dragged themselves to the nearest dry land, the wajū of Nagasuji-guchi, they encountered ropes stretched between stakes which further hindered their progress towards safety. The shoreline was covered by tall, dense reeds, which acted as a magnet to the desperate and demoralized samurai. As they crawled into the reed-beds they discovered them to be swarming with more Ikkō-ikki arquebusiers and archers, who cut them down like flies. The shores of the reed-beds were booby-trapped with old pots and vases, buried up to the necks in the sand, providing a trap for ankles and further slowing down the samurai withdrawal into a sitting target. As night fell the defenders realized that the sole survivors of the Oda army were confined within the next wajū of Ota-guchi,

A mounted samurai warrior with naginata. This is the long-bladed version favoured by the warrior monks.

so the dyke was cut, rapidly flooding the low-lying land and catching the remaining samurai in an inrush of muddy water.

The Ikkō-ikki use of firearms

As noted earlier, the warrior monks were among the first armies to develop the use of the arquebus. The organized and cohesive nature of the Jōdo Shinshū communities also enabled them to develop firearms production in a way that

An itinerant monk begging in Nara. His costume is not very different from what might have been seen in the days of the warrior monks. He is carrying a shakujo (rattle) in his right hand.

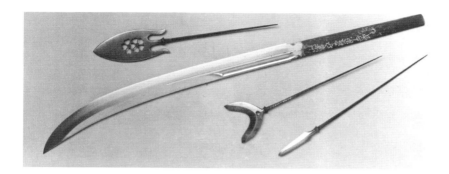

A naginata blade, framed by types of arrowhead.

left most daimyō standing. Tokugawa Ieyasu's battles against the Mikawa monto provide an early example. On one occasion Ieyasu felt a bullet strike his armour, but thinking that it had not penetrated he fought on. It was only when he got back to Okazaki castle when the fighting was over that he realized how near he had come to being killed, because when his servant stripped off his body armour two bullets fell out of his shirt.

A few years later Oda Nobunaga had his first experience of the force of warrior monk gunfire. During his attempt on Ishiyama Honganji in 1570 Nobunaga's army was stunned both by the ferocity of the surprise attack launched against it and also by the use of controlled volley firing from 3,000 arquebusiers. In the chronicle *Shinchōkoki* we read that 'the enemy gunfire echoed between heaven and earth'.

By the time of the second attack on Nagashima in 1573 Nobunaga had created his own form of mass firearm tactics. Covered by an advance from the west under Sakuma Nobumori and Toyotomi Hideyoshi, Nobunaga sent his gunners on ahead along the main roads into Nagashima, hoping that the volley fire would blast a way through for him. Unfortunately, as soon as his men were ready to fire, a fierce downpour soaked the matches and the pans, rendering nine out of every ten arquebuses temporarily out of action. The Ikkō-ikki took this as a sign from heaven of divine favour, and launched an immediate counterattack for which Nobunaga's army was ill prepared. They began to fall back, and as the Ikkō-ikki pressed forward they received a further sign from heaven as the clouds parted and the rain stopped, enabling them to employ their own arquebuses because their pans had been closed and the fuses had been in dry bags. The defenders advanced perilously close to Nobunaga himself, who was in the thick of the fighting astride a horse. One bullet narrowly missed his ear and another felled one of his retainers through the armpit.

In a further action against the Ikkō-ikki in 1576 Nobunaga received a bullet wound in his leg, and it is interesting to note that this incident occurred one year after his great victory at Nagashino. That was the battle where Nobunaga won renown for using tactics very similar to those he had experienced at the hands of Japan's most fanatical fighters: the Ikkō-ikki – Japan's latter-day warrior monks.

結論 *Conclusion*

*I*n this book I have tried to present the wide range of social class and personal motivation that contributed towards the making of the warriors of medieval Japan. I hope to have shown that the catch-all term samurai is woefully insufficient to describe both the breadth and depth of involvement in two centuries of civil war. Participation ranged from the absentee landlord Kujo Masamoto, rudely forced to leave a privileged and sheltered life in the imperial court because of the disorder in his estates, to the anonymous wife whose headless body appears on the painted screen of the defence of Hara.

Between these two extremes we have a complete spectrum of personal and social commitment. The samurai, inspired, brainwashed even, by the deeds of the ancestors whose exploits were constantly dangled in front of them like a carrot for a donkey, but whose earthly rewards of power, fame, glory and wealth were often the primary motivation. The ashigaru, who saw in military glory the chance to escape from the humdrum world of the farmer and who, from 1591 onwards, were constantly reminded how lucky they were when they saw hundreds of peasants from similar backgrounds to their own bent double under heavy packs and driven on by samurai's blows. The ninja, who in other circumstances would have been little more than an ikki of jizamurai, but in Iga and Koga became the directors of a thriving business in mercenary warfare, whose success and mystique, one feels, were deliberately exaggerated for commercial purposes long before they were discovered by Hollywood. The warrior monks, as grasping and ruthless as any samurai, who relied just a little too much on the fear of the gods they represented instead of moving with the times, and finally the monto of the Ikkō-ikki, who present the most confusing images of all. Religious fanatics or vermin to their enemies, proto-Marxists or proto-democrats to modern admirers from opposing political persuasions, they set up independent, self-governing model communities, and then spoiled it all by attacking the Nichiren settlements in Kyōto who were doing exactly the same.

This book has concentrated on the ordinary warriors of medieval Japan. Their commanders are dealt with elsewhere, but their development was moulded totally by the changes in Japanese society that the great unifiers of the nation brought about, and if there is one man whose life profoundly affected each of the four groups discussed here, that man is Oda Nobunaga. Several samurai families were totally annihilated by his campaigns. His destruction of the Ikkō-ikki in Echizen in 1575 was accompanied by the worst massacre in Japanese history, while his scorched-earth march through Iga Province in 1581 destroyed the original ninja organization. Only ashigaru, one feels, whom he lifted from being military appendages to entering the core of a samurai army, would have a good word to say for him, a situation illustrated by the fact that they were the only warrior group covered here who did not actually try to kill him. A ninja tried to assassinate Nobunaga in 1573 and an Ikkō-ikki marksman put a bullet into his leg in 1576. His end finally came in 1582 when his lodgings at the Honnoji temple were surrounded by his own supposedly loyal and devoted samurai, an ironic comment on the popular view of the best known warriors of medieval Japan.

This statue of Oda Nobunaga stands on the site of his castle of Kiyosu. He is wearing a dō maru style of armour with haidate and an eboshi on his head.

Glossary

Akuso	'Evil monk', a pejorative term for sōhei
Ashigaru kashira	Captain of foot soldiers
Ashigaru ko gashira	Lieutenant of foot soldiers
Ashigaru taishō	General of foot soldiers
Bokutō	Wooden sword
Bushidō	'The way of the warrior'
Chō	A distance of 109m
Daimyō	Feudal lord
Daishō	Pair of swords
Dō	Body armour
Dō maru	Style of armour wrapping round the body
Futon	Folding mattress
Genin	Ordinary ninja
Geta	Wooden clogs
-Gumi (kumi)	Military unit
Gunkimono	War tale
Habiki	Edgeless sword
Hachimaki	Head band
Haidate	Thigh guards
Hakama	Wide trousers
Hamagari	A long, thin folding saw
Haori	Jacket
Hara kiri	Ritual suicide
Haramaki	Style of armour opening at the rear
Hata-jirushi	Flag streamer suspended from cross-piece
Horō	Cloak worn stretched over a bamboo framework
Ichiryo gusoku	Owners of one suit of armour
Ikki	League or organization
Jinbaori	Surcoat

Jingasa	Foot soldier's light helmet
Jinja	Shintō shrine
Kamayari	A spear with a crescent-shaped crossblade
Kami	A Shintō deity
Kancho	A spy
Kannushi	Shintō priest
Kashira	Officer of ashigaru
Katana	The standard fighting sword
Ken	Length of 1.8m
Kenjutsu	Sword techniques
Kesa	The ceremonial scarf worn by Buddhist monks
Kimono	Garment like a dressing gown
Ko uma jirushi	Smaller of a lord's standards
Koku	Measure of 180 litres of rice
Kote	Sleeve armour
Kusazuri	Skirts of armour, tassets
Maedate	Crest on the front of a samurai's helmet
Maku	Curtains enclosing a general's headquarters on a battlefield
Mikoshi	Portable shrine
Mitama	The spirit of a Shintō kami
Mochi-yari	Hand spears
Mochiyari gumi	Spear bearer
Mogami-dō	Multi-plate armour in hinged sections
Mon	Heraldic badge
Monme	Weight of 3.75gms
Monto	Adherent of Ikkō-ikki
Mune ita	Upper section of breastplate
Nagae yari	Long-shafted spear
Naginata	Glaive or curve-bladed spear
Nembutsu	Literally 'Buddha-calling', a prayer sequence
Nobori	Vertical banner
Nō dachi	long sword with very strong, long handle
Okashi gusoku	Loan armour provided for ashigaru
Okegawa-dō	Smooth surfaced armour for ashigaru
Ō uma jirushi	Larger of a lord's standards
Rōnin	Samurai whose daimyō had been killed
Sahai	Baton of command
Sake	Rice wine
Sashimono	Flag or other device worn on the back of armour
Sengoku jidai	Age of Warring States (1467–1600)
Sensei	Teacher

Shaku	Length of 30.3cms
Shashu no ashigaru	Archer foot soldiers in the 14th century
Shinai	Practice weapon made of bamboo
Shinobi	Alternative reading of 'nin' in ninja
Shinobigama	Ninja sickle and chain weapon
Shōgun	Military dictator
Shugo	Military governor
Sode	Shoulder plates
Suneate	Shinguards
Tabi	Socks with separate compartment for big toe
Tachi	Long sword worn slung from a belt
Tanto	Dagger
Tasuki	Sash
Teppō ko gashira	Officer in charge of arquebusiers
Tozama	Outer lords
Tsuba	Sword guard
Tsukai ban	High-ranking elite messenger corps
Tsumeru	Technique for practising sword combat
Uma jirushi	Standard used by samurai
Umamawari	Daimyō's bodyguard
Uwa-obi	Belt
Wakizashi	Short sword
Waraji	Straw sandals
Yamabushi	Wandering mountain monk
Yamashiro	Mountain castle
Yari	Spear
Yarijutsu	Spear techniques
Yari kashira	Captain of spears
Yashiki	Mansion
Yumi	Bow
Yumi kashira	Captain of bows
Zori tori	Sandal bearer, equivalent to a batman

Museum collections and places to visit

Samurai arms and armour of the Age of Warring States may be seen in some of Japan's greatest museums, although the Japanese practice of rotating collections means that materials are displayed for only short periods, so it is wise to check before making a visit. There are also numerous temporary exhibitions. Tokyo National Museum and the Tokugawa Art Museum in Nagoya are two of the best collections.

The most dramatic example of a large-scale and permanently displayed collection is the Watanabe Museum in Tottori on the Japan Sea coast, which has a remarkable collection that features rank after rank of armour, including many ashigaru suits, arranged like a football terrace. There are also numerous weapons and flags. The Ii collection in Hikone is now housed in a purpose-built museum at the foot of the castle hill, and even though the exhibits are rotated, the chances are that any casual visit will yield several examples of the red devils' armour (so called because of the colour of the lacquer). The Takeda Museum at the Erin-ji near Kōfu contains all the Takeda war banners, while the Date Museum in Sendai has several examples of their renowned bullet-proof armours.

Outside Japan outstanding places are the Museo Stibbert in Florence and the Royal Armouries Museum in Leeds, which has splendid armour and several arquebuses and spears. Several other museums have smaller collections of armour. For good mixed displays of samurai and ashigaru equipment visit Snowshill Manor near Broadway in Worcestershire, or the Metropolitan Museum in New York.

There are several places in Japan where the ninja's tourist potential has been very well realized. The centre of the popularization of ninja in Japan is undoubtedly Iga Ueno in Mie Prefecture. The park in the castle grounds boasts a ninja house and a ninja museum. The house, moved from a nearby village and rebuilt, is very convincing. It contains several trap doors and concealed

entrances, which are demonstrated to the visitor by two fetching young lady ninja, dressed in all-concealing ninja costumes, the effect of which is spoiled by the choice of bright pink or purple as a colour. The museum is also very interesting. Koga, the rival to Iga in its supply of shinobi mercenaries, boasts two ninja tourist attractions. One is a ninja house very similar to the Iga version. The other is a preserved ninja village, complete with temple and shrine. Both are well worth visiting, but are not quite as accessible as the Iga sites.

Nijo jinya, the house in Kyōto used for the hypothetical assassination attempt related earlier, is well worth a visit. All the features noted in the fictional account actually exist in the house. Also worth seeing are all the fire precautions that enabled Nijo jinya to survive the Great Temmei Fire of 1788. A visit can be combined with nearby Nijo castle, where the sound of the famous 'nightingale floor' accompanies the visitor round the spectacular palace.

A further example of authenticity is found in the Teramachi district of Kanazawa. The Myoryuji was one of a number of temples relocated to the outskirts of the city by the third daimyō, Maeda Toshitsune, to provide an outer defence for Kanazawa. The Myoryuji possesses a number of secret rooms, concealed doors and secret passages, and is now inevitably known as 'Ninja-dera' or the 'ninja temple'. It is not the less worth visiting for that,

The Kōfukuji of Nara viewed from across the pond of Sarusawa which provided some defence. We can see the famous five-storey pagoda.

because like Nijo jinya all the features are original. Finally, it is possible to visit a genuine ninja's grave without leaving Tokyo, because the famous Hattori Hanzo is buried in the garden of the Seinenji temple, which lies near to Sophia University in Chiyoda-ku. Inside the temple hall is Hanzo's spear.

For warrior monks, the Tōdaiji and the Kōfukuji, the two great temples of Nara, remain among Japan's finest tourist attractions, and although most of their wooden buildings have been rebuilt and restored over the years, it is easy to conjure up images of sōhei marching through their courtyards. Nearly all of the Tōdaiji/Kōfukuji/Kasuga area is virtually traffic free, and much of it is parkland. The same Buddhist statues and images that inspired the sōhei are still there in the dimly lit temple halls, and the great gates and the pool of Sarusawa cannot have looked very different. The only problem the visitor has is avoiding the inquisitive deer!

Mount Hiei, which dominates the city of Kyōto from the north-east, still presents the same duality of security and menace that met the eyes of the imperial courtiers. It is easily reached by public transport, and it is possible to make a complete circuit of the Enryakuji complex beginning at Sakamoto near Lake Biwa, where the Hiyoshi shrine of Sanno the mountain king still exists, and descending into Kyōto. The Hiyoshi shrine displays the latest equivalent of the sacred mikoshi that were carried into Kyōto. A cable car from Sakamoto whisks you up to Enryakuji in a few minutes, where there is much to see and the view is magnificent. Onjōji (Miidera) is nearby and also worth a visit. You can see Benkei's famous bell, and also the cauldron used to make the bean soup that he demanded as compensation.

In Kyōto the Nishi Honganji and Higashi Honganji are open to the public, as are Kyōto's famous Zen temples, many of which have wonderful gardens. The battlefield of Uji is not far away. Kobo Daishi's foundation of Koya-san is another monastic complex well worth a visit. It is famous for the mausoleums of famous samurai, and at least one temple takes in guests. It is a wonderful opportunity for a visitor to share in a little of the monastic life.

At the Negoroji in Wakayama Prefecture is the Daito (great pagoda), the only building that survived Hideyoshi's attack. It was built in 1496 and bullet holes from the 1585 attack can still be seen. The rest of the complex is also very interesting, and there are some fine gardens. Wakayama castle, built on the site of the Saiga-ikki's Ota castle, is nearby. The *hondo* (main hall) of Negoroji was rebuilt at Daigoji near Kyōto.

As for the Ikkō-ikki, the topography of Nagashima has changed much over the centuries but retains an atmosphere of sea and reed-beds that still has the power to evoke impressions of the 16th century. The land is flat and not unlike Holland in appearance, because much of it has been reclaimed, and the rice fields are bordered by reed-beds as they reach the shore. One gate and part of the moat is all that remains of Nagashima castle. Its keep survived until 1959,

when it was struck by lightning. The Ganshoji lost its original location to the sea and has been rebuilt further inland, but it still boasts a stone wall that gives it the appearance of a fortified place. Within its courtyard is the most interesting feature of all: a stone stupa erected recently as a memorial to the martyrs of the Ikkō-ikki.

Osaka castle holds few traces of the former Ishiyama Honganji, but an idea of its impregnability may be gained by the view from the top of the castle tower. There is also a memorial stone to the Ikkō-ikki, and the excellent museum inside Osaka castle's keep contains several interesting items relating to the Ikkō-ikki. There are flags and a suit of armour associated with Shimotsuma Nakayuki. Apart from Osaka, it is rare to find arms and armour in Japan specifically linked to warrior monks. Nearer to home, the Royal Armouries Museum in Leeds has some naginata on display, along with dō maru types of armour, arquebuses and swords.

Finally, in Torigoe, near Komatsu in Ishikawa prefecture, the Ikkō-ikki's fortified temple has been excavated and partly restored. This, together with the Ikkō-ikki Museum in Torigoe village provides an excellent visual introduction to the Kaga Ikkō-ikki. Across the border in former Echizen is Yoshizaki, with a museum and the attractive landscaped site of the Ikkō-ikki headquarters.

Hideyoshi's attack on Negoroji in 1585. This print shows the defence of the pond on the west of the complex.

277

Bibliography and further reading

Apart from general works listed elsewhere the source for several quotes in the samurai section is *Hagakure*, translated by W. S. Wilson (Kodansha, 1979). Thomas Conlan's *State of War* (University of Michigan, 2003) deals with the 14th century, but much is applicable to later times. The information about the operations in Korea is largely taken from Kuwada et al. (editors), *Chōsen no Eki* (*Nihon no senshi* Volume 5), which has an extensive appendix of primary source material. For Korea see also the bibliography in Turnbull's *Samurai Invasion: Japan's Korean War 1592–1598* (Wiedenfeld & Nicholson, 2002). Some of the primary source material referred to here may be found in translation in Turnbull's *The Samurai Sourcebook* (Cassell, 1998). For two thorough case studies of battles see Turnbull's Campaign 69: *Nagashino 1575* (Osprey, 2000) and Campaign 130: *Kawanakajima 1553–1564* (Osprey, 2003).

The main sources for the ashigaru section are two works by Yoshihiko Sasama entitled *Ashigaru no Seikatsu* (1969) and *Buke Senjin Sahō Shōsei* (1968). The first is the standard work on the history of ashigaru and contains long sections from *Zōhyō Monogatari*. The second, which is concerned with the entire samurai class, also contains much from *Zōhyō Monogatari* and other essays and primary source material on ashigaru. The ashigaru are also covered in two recent volumes in the series *Senryaku, senjutsu, heiki jiten*. Volume 2, *Nihon Sengoku hen* includes many drawings of ashigaru in action, while Volume 6, *Nihon Johaku hen* concentrates on their role in sieges. Kurosawa's films *Kagemusha* and *Ran* give very accurate depictions of ashigaru warfare. *Throne of Blood* also shows ashigaru in action during a siege.

A Japanese book entitled *Ninja*, by various authors, in the series *Rekishi Gurafiko*, published by Shufu to Seikatsusha (Tokyo, 1993) is very good. Two more recent books are *Ninja to Ninjutsu* (Rekishi Gunzo, Volume 71, Gakken, 2003) and *Iga Koga Shinobi no subete* (2003). There are also a huge number of popular works on the market dealing with ninja fighting arts and ninjutsu. Details of the operation of Chinese explosive devices may be found in Turnbull's New Vanguard 43: *Siege Weapons of the Far East (1)* (Osprey, 2001) and New Vanguard 42: *Siege Weapons of the Far East (2)* (Osprey, 2002).

For the environment of the warrior monks see Turnbull's Fortress 34: *Japanese Fortified Monasteries AD 949–1603* (Osprey, 2005). The standard history of the early warrior monks is *Sōhei* by Katsuno Ryushin (Tokyo, 1955), and for the Jōdo Shinshū armies it is *Ikkō-ikki no kenkyu* by Kasahara Kaguo (Tokyo, 1982). The works of Sasama Yoshihiko, such as *Buke Senjin Saho Shusei* (Tokyo, 1969), also have sections on the warrior monks. The most complete account in English of the development of Buddhist monasticism in Japan, and particularly the political context that led to the warrior monks, may be found in Volume 2 of *The Cambridge History of Japan* (Cambridge University Press, 1984). *The The Origins of Japan's Medieval World: Courtiers, Clerics, Warriors and Peasants in the Fourteenth Century*, edited by Jeffrey Mass (Stanford University Press, 1998) contains an interesting chapter on 13th and 14th-century developments. The warrior monks of Nara and Kyōto are discussed in Turnbull's *Samurai Warfare* (Weidenfeld & Nicholson, 1996).

Index

Figures in **bold** refer to illustrations